The CopperSpoon Chronicles
Cookbook

A Tavern-Inspired Adventure
with Good Food and Cozy Vibes

Emily Teuscher

Skyhorse Publishing

Copyright © 2025 by Emily Teuscher

All rights reserved. No part of this book may be reproduced in any manner without the express written consent of the publisher, except in the case of brief excerpts in critical reviews or articles. All inquiries should be addressed to Skyhorse Publishing, 307 West 36th Street, 11th Floor, New York, NY 10018.

Skyhorse Publishing books may be purchased in bulk at special discounts for sales promotion, corporate gifts, fund-raising, or educational purposes. Special editions can also be created to specifications. For details, contact the Special Sales Department, Skyhorse Publishing, 307 West 36th Street, 11th Floor, New York, NY 10018 or info@skyhorsepublishing.com.

Skyhorse® and Skyhorse Publishing® are registered trademarks of Skyhorse Publishing, Inc.®, a Delaware corporation.

Visit our website at www.skyhorsepublishing.com.

Please follow our publisher Tony Lyons on Instagram @tonylyonsisuncertain.

10 9 8 7 6 5 4 3 2 1

Library of Congress Cataloging-in-Publication Data is available on file.

Cover design by Kai Texel
Cover and interior images by Emily Teuscher and Julia Bland

Print ISBN: 978-1-5107-8198-6
Ebook ISBN: 978-1-5107-8199-3

Printed in China

Acknowledgments

Hello travelers and all of my little spoonies! Thanks for joining me again and for all your support. I am so excited to share my very first cookbook with you! For those who don't know me, I've been making content online as "The CopperSpoon Inn and Tavern" for five years, and now we are finally sharing a book packed with not only your favorite recipes, but also the stories behind them.

First off, let's get into how this book works. This is not your average cookbook, but, instead, a journey of self discovery and good food. The table of contents will list out each chapter of the enthusiastic Cob CopperSpoon's coming-of-age story and all the recipes she discovers along the way. Each dish has a story, and those stories make the recipes what they are. If you're not interested in the story and just want to get to the food, there's a list of recipes sorted by dish type if you check out the index on page 333.

I, Emily Teuscher, am the face behind the recipes, the local tavern-keep you see online. However, none of this would have been possible without my incredible storyteller, Julia Bland. Julia worked with me as a ghostwriter through this whole process, taking my ideas and turning them into a living, breathing world. She's a writer and illustrator based outside of Toronto, Canada—she even contributed many of her artistic skills to this book.

When I decided to make a cookbook, I knew that I wanted to make something really special, and I am so grateful for all of the love and effort Julia has put into this project with me.

Bethany Jett, my literary agent, has been so helpful throughout this process, and I am so lucky to have her. She has believed in my vision since the very beginning. I remember meeting with her for the first time and feeling so touched by how enthusiastic she was about my crazy idea. After many emails of agents telling me the cookbook "wasn't the right fit," or that they wouldn't know how to market my idea, her belief in the CopperSpoon cookbook gave me hope.

I also had the pleasure of working with the incredible Kyle Weiss. He is (in his words) "a kind emulsification of awkward confidence and daily confusion." He is an autistic public speaker, advocate, author, and has been working in the restaurant industry for fifteen years, achieving the title of sous chef. Above all else, though, he's a friend. He used his years of knowledge and his special interest in culinary history to make our substitution section. No matter who you are or what your dietary restrictions are, you can still enjoy a CopperSpoon recipe thanks to Kyle. I am so extremely grateful he was so willing to share his knowledge with me and our CopperSpoon Family.

While I developed all of these recipes on my own, my family are the ones who truly taught me to love food. I remember the days of sitting at a counter with my sisters and watching my grandma cook—we would constantly fight over who got to make the guacamole and watch hours and hours of the Food Network. My dad instilled in me a love for smoking meats, and my mom knew all sorts of tips and tricks from her years of working in the restaurant industry. My sisters and I would take turns cooking full blown meals for each other by the time we were ten. My nana made pancakes that I absolutely hated, but she redeemed herself with her peanut butter-honey popcorn and the best sweet treats. My whole life I have been surrounded by the love of food, and I am so grateful for each family member that taught me something new.

I can't just thank my family, though; I also have to thank the family I made along the way. To two of my best friends, Autumn and Gracie, thank you for helping me test recipes and always supporting me in this journey. To my bestie, Sean, I never could have conjured up some of these tea creations without you. Drinks were never my specialty but you sparked a love for herbal blends in me. I am also so lucky to have my fiancé's family. They so easily made me one of their own and I can't express how much their love and support means to me. To my second mom, Ann, thank you so much for all of the support you have shown Brett and me. I know you would move mountains for your son, but you have also cared for me in a way not many would. We could not have done this without you, and I am so grateful for the role you play in our lives.

To my fiancé, Brett. You all know him as Karn from the CopperSpoon, but to me, he is the love of my life. I am extremely confident in the fact that I would have never made it here today without him. He has always believed in me and has always loved me in a way nobody ever has. Brett has been telling stories and playing RPGs for over sixteen years. He taught me the love of storytelling, and he helped come up with how The CopperSpoon's story would lay out. He never once doubted me and has always been by my side to hold my hand through the good and the bad. I love you so much Brett, and thank you for making my life so, so, so much better than it's ever been before.

And finally, to all of my little spoonies. None of this would have been possible without you. I cannot thank you enough for supporting me throughout these years of creation. I have never felt the love of a community like ours and I am so lucky to have all of you.

In conclusion, I will say this: never stop exploring, always remember to be kind, and of course, I hope you enjoy, traveler.

Contents

Acknowledgments III

CHAPTER ONE:
Preparing for the Journey 1
Internal Temperature Guide   2
Substitutions   3
Smokey Copper Spice Blend   13
Cyclops Bane   14
How to Perfectly Roast Garlic   15
Roasted Garlic Butter   16
Garlic Confit   17
How To Butterfly   18
Gluten-Free Flour Blend   19

CHAPTER TWO:
Family Traditions 20
Copper Cockatrice Caprese   22
Not Your Papa's Bread Rolls   24
Nana's No-Wheat Bread (Gluten-Free)   26
Lemony Toadstools with Salty Cheese   27
Nana T's Copper-Pop   29
Grammy Linda's Spoon Tacos   30

CHAPTER THREE:
First Taste of the World 32
Hen and Hearth Stew   33

CHAPTER FOUR:
A CopperSpoon Quest 35
Ole Bessy's Legacy   37
Forest Fromage Soup   40
Sampler Spuds   42
The Adventurer's Comfort   45
Pillow Bread   47
The Tavern Classic   49

CHAPTER FIVE:
Some Heroes Bake Chocolate Cakes 51
100 Gold Chocolate Cake   54

CHAPTER SIX:
A Night at The Rusty Dog 56
Smoked Centicore Sandwich   59

CHAPTER SEVEN:
Trial of Might 62
Forager's Impy Rolls   68
Crispy Roasted Spuds   70
Cheesy Garlic Swirls   72
Fudgy Brownies (Gluten-Free)   74
Dwarven Float   76

CHAPTER EIGHT:
Feeding the Grumpy 77

CHAPTER NINE:
Misfits of the Bastion 80
Surprise Fries 86

CHAPTER TEN:
Mysteries of the Deep 89
Ocean's Embrace   91

CHAPTER ELEVEN:
A Taste of the Tropics 93
Colossal Crab Cheese Dip   95
Cheesy Harvest Wands   97
Bayberry Taffy   98
Chewy Gnome Bread and Cheese Sauce   100
Huntsman's Hoagie   102
Tropical Cream   105
Siren Fry   106

CHAPTER TWELVE:
Sick at Sea 108
- Harold's Ginger Peppermint Tea 114

CHAPTER THIRTEEN:
Discourse on Ivory Shores 115
- Sea Bullet Rice 123

CHAPTER FOURTEEN:
Plans on Plans 126
- Sea Moon Charcuterie 128

CHAPTER FIFTEEN:
Destined for Doom 130
- Honey-Glazed Pink Lance 133
- Roasted Coral Bulbs 134
- Kelpie Cookies (Gluten-Free) 135
- Sea Dandelion Lemonade 136

CHAPTER SIXTEEN:
Revenge of the Gnomes 138
- Aunt Jo's Alligator Ranch Biscuits 143
- Chimera Roast and Root Veggies 144

CHAPTER SEVENTEEN:
Menagerie of Monsters 147
- Stuffed Dragon Scale 148
- The Tea Witch Soup 151
- Gold Coins 153
- High Elven Garden Tacos 155
- Uni-Fruit Cheesecake 157

CHAPTER EIGHTEEN:
Dongle the Troll 159
- Gnomebalaya 164

CHAPTER NINETEEN:
Missing Villagers 166
- Pixie Pie 168

CHAPTER TWENTY:
Trouble Afoot 171
- Moorhsum Cap Sandwich 174
- Terra-To Salad 176

CHAPTER TWENTY-ONE:
The Web 178
- Red Ruby Spiced Cider 184
- Squashling Soup 185

CHAPTER TWENTY-TWO:
Markings 187
- Melodious Mushroom Soup 189

CHAPTER TWENTY-THREE:
Irabel's Journey 191
- Crimson Berry Soup 193
- Everything-but-the-Dragon's-Hoard Scones 195
- Gruble Kebab and Cucumber Salad 197
- Sweet Dream Soup 201

CHAPTER TWENTY-FOUR:
Maps and Mushrooms and Bears, Oh My! 203
- Braised Dire Bear Belly and Eggs 205
- Forager's Pillows 207

CHAPTER TWENTY-FIVE:
Stepping into the Darkness 210
- Wildwinter Tea 214
- Kappa Cookies (Gluten-Free) 215

CHAPTER TWENTY-SIX:
Something More 217
- Piggy and Onion Cheesy Melt — 222
- Scrumptious Scholars Pasta Salad — 224

CHAPTER TWENTY-SEVEN:
Code Name: Bread Pudding 226
- Chocolate Cherry Allure — 231

CHAPTER TWENTY-EIGHT:
How to Cheat the Heat 234
- Firebird Stew and Rice — 240

CHAPTER TWENTY-NINE:
Into the Flames 243
- Boar Butt Sliders — 249
- Changeling Chili — 251
- Phoenix Feathers — 253
- Golem Grub — 254

CHAPTER THIRTY:
The Twelfth Knight 256
- Rancheros Adventeros — 259

CHAPTER THIRTY-ONE:
Beacons of Hope 262
- Crispy Lava Lizard Tacos — 264

CHAPTER THIRTY-TWO:
Bitter Ends 266
- Karn's Comfort — 273

CHAPTER THIRTY-THREE:
Unwinding 274
- The Tag-Along's Clouds and Cream — 276
- Harold's Late Night Comforts — 278

CHAPTER THIRTY-FOUR:
A Big Blur 279
- Burnt Sugar Harvest Brew — 281
- Manticore Noodles — 283
- Island Burger — 285

CHAPTER THIRTY-FIVE:
An Old Frenemy 288
- The Meal — 290
- Toadstool and Leaf Pockets — 292
- Broccoli and Dire Bull — 295
- Farvenor's Autumn Harvest — 297
- Baked Apple Cheese — 300

CHAPTER THIRTY-SIX:
The CopperSpoon Inn & Tavern.... 302
- Roasted Thunderbird Thighs with Zucchini and Squash — 305
- Wanderer's Savory Porridge — 307
- Twinebrush Onion Soup — 309
- Baklava in Bloom — 311
- Sea Dragon and Noodle Stew — 313
- The Copper Shepherd — 315

CHAPTER THIRTY-SEVEN:
And Then There Were Five 318
- Cheesy Vine Fruit Manicotti — 323
- Dryad's Crunchy Morsels — 326
- Blackberry Honey Crumble and Ice Cream — 328

CHAPTER THIRTY-EIGHT:
Onward, Onward 330

Metric Conversions 332
Index 333

Frostcreep Tundra
Ebon Woods
Terrolecki Swamp
The Violet Bastion
Honey Star
Twinebrush
Farvenor
Wildflower Plains
Newelin
Arvilia
Scoterra Desert
Marlin's Shore
Nautinara

CHAPTER ONE
Preparing for the Journey

Hey, Journal, It's me, Cob!

  I've been waiting so long to crack you open and start writing, and now the time has finally come! Well . . . <u>sort of</u>. I leave in a few days. I'm finally old enough to set off on the traditional CopperSpoon family adventure. Yup, you heard me right, the very same adventure I've spent the last <u>seventeen</u> years dreaming of! Now, I know what you're wondering: am I <u>really</u> ready for such a big undertaking? You bet your butt I am!

  Countless hours have been put into planning, researching, and then re-planning all of the things I want to do and see. Not to mention I've quadruple—no, <u>quintuple</u>—checked that I've packed all the essentials I need.

  Bedroll? <u>Check</u>!
  Clothes? <u>Check</u>!
  Toothbrush? <u>Check</u>!
  Cinnamon? <u>Check</u>!
  You name it, I got it.

  And that's not all, I've been brushing up on all my cooking techniques, too. Why? Because this isn't just about the adventure <u>or</u> even all the stories I'll be able to tell. Nope, It's about the <u>food</u>—the delicious, wonderful, scrumptious food that I'll learn how to cook along the way. My mouth is watering already.

  Anyway, here are all the CopperSpoon fundamentals, techniques, and tips that I'm tucking away in my brain just in case I need them on the road. I figure it'll be best to write them down here, just in case!

Internal Temperature Guide

When checking meat temperatures, always probe into the center of the thickest part of the meat, avoiding super fatty areas and the edges.

Beef:
Rare: 125–130°F
Medium Rare: 130–135°F
Medium: 135–145°F
Medium Well: 145–155°F
Well: 155°F

Pork:
Medium Rare: 145–150°F
Medium: 150–155°F
Medium Well: 155–160°F
Well: 160°F

Chicken/Turkey:
165°F

Seafood:
145°F

Substitutions

(I asked my cousin Kyle to write out a substitution guide for me. He is really, really smart, and I just know this will help me on my journey!)

*(Please keep in mind information in this book is not intended as medical advice, a nutritional guide, nor for diagnosis of any medical condition. These substitution ingredients and methods are suggestions and as a guide only; please seek a qualified doctor's advice if you are concerned you may have an undiagnosed condition or have other concerns about any substitution ingredient. Always double-check allergy statements on any products you purchase. Food manufacturers may change their ingredients at any time.)

These substitutions are just that, substitutions. Not every ingredient will taste the same, but this is a good start for altering recipes to fit any diet.

Whether you're due for a trip to the market, you want to eat healthier, or someone could be in discomfort or danger from consuming a particular ingredient, substitutions are for *everyone*! Here's a general guide to get you started!

Allergies*

Recipes in this tome may call for certain ingredients that cause problems for some people. According to the real-world FDA, the most common allergens are milk products, eggs, fish/fish products, shellfish/crustaceans, tree nuts, peanuts, wheat and related grains, and soy nuts/soybeans. If any adventurers happen to need alternative suggestions to any of these ingredients, fear not, you'll not be taken out of the story! Here's a quick guide to make sure your blade stays sharp, your magic keeps its mana, and your lute holds a tune when cooking for your favorite heroes and villains.

Really, I'm including this information to bring awareness and inclusivity of basic food allergies and substitution info, with maybe a few hints along the way: I want to get you cooking for your main quest!

Milk/Dairy

The two main concerns are lactose (the sugars) and milk proteins in typical cow's milk. Milk can be sneaky in making its way into food you wouldn't necessarily suspect. Certain products, like some cured sausages (salami), have whey and other dairy in them. Some people can be allergic to more than cow's milk. Depending on you or your inn guest's needs, here are a few common substitutions that can be used by themselves in equal measurement in most recipes:

- **Lactose-free (cow) milk:** Same as the real thing, minus the lactose. Be sure the person getting this substitution does not have a protein allergy!

- **Ghee/clarified butter:** This is cow butter, but with only the fat remaining. Please note this to anyone with any allergies; some can tolerate it, others cannot.
- **Goat milk:** No bovine here! Use as one would use cow milk. Sometimes adding a little water can thin this richer substitute out, but works great in place of regular cream. Unless whipping, of course.
- **Goat butter:** Same as goat milk, no cows involved. Goat butter is very rich and flavorful, and some even make the swap simply for that reason alone.
- **Goat cheese/chevre:** Chevre is a soft goat cheese that is great for cream cheese substitution.
- **Almond/Soy/Cashew milk:** If you aren't allergic to these, they're a great substitute. Most have enough oils to make for a direct substitution.
- **Oat milk:** Oat-derived, good thickness. Add ¼ teaspoon oil of your choice if needed due to the thinner nature or use as-is.
- **Sheep cheese (and other sheep products):** It's possible to use this as a substitution, however, some may still have a reaction to it! Naturally, ask them first.
- **Mayonnaise:** It's true, typical mayo is just eggs and oil. Provided peanut oil isn't used, and someone isn't allergic to eggs, this can be used as a savory cream/sour cream substitution!
- **Vegan options:** There are a *lot* of vegan "dairy" products from sour cream to cheeses, mayo, milks, ice cream, and dessert toppings. They often need to be experimented with for best results, as their properties do not always yield the same texture/flavor/chemistry as their animal counterparts. So I wouldn't host a banquet without doing some proper testing first. Not to mention, they can be made from ingredients where other allergens may be present, such as soy and tree nuts and other proteins. The bottom line? They're not going to cause dairy concerns!

There are a lot of dairy-alternative products out there in the realm, from frozen treats to candies and snacks. Your best bet would be to do some research, find who sells the ideal stuff, and experiment with dish results.

Eggs

Eggs, mainly from the humble chicken, are a common ingredient in many recipes. Like milk, they can even be in unlikely places, such as certain noodles and ice cream. Fear not, provided it's okay with you and your guest, here's a few suggestions for alternatives:

For Whole-Egg Applications:

- **Quail eggs:** sure they're tiny, but 4 quail eggs equal 1 medium chicken egg, and 5 equal 1 large egg.

- **Duck eggs:** 1 duck egg will equal 2 medium, regular chicken eggs. They are a bit richer and fattier, so adding an extra tablespoon of water might help in some instances.

For Baking:

- **Flaxseed "egg":** Use 2 teaspoons of ground flaxseed and 5 teaspoons of water to replace 1 large egg. Has a decent flavor, too.
- **Psyllium "egg":** What is psyllium? It's a plant grown for mucilage fiber, found in many health stores. It can be a good ingredient to have on hand. Two teaspoons of psyllium husk with 4 tablespoons of water, whisked and rested, equals 1 large egg. Some ideas out there suggest using sparkling water and a dash of oil for extra weight and "lift."
- Like milk alternatives, other egg product alternatives are all over the place. Even ¼ to ½ cup of mashed banana has been known to take the place of a medium or large egg.

Fish (any vertebrate or finfish): Seafaring adventurers, ye are warned, there be things swimming in these depths. They're called fish allergies, and they're not fun. Here's a few fish-free things you can try as substitutions:

- **Tofu:** A firmer tofu can, ounce for ounce, replace fish relatively easily. There's even been tales of people soaking it with nori (sushi seaweed) for a more oceanic taste.
- **Gardein:** It's a ready-made product that does fairly well in place of many called-for fish in appropriate recipes.
- **Seitan:** No fins, no frills, no problem. It is wheat gluten, but there's a lot of versatility with this product. Seasoned right, it might not be fish, but it has a good texture when cooked similarly.
- **Vegetables:** Seems strange to suggest this, but eggplant can make for a good, softer whitefish alternative. (You could use carrot and parsnips even, for firmer textures.) Softened by a little pre-cooking or marinating, they're sponges for whatever flavors you like. They're kind of shaped like fish, too. Kind of.

Crustacean/Shellfish (Crawfish, Crab, Lobster, Shrimp, Oysters, Etc.)

Bards aren't always the best hunters, they're more… gatherers. While some wild onions might be fine, if they come back from a beach trip with a basket of things they picked off the rocks, it could mean a trip to a healer for them and their friends. What can be used instead? Try these:

- **Tofu:** Once again, tofu is the blank palate. Softer tofu can really do wonders with some acidity, oil, garlic, and herbs. They might not be clams or shrimp, but they taste good.

- **Mushrooms:** Dried oyster mushrooms, in particular, can be marinated in a light seaweed brine for a bit and develop great flavor. They can be used, gram for gram, ounce for ounce, for many shellfish and crustacean recipes! As long as the mushroom is light in color, buy 'em and give 'em a try.
- **Finfish:** Wait, didn't we just cover this? Some people that have crustacean/shellfish allergies do okay with regular fish. As is the rule, if in doubt, ask if you aren't sure of your friend's allergies (please!). Cod, tilapia, bass, snapper—any light-fleshed, light-tasting fish can usually replace shrimp, lobster, and crab in recipes.

Tree Nuts (walnuts, almonds, walnuts, pecans)

Ah, trees. If they're not magical and chatty, they're silent and love to offer things that might harm someone. Tree nut allergies exist in obvious and not so obvious places, so here are some alternatives:

- **Sunflower seeds:** Shelled/hulled roasted sunflower seeds can mostly be used with allergen concerns of this category. There are even sunflower seed butters out there that are really tasty, and can be used in place of other nut-butters.
- **Pumpkin seeds:** Roasted pumpkin seeds are delicious. Chop, grind, or break out the mortar and pestle. The outer shell can be a little tough, and a bit of steaming can loosen them up for varied usefulness.
- **Pepitas:** Are you seeing a trend? Seeds aren't nuts! Pepitas are a hull-less seed from a specific pumpkin variety. If you are lucky enough to live in an area with a store catering to the Hispanic population, you're sure to find them. They're so good, you might wanna use them as a substitution anyway.
- **Hard pretzels:** Odd as this may sound, they do well in place of a lot of nuts. Some of the peanut suggestions below may work, too!

Peanuts

Peanut allergies can be *very* severe. Some people can't even breathe the same air where peanuts or peanut products are frequently used. Be sure to let a person with a peanut allergy know even if any equipment you used has come into contact with peanut-related products. That aside, here are some alternatives:

- **Roasted edamame/soybeans:** Soy nuts, provided one doesn't have a soy allergy as well, can be used effectively for peanuts. Due to their lighter weight, it might be advisable to increase what the recipe asks for by 50 percent or so.
- **Pistachios:** They can, weight for weight, be a good substitution for those with a peanut allergy.
- **Chickpeas/garbanzo beans:** Roasted, they're super good. There are various easy recipes online

(whatever that is) to make a peanut or peanut butter-like substitution.
- **Sesame seeds and paste (also known as "tahini"):** These add a depth of flavor that's distinct, nutty, and tasty.

All this to say, nut concerns being stressful enough, if in doubt, just skip the nuts and seeds.

Wheat (including rye/triticale)

Wheat is everywhere in the modern world. Wheat allergies, like celiac, are another awful one. Nothing will take the pep out of a hero's step quite like a bit of gluten if they suffer from this disease. However, there are many alternatives in case of an allergy. Breadcrumbs, if needed, can be made from gluten-free bread; there is gluten-free beer, gluten-free noodles, and other products.

Like peanuts, if there's a wheat allergy, it's extremely difficult to make something gluten-free if your kitchen and equipment isn't already cleaned and set up to accommodate a wheat allergy. Not all are created equal, so the quest becomes: which is best? Please be careful, but here are some alternatives:

- **Gluten-free flour:** Seems obvious, sure! Many stores carry various quality flours that are designed to emulate real wheat flour. The best advice here is to do research not only for your recipe but ask anyone you may know with celiac what their favorite is. They'll know best!
- **Corn starch:** If you're just thickening a sauce or making a gravy or some other secondary need, corn starch is gluten-free and readily available.
- **Rice noodles and flour:** Much stickier when wet and occasionally hard to handle, rice flour and noodles can have certain applications that make them useful—noodles being one, of course. The flour is a safe alternative and good for baking when instructions are followed.
- **Almond flour:** If there's no tree-nut allergies, almond flour not a bad way to go. Makes a tasty roux and has a nice, nutty flavor.
- **Coconut flour:** As with other non-wheat flours, coconut flour is gluten-free and has many applications. It works well as a batter and is also good in sweeter things like breakfast foods and desserts.
- **Psyllium husk:** Here we go again! It's a great thickener if pulverized to a powder and it's a good source of fiber. It can be added to things like almond and coconut flour to really give some chew to certain baked goods.

Soybeans/Soy Nuts

All allergens are sneaky, but soy is one of the worst. It's a crop that's easy to grow worldwide, has significant nutrition per yield, and due to this, soy allergies are common. Besides tofu, edamame, and soy sauce, there are not many calls for the direct use for soy. But here are some alternatives in the event you need a substitute:

- **Balsamic vinegar:** Soy sauce has soy in it. Who knew? Vinegars overall are from fermented fruits, so this could be a good way to go. Add a bit of water to reduce acidity, and salt to taste.
- **Monosodium glutamate:** MSG got a bad name for itself due to some rather ignorant opinions some years ago about Chinese culture and cooking. Once made from seaweed, it now comes from sugarcane. Tomatoes are naturally high in MSG, as is cheese. This amino and glutamic acid is best known as the "umami" flavor that soy can be attributed to.
- **Coconut aminos:** There are many different varieties of aminos out there, but they all serve as a flavor-adding component. Some varieties do contain soy, so check carefully. The coconut amino variety is derived from tree-sap!
- **Mushrooms:** Dried mushrooms, chopped small, can taste even better than dried or roasted soybeans.
- **Lima beans:** Edamame alternative? Beans can work. If they're green, fresh, and tasty to you, they are still beans!

Fruits

By the numbers, kiwis, peaches, and apples are the most common fruits with concerns to food allergies. Ten percent of food allergies are from fruits! It may be tempting to cross less-hostile lands and sneak into an orchard and pick a few ripe ingredients, but not all travelers can enjoy these!

If you need to substitute these common ingredients, consider pears for apples, apricots or plums for peaches, and bananas for kiwis. They may not have the exact flavor/texture profile, but especially in baking, they won't significantly change moisture or pH levels. You will receive +1 intelligence for preparing with skins off the fruits, too. There are people who suffer with allergies to specific groups of fruits, like tropical fruits and those that are from more northerly climates. Sneaky berries and citrus, for example, can be in certain processed ingredients, so be careful! Melons are another one, which are in the cucurbit family, which also includes some vegetables! (See the notes on the vegetables below.) Best practice? Research the family groups of related fruits before making an assumption. Ask the adventurer who may have allergy concerns what they are safe and comfortable with.

One way to get tartness without the fruit or citrus component is lemongrass! A tea made from this herb goes a long way.

Vegetables

Whether grown on a stalk, in the ground, or on the vine, vegetables make up an important part of our health as well as our flavor profiles across the land!

Allium

Garlic, onions, shallot, chives, and leeks are all in the *allium* genus, a food gathered and cultivated worldwide for thousands of years. These plants, related to lilies, also are responsible for quite a few allergies and upset tummies. Whether it's discomfort for the eater (or those around them) or a trip to the healer, here's a few suggestions:

- **Skip them:** Many recipes do quite well simply omitting alliums altogether without too much of a flavor change.
- **Use herbs:** Thyme, sage, and tarragon are a few examples, used separately or together to taste, that can boost flavor without sacrificing the character of a dish. Laurel leaves—more commonly known as bay leaves—also work great in soups and stews. They're even more delicious when fresh!
- **Fennel bulbs:** While celery may be an obvious choice for some texture, there's a more adventurous choice: fennel bulbs! They do have a slight anise nose and flavor unless slow-cooked—however, they can be delicious!

Nightshade Plants

Tomatoes, peppers, eggplant, and potatoes are all in the nightshade family: any alchemist or potion maker will tell you that nightshades are not to be trifled with. These plants (not so much the fruits or tubers they produce) contain powerful alkaloids that can cause allergic reactions.

- **Tomato alternatives:** Try using red beets and a little vinegar for acidity and to get some color and thickness in a sauce or red fruits or berries. Another interesting substitution could be hibiscus or tamarind!
- **Pepper alternatives:** This is a tough one, because those sensitive to spice might appreciate leaving these out completely, yet there may also be someone with a food allergy that likes to turn up the heat. Black peppercorns and some goji berries mixed together or Szechuan peppercorns mixed with carrot could be an option.
- **Eggplant alternatives:** Sliced squashes or sweet potato can be used with some trial and error, but keep in mind these substitutes will require additional cooking and treatment beforehand to get that soft texture eggplant is known for!
- **Potato alternatives:** Many root vegetables are not nightshades. Sweet potato, celery root, turnips, rutabaga, and parsnips make fantastic substitutions across the dining table!

Other allergies to be aware of:

Squash, zucchini, and pumpkins are related to melons! The cucurbit family has a cute name, but if a person has a sensitivity or allergy to one, it's common for problems to cross into other members of this food family. Consider other tuber replacements listed above as an alternative.

Asparagus, corn, lettuces, turnips (and their relatives), mushrooms, anything in the brassica family (broccoli, cabbage, cauliflower, brussels sprouts) make up many, but not all, of the rest of the vegetable allergy concerns. We encourage readers to search information from reputable sources to find substitutes for these:

For anything we left out, unfortunately, there are not enough pages in this book. But fear not, adventurer, there's plenty of recipes in this book that you can use!

Sensitive Tummies

Gut health can be a challenge for some travelers. Certain conditions from irritable bowel syndrome, ulcerative colitis, and Crohn's can lead to flare-ups and embarrassing dining situations for people. For someone who may have also experienced gallbladder surgery, gastrointestinal procedures, and other gut concerns, the amount and type of fats, oils, fibers, sugars, and spices can make or break someone's meal at the local tavern. If you yourself are recently diagnosed, please refer to your doctor's or health practitioner's advice! If you know someone who may have these concerns, they will be able to best guide and educate you on their needs.

Diabetic Concerns

If you are new to a diabetic-friendly diet, please consult your nutritionist, physician, or doctor, as their professional healing spells, advice, and potions will be your best option. For those more familiar with diabetes, it is likely we cannot impart better information about substitutions than you already know! Cooking for someone else? Feel free to show them a recipe before cooking in this book to get their input.

Meat Products

Some adventurers and travelers, whether for ethical or religious reasons, may not be able to eat some of the ingredients listed above. There are plenty of meat substitutes available that are plentiful in other sources. All recipes in this book can be easily substituted with your favorite protein alternative. Mix and match to your heart's content!

Herbs & Spices

Once in a while, the apothecary, market, or bazaar may be out of an ingredient. Perhaps you don't like certain flavors or you may be sensitive to spices. Fret not, wary adventurer, there are alternatives you can use instead! Here's a few things to consider:

- **Quality of Herbs & Spices**: If it's been a while since you've opened up a particular ingredient on your shelf, consider checking the date. Any dried ingredient is most potent up to a year from date of purchase and diminishes by as much as 20 percent per year after. If you're not getting results from measured ingredients, they may need to be replaced. This is especially true if they are pre-ground. Try buying certain things in smaller quantities to save waste and money!

- **Whole vs. Pre-Ground:** Some herbs and spices come processed; others can be whole leaves and seeds! The more they are broken down initially and stored, the faster they lose their flavor, so go whole if you can! There's nothing more satisfying than grabbing a mortar and pestle and letting out your inner warrior by grinding them yourself.
- **Fresh vs. Dried:** Some of you may have magical gardens either on a window ledge or even in a plot of land to call your own! Of course, put them to use! The equivalency of freshly picked herbs is 1 tablespoon vs. 1 teaspoon of a dried ingredient.
- **"Sweet" Spices:** Allspice, cinnamon, cloves, nutmeg, and mace tend to have similar spirit when in use, especially in various baked goods. All of these distinct spices have a pungent flavor that can be substituted for each other. Don't be afraid to measure with your heart, but start small and taste as you go!
- **"Less-Sweet" Spices:** Cardamom, turmeric, coriander, and even ginger lean toward a slightly warmer/savory flavor. They can easily pair with sweet, savory, and umami flavors. Fennel seed and star anise can have a more licorice or even slight vanilla undertone to them with an adept hand. Cumin is famous for adding a "meatier" flavor if used very sparingly and becomes very distinct—even sour—if used in excess. Cardamom is a favorite for adding a smoke-like, earthy flavor.
- **"Spicy" Spices:** As one would imagine, black pepper, white pepper, and red pepper can really add a kick faster than a centaur in a tavern brawl. Sometimes omitting these spares the mouths and tummies of your guests. Fortunately, things like sweet or smoked paprika or even annatto (achiote) can be used to replace various peppers! Be sure there isn't someone with a capsicum allergy at your table.
- **"Sweet" Herbs:** Mint, basil, and tarragon are often the main "sweeter" herbs available. Tarragon has a slight anise hint while basil tends to have a light freshness and mint has a coolness. They can be experimented with if one or the other is not available or not palatable.
- **"Savory" Herbs:** Herbs are wonderful in part because of their milder attitude and agreeable flexibility. Even the "sweet" herbs like mint, basil, and tarragon can find a home alongside the "savory" herbs: sage, thyme, marjoram, bay (laurel) leaf, oregano, and rosemary. Many of these herbs are related in nature, too. For example, bay leaf can be substituted with thyme. Oregano for basil or rosemary, or in any combination you like. Cilantro sometimes tastes soapy to

people so a perfect substitution is Italian parsley. It has a wonderful fresh flavor that's the perfect replacement.

- **Saffron:** Delicately and painstakingly harvested from the crocus flower, it's *very* expensive. An alternative is "safflower," from the daisy family, that can add nearly the same color but doesn't add the flavor... or the cost.

Salt

Salt is salt, right? An alchemist might say sodium chloride is all the same, and they'd be correct. Salt, however, is a generic term, and their trace minerals give them distinct flavors. There are many different colors and varieties. Table salt can contain iodine and has fine granules. There's also smoked salt, which is for finishing a dish. Kosher salt is a staple of most professional kitchens. It's cheap and dissolves easily. Sometimes, however, a low-salt diet is needed.

- **Monosodium Glutamate/MSG:** Speaking of salt, MSG is a salt, too! It gives food a lovely umami flavor as mentioned in the allergy section and makes a great substitute for salt. Unless one has a specific reason for not using it, MSG is a great thing to keep around, with or without salt concerns.

- **Potassium Chloride:** While not quite a salt, it has salty properties. Whether by itself or in a product mixed with sodium chloride, it can be used in place of regular salt.

In closing, the purpose of this grand, gastronomical writ is not to be an exhaustive list of all the possible substitutions for every scenario. Whether you are looking at the subject through the lens of medicine, health, lifestyle, allergies, or even religious observation, there are myriad books, papers, and nuanced websites with suggestions that will provide more detailed information.

Just remember, when in doubt, experiment! If you're an old sage with the hob or have never seen a whisk in your life, some final advice and wishes for you:

- Keep your knives sharp
- Keep a spoon handy
- Always have two towels
- Work clean
- *Mise en place* (prep your ingredients)

It's about family, friends, full bellies, and fun—no matter where your adventure takes you.

—Kyle Weiss

Smokey Copper Spice Blend

This spice blend is something my papa came up with and we put it on everything! Steak, chicken, fish. My papa says he first tried it on grilled griffin! I wonder if I will get to try griffin?

SERVES 1-2, DEPENDING ON MEAL

Prep time: 5-10 minutes

INGREDIENTS

- 3 tablespoons paprika
- 1 teaspoon cayenne (double, triple, or more for a spicier rub!)
- 1 tablespoon garlic powder
- 2 teaspoons whole coffee beans
- 2 teaspoons whole black peppercorns
- 2 teaspoons white pepper (optional)
- 2 teaspoons basil
- 2 teaspoons oregano
- 2 teaspoons rosemary
- 1 tablespoon onion powder
- 1 teaspoon ground mustard
- 2 teaspoons coriander
- 3 tablespoons salt
- ½ cup dark brown sugar

INSTRUCTIONS

1. Put all your spices—except for the salt and brown sugar—into a coffee grinder, spice blender, or mortar and pestle. Grind it all up until a fine powder is formed. (If you don't have whole spices, you can use ground ones instead!)

2. Combine your mix with the salt and brown sugar, and store in an air-tight container until ready for use.

This works great on beef, pork, chicken, and even fish! I especially like using it for ribs. For optimal flavor, rub down your meat of choice using mustard, before generously applying your BBQ rub. The mustard will help tenderize your meat *and* help the seasoning stick to it too! (I promise it doesn't taste like mustard either!)

Whether you are roasting, smoking, or grilling, this seasoning will bring a world of flavor to whatever you cook with it!

Cyclops Bane

This is an old remedy Mama Copper used on her adventure. Its basically just a chili oil but apparently cyclopes <u>hate</u> the stuff!

Cook time: 5 minutes

Ingredients

- 3 tablespoons fresh Thai chili peppers, minced
- 2–3 tablespoons minced garlic
- ½ cup neutral oil (avocado, canola, etc.)

CAUTION: Be very, VERY careful while doing this. The oil is extremely hot. To avoid accidents, use a large, heat-safe bowl and make sure you pour very slowly. If you pour too fast, the oil could splash up and burn you. Hold the pan away from your body as you pour.

Instructions

1. First, place your chili peppers and garlic into a large, heat-safe bowl.
2. Place your oil in a medium-sized sauce pan. Heat your oil over medium-high heat until it is screaming hot. This should take 2 to 3 minutes at most. Your oil will become shiny and may begin to start smoking.
3. Once your oil is fully heated, remove your pan and carefully pour over your peppers very slowly, holding the pan far away from you as you pour.
4. Let your chili oil cool and store in the fridge.

How to Perfectly Roast Garlic

Prep time: 5 minutes | Cook time: 2 hours

Ingredients

Full head of garlic
½ tablespoon olive oil

Instructions

1. Snip or slice the tip off your bulb of garlic, and remember, *just the tip*! (You don't need to slice off a lot here, just enough to get the olive oil into the garlic.)

2. Place the garlic on a sheet of foil big enough to fully wrap it up. Pour your olive oil directly over the top where you trimmed the garlic. You will have some overflow, but that's ok!

3. Wrap the garlic tightly in your foil. Repeat all of the above steps for however much garlic you plan on roasting… so, if you're anything like me, it's a *lot*! Don't forget you can always make extra and freeze the leftovers!

4. Place all of your garlic into an oven-safe dish and put it in your cold oven. I know this sounds weird, just trust me!

5. Now turn on the oven to 350°F with your garlic babies inside! Once the oven has fully heated, start a timer for 1 hour.

6. After your timer has gone off, turn off the oven, but leave the garlic inside for at least 30 minutes, preferably an hour. This is where the magic happens!

7. Carefully remove your garlic from the oven and unwrap them from their foil blankies. Let them fully cool before squeezing the soft, caramelized garlic from its shell. And for those who refuse to let it cool all the way (me), you can use a pair of tongs to safely squeeze the garlic from the husk. Just be careful not to burn yourself! (Beware: The garlic is very sticky and will stick to your hands during the squeezing process.)

> If you just want to buy pre-peeled garlic cloves to roast, you can use this same method by placing the cloves with oil in a foil boat, just make sure to check them every 30 minutes to make sure they're not burning.

Roasted Garlic Butter

Prep time: 5-10 minutes

Ingredients

1 tablespoon fresh rosemary
1 tablespoon fresh thyme
1 tablespoon fresh parsley
1 cup softened salted butter
1–3 bulbs roasted garlic (see page 15)
Salt and pepper, to taste

Instructions

1. Make sure all of your fresh herbs are finely chopped then mix them together.

2. Add your softened butter and roasted garlic to your herbs. Gently mix until all of the herbs and roasted garlic are evenly distributed in the softened salted butter.

3. Taste your roasted garlic butter and add salt or pepper as needed. This is all up to personal preference, so go with your heart here!

4. Store in the fridge for up to 2 weeks! For easiest use, you can shape your butter into a log using some plastic wrap.

Garlic Confit

Prep time: 5 minutes | Cook time: 1-3 hours

··········· INGREDIENTS ···········

- Whole peeled garlic cloves (as many as you want to make)
- Olive oil (enough to cover your garlic)
- Herbs/peppers (optional)

INSTRUCTIONS

1. Place all of your garlic cloves in an oven-safe dish. You can use as much garlic as you want to prepare, you just need to have enough oil to fully cover all of your garlic.
2. Add in your olive oil until your garlic is fully covered.
3. Add any herbs or flavor additives you want at this point. I typically use whatever herb is in abundance from the garden, but you can also add spicy peppers to give it a little kick.
4. Bake your garlic in a 225°F oven for 1 to 3 hours, just until the garlic is golden brown and soft.
5. Remove from the oven and let cool for at least 1 hour.
6. Store the olive oil and garlic together in airtight containers. This will last 2 weeks in your fridge or longer frozen.

How to Butterfly

Prep time: 10-15 minutes

Instructions

Chicken Breast:
1. Place your chicken breast flat on a cutting board.
2. Holding your knife parallel to the cutting board carefully, start cutting the chicken horizontally through your chicken breast, making sure not to fully cut through to the opposite side.
3. If done correctly, you should end up with one large, thin piece of chicken.

Pork Roast:
1. There will be a smooth top side to your pork roast. Place your pork facing with the smooth side up on a cutting board.
2. Starting from one side, cut about 1 inch into the pork. Making small slices, filet the pork until about 1 inch away from the opposite side of the roast.
3. From there, flip the pork open like a book and repeat the same process, starting from where you previously cut. Once finished, it should lay out to be one long flat piece of meat.

Gluten-Free Flour Blend

Prep time: 5-10 minutes

Ingredients

3 parts brown rice flour
3 parts cornstarch
2 parts soy flour
1 part masa harina

Instructions

1. This one's easy! Just combine all of your ingredients in a large bowl, transfer to a container, and store in the freezer!

CHAPTER TWO
Family Traditions

Hey Journal!

    Now that that's out of the way, let me explain myself a little more. Food has always been important for us CopperSpoons. I mean, look, we even have the word "spoon" in our name! (Wait, and "copper," too, I guess . . . but that's not very foodsy.)

    My family has lived in the quiet village of Honeystar for generations upon generations. This little halfling village's name is what I imagine you'd find under the definition of the word "home." I really couldn't be more grateful that my ancestors found such a beautiful place for us to settle. Honeystar has everything that anyone could ever need: a loving community, fruitful harvests, a river of fresh water, and the Ebon Forest, which surrounds the village like it's embracing it in a great big hug.

    I grew up in a family full of chefs, cooks, bakers, and everything in between. Food is such an important thing to our family—so important, in fact, that it's deeply ingrained in all of our traditions. My upcoming journey is an excellent example of this, actually! After a certain age, members of the CopperSpoon family head out in the world all on their own to fill up their cookbooks with recipes and bring new knowledge back to the rest of the family. Cool, right?

    Whoever sets out on their big journey gets to bring the family's ancient, legendary copper spoon with them, too. It's not just any spoon, though—it's enchanted! You can turn that thing into any utensil you could ever need. It even cleans itself when you're all done!

    Not only that, but we have a big stash of spices at home that I'll have access to all throughout my adventure! That's right, no matter how far away from home I am, I'll always be able to get my hands on the family's BBQ seasoning or some delicious basil leaves.

    Huh? How is that even possible? Well, my mom gave me a magical little pouch called the pantry pouch. All I have to do is reach inside of it, think of the spice I need, and then there it'll be!

    Oh! Speaking of spices, it's another tradition at home for everyone to check the spice stash each night and see what the most recent adventurer's using. And this time, they'll be looking to see what <u>I'm</u> using! Sorry I keep mentioning the adventure, but I'm <u>so</u> excited!

And . . . honestly, so nervous, too. I'm thrilled to explore the world, but I've never been away from my family for very long. I'm really gonna miss them. . . .

I know, I know, I'm twenty now and that's _way_ too old to get homesick. I can always write a letter or head home if I really need to. I guess what I'm trying to say is that it'll be strange to be out in the wide world without them by my side.

That's one thing that's really great about food, though, isn't it? With the right ingredients, and some happy memories, you can feel close to your loved ones with the taste of just one warm, nostalgic meal! I have a few classic CopperSpoon recipes I'm going to bring along with me for that very reason. Here they are!

Copper Cockatrice Caprese

Papa Copper came up with this one on his adventures! This was my favorite, not only because of the delicious recipe but because of the story that came along with it. Papa Copper has always been a big fisherman so imagine his surprise when a fishing adventure turned into a battle with a half serpent dragon, half rooster! This recipe was the aftermath of his victory! We don't have many cockatrice around here so we normally just use chicken.

Makes 4 Sandwiches

Prep time: 15 minutes | Cook time: 15-20 minutes

Ingredients

- 4 chicken breasts (or cockatrice if you can get your hands on some!)
- Salt
- Pepper
- Garlic powder
- Onion powder
- Paprika
- 1 tablespoon olive oil
- 2 tomatoes
- 1 (16-oz) package fresh mozzarella
- ½ cup fresh basil
- ½ cup mayonnaise
- ¼ cup balsamic vinegar
- 4 ciabatta bread rolls

Instructions

1. You are going to start by butterflying your chicken. Once butterflied, slice down the middle to make two even pieces (see page 18).

2. Once all your chicken is cut, season to taste with salt, pepper, garlic powder, onion powder, and paprika.

3. Heat a large skillet or cast iron over medium-high heat with your olive oil. Alternatively, you can smoke/grill these if you prefer that cooking method.

4. Once the pan is searing hot, add in your chicken. Cook until golden brown, about 5 to 7 minutes on each side.

5. While your chicken is cooking, slice your tomatoes, mozzarella (if desired), and basil. For the basil, stack a pile of leaves on top of each other and roll up for easy slicing.

6. Mix your mayonnaise, balsamic, and a pinch of salt and pepper to make your sauce. Taste this as you go. If you like a super vinegar-y punch, add extra vinegar. If it's *too* vinegar-y, just add a little more mayonnaise.

7. Once the chicken is fully browned, add 1 to 2 slices of your mozzarella. Cover your pan with a lid or place in a 350°F oven. Leave until your cheese is fully melted and the chicken has reached an internal temperature of 165°F. (If you're on a grill, just close the lid and let the cheese melt.)

8. Toast your ciabatta. This step is optional, but I think it makes the sandwich way better!

9. To assemble, I recommend putting the balsamic mayonnaise on both sides of your bread. Add 1 to 2 pieces of chicken and tomato (with an optional pinch of salt and pepper on top), then a sprinkle of your sliced basil.

10. Enjoy! Be sure to bring your napkins for this one—it's a messy sandwich, but it's so worth it.

Not Your Papa's Bread Rolls

Papa Copper isn't much of a baker, so I came up with this recipe to use for his sandwiches!

MAKES 4 SANDWICH ROLLS

Prep time: 2½–3½ hours | Cook time 20 minutes

Ingredients

- 1¼ teaspoons active dry yeast
- 1 cup warm water
- 2⅓ cups bread flour (can substitute with all-purpose or high-gluten flour)
- 1 teaspoon salt

Instructions

1. Add your yeast to warm water. Mix and set aside to let the yeast bloom. Your water should be warmer than room temperature, but not hot.
2. In a large bowl, mix your flour and salt together.
3. Once the yeast mixture has rested for 5 minutes and bloomed, add to your flour and start mixing until there are no dry spots left in your dough. You may need to get in there with your hands to fully mix it. This dough is a bit on the wet side, so don't be afraid to add some flour to your hands.
4. Leave your dough in the bowl, but keep it covered with plastic wrap or a clean dish towel. Leave at room temperature for 45 minutes to 1 hour to rise.
5. After you have let your dough rise for at least 45 minutes, fold the dough in on itself. It really helps to get a little bit of water on your hands to avoid the dough sticking to your fingers. Starting on one side, grab the edge of your dough ball and stretch it out as much as you can without ripping it. Then, fold it into the middle of the dough ball. Repeat this process for all 4 sides of your dough.
6. Re-cover your dough and rest for another 30 minutes. Repeat this process 2 to 3 more times until your dough has doubled in size.
7. Place an oven-safe baking dish filled with 2 cups of water on the bottom rack of your oven, and preheat to 420°F. This is going to fill your oven

with steam as the water heats, so be aware and very careful as you open and close your oven.

8. Lightly flour a large surface and place your dough ball on it seam-side down, making sure that only one side of the dough touches the floured surface.

9. Divide your dough into 4 even pieces using a pastry cutter or sharp knife. Be sure to flour whatever you use because the dough will stick to it.

10. To shape your rolls, gently fold the sticky side of your dough pieces into each other. Hold the floured side of the dough in the palm of your non-dominant hand. Being very gentle as to not pop any air bubbles in the dough, gently fold in each corner until a loose oval shape forms. Place seam-side down on a parchment-lined baking sheet. They should be about 1 inch thick once you are finished.

11. Once the oven is fully preheated, place your baking sheet on the middle rack above the water basin. Using a spray bottle (or even by just flicking some water from your hands), spritz the tops of the rolls right before you close the oven. You don't need a lot here, just enough to add some moisture to the dough.

12. Bake for 20 minutes, then let your rolls cool for a bit. Make sure to let the pan of water inside the oven cool before you try taking it out. It will be very hot!

13. Enjoy! This is the perfect bread for sandwiches, or even just to eat cheese with!

Nana's No-Wheat Bread (Gluten-Free)

My nana is <u>the best</u> baker. Her adventures took her to the far corners of the Scovterra Desert where wheat is in low supply. No problem for Nana though! She used her expert baking skills to create delicious baked goods without using any flour at all! What. A. <u>Legend!</u>

Makes 1 loaf

Prep time: 1½ hours | Cook time: 1 hour

Ingredients

- 1½ cups warm water
- 1 tablespoon sugar
- 1 tablespoon yeast
- 2½ cup Gluten-Free Flour Blend (see page 19)
- 2 teaspoons xanthan gum
- 1 teaspoon salt
- 3 eggs
- 1 teaspoon apple cider vinegar
- 1½ tablespoons olive oil

Instructions

1. Combine your warm water, sugar, and yeast in a small bowl. Let sit to get frothy while you mix your other ingredients.
2. Combine your flour, xanthan gum, and salt in a large bowl and mix well.
3. In a third bowl, whisk your eggs, vinegar, and oil until the eggs are a bit frothy.
4. Combine both of your liquid mixes with your dry ingredients. Mix together until a smooth batter-like dough forms. It will not look like a regular bread dough, but this is normal! Mix your dough for 4 minutes until it's nice and smooth.
5. Scoop your dough into a greased loaf pan and let rise until it is about ½ inch away from the top of the pan. This should take about 30 to 60 minutes.
6. Bake at 375°F for 50 to 60 minutes until fully baked. The loaf should look golden brown and not sink or bow when you tap the top.

Lemony Toadstools with Salty Cheese

My older sister came home with this recipe from a group of forest-dwelling fairies. She told me how they used their nature magic to grow a perfect cirle of mushrooms before her very eyes. As any logical person would, she plucked them right then and there to make this recipe! It's my absolute favorite way to eat mushrooms now!

MAKES 1–2 SERVINGS

Prep time: 20–30 minutes | Cook time: 10–15 minutes

Ingredients

- 1 pound button mushrooms
- 4–5 cloves garlic
- 1 lemon
- Baguette
- Olive oil
- Salt and pepper
- 6 tablespoons butter
- Fresh rosemary and thyme
- ¼–½ cup freshly grated Parmesan cheese

Instructions

1. Using a damp paper towel, gently wipe any dirt off of your mushrooms. Once they are fully cleaned, halve and quarter your mushrooms so they are bite-sized pieces.
2. Crush and peel your cloves of garlic, setting one aside for later.
3. Cut your lemon in half and set aside.
4. Thinly slice your baguette. Drizzle the slices with some olive oil, salt, and pepper.
5. Heat a large cast iron or non-stick skillet over medium heat. Add a medium glug of olive oil then toast your bread in the pan for 1 to 2 minutes per side or until golden brown.
6. Once you remove your bread from the pan, immediately take your extra clove of garlic and rub it directly on the warm toasted bread.
7. Add your butter to the hot pan and melt completely.

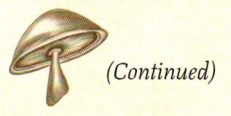

(Continued)

8. Once your butter is fully melted, add in your crushed garlic and fresh herbs. Sauté garlic and herbs for 2 to 3 minutes or until the garlic and butter starts to turn a golden brown.

9. Add in all of your mushrooms. Sauté until they start becoming soft and juicy, about 4 to 7 minutes.

10. Remove the sprigs of your fresh herbs and add in juice of one half lemon. At this point, you'll want to taste a mushroom and add salt, pepper, and/or extra lemon juice to your taste preference.

11. Turn off the heat and grate in your cheese. Mix thoroughly before serving.

12. Arm yourself with some of your toasted bread for scooping and enjoy! This is a great appetizer to share with a friend or the perfect meal for one.

Nana T's Copper-Pop

Did I say Nana was the best baker? Well, she's the best popcorn maker, too! She developed this recipe upon visiting three farmers in the middle of a generational rivalry. One grew corn, another peanuts, and the third kept honey bees. All with one recipe she ended a century-long feud <u>and</u> created a very successful popcorn business along the way!

Makes 8 servings

Prep time: 5-10 minutes | Cook time: 5-10 minutes

Ingredients

- 10 tablespoons unpopped popcorn (about 2 bags)
- ½ cup peanut butter
- ½ cup honey
- ½ cup sugar

Instructions

1. Pop your popcorn. If you are using loose kernels, add about 1 tablespoon of oil and 2 tablespoons of butter to the bottom of a large pan. Add in all of your kernels and cover with a lid. Heat your popcorn over medium heat until your popcorn is fully popped, shaking your pan every once in a while. If you're up to the task, it might be worth spending some time picking out the kernels before pouring in the peanut butter mixture.

2. Heat a small saucepan over medium heat with your peanut butter, honey, and sugar.

3. Bring to a boil and cook for about 5 minutes at a boil, stirring constantly.

4. Once sugar has dissolved and the peanut butter mix has been heated, pour evenly over your popcorn.

5. Stir in the peanut butter mix carefully—it's very hot.

6. Enjoy, but be careful when eating! Hard kernels may stick to the popcorn pieces and hurt your teeth if accidentally bitten down on—I've done that *a lot*—not fun!

Grammy Linda's Spoon Tacos

Every single time we would go over to the grandparent's house it was a requirement that we had spoon tacos. Of course, everybody would get into the kitchen to help. One of us got to brown the ground beef, another crushed the chips, and one lucky sibling got the honor of making the guacamole! Grammy Linda never told me which adventure she learned this on, only that if the secret gnome society every found out she swiped their recipe the whole town would be in <u>big</u> trouble.

MAKES 4-6 SERVINGS

Prep time: 15-20 minutes | Cook time: 10-20 minutes

Ingredients

- 1 pound ground beef
- 1 (16-oz) can kidney beans
- Salt, to taste
- Pepper, to taste
- Garlic powder, to taste
- Onion powder, to taste
- 2-3 handfuls tortilla chips
- ½ cup sour cream
- 1-2 heads of lettuce
- 1-2 tomatoes
- ½-1 cup shredded cheddar cheese
- Chips and guacamole (optional)

Instructions

1. In a large pan, cook your ground beef over high heat. The meat will release some juices, so make sure to cook your beef until all of that liquid has evaporated.

2. Add your beans and a hefty amount of salt, pepper, garlic powder, and onion powder to your ground beef. Cook until your beans are fully heated through.

3. Put your ground beef and bean mix into a large oven-safe dish.

4. Crush up your chips and layer over the beef and beans.

5. Chop up your lettuce and tomatoes and spread it evenly over your chip layer.

6. Heat your sour cream until it's just runny and spread over your lettuce and tomato.

7. Top with your shredded cheddar and broil for 4 to 5 minutes until your cheese is just melted.

8. Serve with some guacamole and enjoy!

CHAPTER THREE
First Taste of the World

Journal!

I did it, I <u>finally</u> did it! I've left home and set off on my great adventure! Where am I going? Well, I've decided to make my way south-west to the Violet Bastion. It's the biggest city on the whole continent! I'm absolutely positive that this will be an excellent place to soak up a bunch of inspiration and knowledge for my recipes. My family's gonna be so proud.

I don't want to get too far ahead of myself, though—it's important to focus on where I am right now so I can write down every single detail. Hmm . . . where to begin? What do I see? What do I feel?

Well, for starters, I'm technically still in the Ebon Woods—but I'm hours and hours away from Honeystar, so don't worry about me chickening out. Things have actually been pretty great so far! I've managed to do some sightseeing, foraged some of my first herbs to add to my travel ingredient list, and I've found a beautiful place to set up camp. It's an incredible little clearing that's filled with flowers that glow golden under the moonlight! I love it here! Love it, love it, love it!

Yay . . .

Okay, <u>fine</u>. I'm a little lonely.

I keep finding myself turning over my shoulder to talk to somebody, but of course there's no one there—all I ever see is the forest. It's a little embarrassing, but luckily there's no one here to see it happen. Well, except for the forest animals, of course. Hey, maybe I'll make friends with a deer or a bunch of little chipmunks. Imagine if I befriended a cranky old badger or some type of forest spirit? That would be so cool.

Anyway, that's enough of that. Tonight I'm gonna treat myself to the hen and hearth stew that my mom sent along with me. It's the perfect way to end a perfect day. I'm so excited about tomorrow that I don't think I'll be able to get a wink of sleep!

Hen and Hearth Stew

Have you ever chased down a chicken before? I have! Me and my cousin used to compete to see who could catch the most chickens in our neighbor's yard. My cousin even told me about a chicken who roams the woods that is twenty feet tall and weighs eight hundred pounds! I wonder if I will find the elusive twenty-foot tall chicken on my travels?

MAKES 4-6 SERVINGS

Prep time: 15-20 minutes | Cook time: 1-1½ hours

Ingredients

Soup Base:
- 1 medium yellow onion (optional)
- 2 medium-large carrots (optional)
- 2–4 stalks celery (optional)
- 5 cloves fresh garlic
- 1 teaspoon fresh thyme
- 2 tablespoons butter
- 2 tablespoons olive oil
- 1 teaspoon salt
- 1 teaspoon pepper
- 5 tablespoons flour
- 1 pound shredded chicken
- 1 can evaporated milk
- 4 cups chicken broth
- 2 bay leaves

Dumplings:
- 1½ cups flour
- ½ tablespoon baking powder
- ½ teaspoon salt
- 4 tablespoons cold butter
- ⅔ cup milk

Instructions

1. First, prep all of your ingredients. Dice up your onion, carrots, and celery into small pieces; and mince your garlic and thyme.

2. Heat a large Dutch oven or pot over medium-high heat with your butter and olive oil. Add in all your veggies and garlic. Sauté until translucent.

3. Once your veggies are fully cooked, add in your thyme, salt, pepper, and flour. Cook for 2 to 3 minutes, stirring constantly so the flour doesn't burn.

4. Add in all of your chicken and mix into the veggies, making sure it's fully coated in the flour.

5. Slowly pour in your evaporated milk and chicken broth, making sure to

(Continued)

mix thoroughly. Bring to a boil and let thicken for 3 to 5 minutes.

6. Reduce heat to low and add in your bay leaves. Cover and let simmer for 20 to 30 minutes while you get your dumplings ready.

7. In a large bowl, mix together your flour, baking powder, and salt.

8. Cut your butter into small cubes and add to your flour. Using a pastry cutter, 2 knives, or your fingers, start cutting your butter into the flour mixture. The butter will flake into smaller and small pieces over time, giving your flour mix a crumbly, sand-like consistency.

9. Add in your milk and mix until there are no more dry spots of flour left.

10. Remove bay leaves. With a large spoon, scoop about a tablespoon's worth of dough into your soup at a time. Do this until all of your dough has been dropped. Cover the pot once again with a lid and let cook for 15 to 20 minutes until the dumplings are fully cooked.

11. Enjoy!

CHAPTER FOUR
A CopperSpoon Quest

Dear Journal,

 Wow . . . I think I might have been a world-renowned explorer in a past life, because I made it to the Violet Bastion like a pro!
 It's so gorgeous. I was always told that buildings could be built taller than trees, but I never believed it until now. Huge towers scatter across the city, dwarfing smaller buildings. The streets are even decorated with lush purple and gold banners, embroidered with the symbol of the crown.
 There are loads of shops filled with everything you can imagine—I passed through so many food markets as I was browsing through the city that I could barely keep up with all the different smells. My favorite was freshly baked bread, of course, but I could also smell new exotic spices that I've never experienced before. I can't wait to actually discover them all.
 Speaking of new experiences, none of this compared to my awe at the sheer amount of people I got to see. Man, everywhere I turned there were hundreds, thousands, maybe even <u>millions</u> of pedestrians out and about—<u>waaaay</u> more than I've ever seen in Honeystar, that's for sure!
 The most interesting part is that everyone here is so unique—and I really mean it! I saw a large sweaty man with green skin at the butchers, and then there was a group of beautiful cat-ladies wandering through a fashion district. I even saw a giant minotaur carrying a huge load of goods into a shop! He almost stepped on me because he couldn't see over the boxes in his arms.
 Anyway, I love the Violet Bastion so far. I want to stop everywhere and see everything! I actually almost got a little overwhelmed when I first

stepped into the city, but I've found myself a nice inn to stay at called The Pampered Pig.

Now that I'm nice and settled I've figured out exactly what I'm gonna do with my time here. There's no shortage of taverns in a city like this and the realization has inspired me to start my very first quest: I'm gonna visit <u>all</u> of them.

Yup! <u>Every.</u> <u>Single.</u> <u>One.</u>

I've got my Journal, and my taste buds, and I'm ready to start making my contribution to the CopperSpoon legacy! I've already made a dent in the list, actually. I've been able to deconstruct and document the ingredients of some of the most delicious meals I've had in the Violet Bastion! This is how adventuring works . . . right?

Ole Bessy's Legacy

First stop, The Scorching Boar. The menu wasn't huge, but they really made up for it with flavor! I talked to the chef, and they're just the sweetest little lizard-person I've ever met—and the very first, too! I'll definitely have to make their beef pot-pie recipe for Grammy Linda when I get home.

Makes 6–8 Servings

Prep time: 15-20 minutes | Cook time: 1-5 hours

Ingredients

- 3 heads garlic + 2 cloves
- 5 medium-small Yukon gold or red potatoes
- 3 carrots
- 1 (8-oz) package button mushrooms
- 1 large onion
- 2 pounds stew beef
- 3 tablespoons flour
- Salt and pepper
- 2 tablespoons olive oil
- ½ tablespoon paprika
- 1 teaspoon Italian seasoning
- 1 cup Guinness or red wine (can replace with black tea or beef broth)
- 2–3 cups beef broth
- Rosemary
- Sage
- Thyme
- 2 bay leaves
- Puff pastry (2 small sheets or 1 large one)
- 2 eggs

Instructions

1. Prep all of your ingredients. Roast your 3 heads of garlic (see page 15), crush the extra 2 cloves, chop up your potatoes, carrots, mushrooms, and onion into bite-sized pieces, and chunk your stew beef into 1-inch cubes if needed.

2. In a large bowl, coat your stew beef in your flour and a big pinch of salt and pepper.

3. Heat your oil in a large oven-safe cast iron pan or skillet over high heat until it's screaming hot. Note: This will be the pan you cook your stew in, so if you don't have a pan large enough to fit all your ingredients, use a large Dutch oven or pot instead.

(Continued)

4. Brown your stew beef in batches. You don't want to overcrowd the pan, so make sure when you add your beef it has some space between each piece. Once your beef has some nice brown marks, remove it from the pan and set aside.

5. Add the crushed garlic, onions, and carrots into your pan. Sauté them until your onions are nice and translucent, making sure to scrape up any stuck-on beef bits from the bottom of the pan while you do so.

6. Once your onions are cooked, add your potatoes, paprika, Italian seasonings, and a pinch of salt and pepper.

7. Make sure everything is nicely coated in the seasoning before adding your stew beef and Guinness. Once again, make sure you scrape up any bits stuck on the bottom of the pan.

8. Add in 2 cups of your beef broth. It is ok if not everything is fully covered with liquid at this point.

9. Add your rosemary, sage, thyme, and bay leaves to the top of your stew, and then cover with a lid. Reduce the heat to a medium-low and let cook anywhere between 1 to 4 hours. The longer you let it cook, the softer and more tender everything will get. Make sure to stir your stew occasionally. If it looks like it is losing liquid or getting too thick, just add in some extra beef broth or water to thin it out and continue to cook it.

10. When you are just about ready to serve, start preheating your oven to 400°F.

11. On a large, lightly floured work surface, fold out your puff pastry. You want to make sure it's going to be big enough to cover your pan or whatever baking dish you are using. If your sheet is too small, you can roll it out with a rolling pin to fit the right size. My pack of puff pastry had 2 sheets that I combined and rolled into 1 large piece about ¼ to ⅛ inch thick.

12. Right before you top your stew with the puff pastry, add in your mushrooms until fully combined and remove your bay leaves and leftover fresh herbs.

13. Top your stew off with your puffed pastry. If you're using an oven-safe pan you can just keep it in the pan. If you are using a pot, transfer your stew to a large baking dish first.

14. Beat your eggs together in a small bowl and lightly brush it over your puffed pastry. Cut 2 small ventilation holes in the center of your pie and bake for about 15 minutes or until the crust is nice and golden brown and the stew filling is bubbling.

15. Let cool for 15 minutes if possible, and enjoy!

MOOOOOO

Forest Fromage Soup

I had the most fabulous time at The Fourth Moon Bar! There was a bunch of people, a bard singing a jaunty melody while playing on their lute, and a fight even broke out! The barkeep didn't seem too happy about that last part, but I was having a <u>great</u> time! Their food was kind of bland, but with a little tweaking I think I've made their signature soup even better.

Makes 6-8 Servings

Prep time: 10-15 minutes | Cook time: 40-60 minutes

Ingredients

- 3 heads roasted garlic
- 1 large onion
- 1 tablespoon rosemary
- 1 tablespoon thyme
- ¼ teaspoon coriander
- 2 heads broccoli
- 1 pound bacon
- 1 teaspoon salt
- 1 teaspoon pepper
- ½ teaspoon paprika
- 4 cups chicken broth
- 2 bay leaves
- 1 pint heavy whipping cream
- ¼ cup corn starch (or flour)
- 1-2 cups shredded cheddar cheese

Instructions

1. To start, prep all of your ingredients. Get your garlic roasting first, dice your onion, mince your fresh herbs, chop your broccoli, and cut your bacon into bite-sized pieces.

2. Heat a 5-quart pot (or larger) over medium-high heat and add in your bacon. Cook until nice and crispy. Once fully cooked, remove from the pan and drain on some paper-towels.

3. Drain about half of the bacon grease from your pot. Once drained, add all of your onions and sauté until translucent. This should take 5 to 10 minutes.

4. Once the onions are fully cooked, add all of your broccoli and all of your seasonings, excluding the bay leaves. Toss everything together and cook for 2 to 3 minutes.

5. Add in your broth and bay leaves. Bring to a boil.

6. Once boiling, reduce the heat to medium-low and cover with a lid. Cook for at least 30 minutes or until broccoli is nice and soft.

7. In a medium-sized bowl, whisk together your cream and cornstarch. Make sure there are no large clumps of cornstarch in the mix.
8. Remove bay leaves. Add your cream mixture and roasted garlic to the rest of the soup and mix thoroughly. Cook until the soup is nice and thick.
9. Add your cheese and cook just until melted.
10. Get yourself a bowl, top with bacon, and enjoy!

Sampler Spuds

<u>Oh! My! Gosh!</u> This place is <u>so</u> fancy! They have pretty white silk fabric on the walls and fancy golden lanterns hanging from the ceiling—oh, and it smells <u>amazing</u> in here! I ordered the potato skin appetizers and they were so good I nearly died! When I make some more money, I'll definitely be coming back to The Gilded Guardian!

I've come up with three different ways to cook potato skins, so I've created a flight of all three! They may not be as fancy as the ones at The Gilded Guardian, but they're still all so good I couldn't possibly choose my favorite!

MAKES 4 POTATO SKINS OF EACH FLAVOR

Prep time: 5–10 minutes | Cook time: 2–3 hours

INGREDIENTS

STORM HAMMER'S JACKET:
2 russet potatoes
2–4 heads roasted garlic
Brie
Salt and pepper
Prosciutto

GOBLIN'S FIRE GLAZED SKINS:
2 russet potatoes
1 head roasted garlic
1 (4-oz) package cream cheese
¼ cup (+ extra for topping) cheddar cheese
4 ounces shredded chicken
2–3 tablespoons sriracha or buffalo sauce
Salt and pepper

SOWBELLY'S YELLOW EYES:
2 russet potatoes
4 eggs
Salt and pepper
2–3 slices bacon
Cheddar cheese

INSTRUCTIONS

1. Preheat your oven to 350°F.
2. Wash and poke holes in your potatoes and if roasting your garlic, snip/slice the tips off of your garlic. Wrap each potato and garlic head in foil with a splash of olive oil and a pinch of salt.
3. Bake your potatoes and garlic for 1 hour. For best results, leave your potatoes and garlic in the oven to cool for an additional hour—you can skip this part as long as your potatoes are cooked all the way through to the center. You can check the tenderness by poking it with a fork or toothpick. If it easily slides in they are ready.

4. Once your potatoes have cooled enough for you to handle, slice them in half lengthwise and carefully spoon out some of the flesh of the potato, leaving about ¼-inch-thick walls.

5. Place your potato skins on a baking sheet and brush with a small amount of olive oil. Place under the broiler for about 5 minutes or until golden brown.

6. Add your toppings! You can add anything that sounds good here, but these are the three I came up with!

Storm Hammer's Jacket (Charcuterie):

1. Add in your desired amount of roasted garlic to the bottom of your potato boat.

2. Add 1 to 2 slices of brie on top of your garlic. You can add as much or as little as you want here, but be aware that when the cheese melts it will sink into the empty boat, so add more than you think you will need.

3. Top off your brie with a pinch of salt and pepper, then add your prosciutto on top.

4. Bake at 350°F until your brie looks ooey and gooey, about 10 minutes.

Goblin's Fire Glazed Skins (Spicy Cheesy Chicken):

1. Mix together your cream cheese, cheddar cheese, chicken, hot sauce, salt, pepper, and garlic in a small bowl.

2. Spoon ¼ of your mixture into each potato and top with extra cheese.

3. Bake at 350°F until the cheese starts getting ooey and gooey, about 10 minutes.

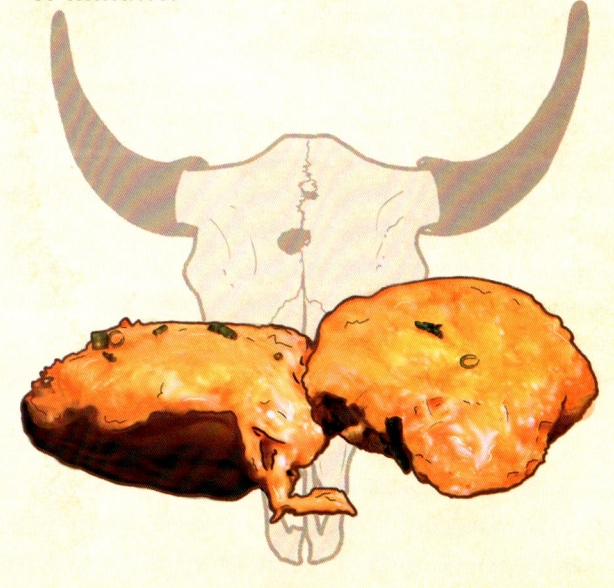

Sowbelly's Yellow Eyes (Breakfast Boat):

1. Crack one egg into each potato skin. (If you like your eggs scrambled, go ahead and whisk before adding them to the potato skin.) Sprinkle with some salt and pepper.
2. Top your egg with your bacon, then top the bacon with cheese.
3. Bake at 350°F until the egg is cooked to your liking, about 7 minutes for a runny yolk and 15 minutes for a cooked one.
4. Top all of these with fresh chopped chives and enjoy!

The Adventurer's Comfort

What can I say, I'm a sucker for some good soup! After asking around, a kind, old gentleman told me about this hole-in-the-wall that served "the best potato soup you'll ever try!" So, I followed his directions, headed down a few narrow alleyways, and finally found this place. Imagine my surprise when I realized that the doorway was just an actual hole in a wall! I ordered the soup and homemade bread, and let me tell you, it did not disappoint! (Plus I think I will be safe from vampire attack for forever! Or at least until I brush my teeth.)

MAKES 6-8 SERVINGS

Prep time: 15-20 minutes | Cook time: 1-2 hours

Ingredients

- 2–4 heads garlic
- 3 pounds potatoes
- 1 large onion
- 2 tablespoons olive oil
- 2 tablespoons butter
- 1 teaspoon coriander
- 1 teaspoon rosemary
- 1 teaspoon parsley
- 1 teaspoon oregano
- 1 teaspoon basil
- 1 teaspoon white pepper
- 1 teaspoon salt
- 1 teaspoon paprika
- 2 bay leaves
- 4–5 cups chicken or veggie broth
- ½–1 cup milk

Instructions

1. Get your garlic in the oven and roast (see page 15).
2. Peel and dice your potatoes and onion, but keep them separate.
3. Heat a 5-quart or larger pot/Dutch oven over medium-high heat. Add in olive oil and butter. Once the butter has melted, drop in the onions and sauté until translucent.
4. Once translucent, add in all of your seasonings and potatoes. Mix everything together until thoroughly coated in seasoning.
5. Next, add in chicken broth until just covering all of your potatoes and onion. Bring to a boil.

(Continued)

6. Once boiling, reduce heat to a medium-low and cover. Let simmer for at least 30 minutes or until potatoes are fully cooked.

7. Once it's fully cooked, remove the bay leaves and add in your roasted garlic and milk.

8. You can stop here and have the soup as is, or you can blend it into a nice creamy soup. To blend the soup, let the soup cool a bit, then, using either an immersion or regular blender, pulse the soup until a nice smooth consistency is formed.

9. Enjoy! You can just eat this soup on its own, but I really like adding cheese or bacon on top. Sometimes both!

Pillow Bread

The soup came with this super soft and fluffy bread I had never even heard of before! They even sell full loaves of it in the back! I asked the chef if I could have the recipe and she directed me to their baker, an enormous, gray-skinned woman covered in tattoos. She told me I could have the recipe but only if I spent the day working for it. I happily agreed and spent the whole day measuring, kneading, and poking fluffy dough! It was amazingly fun! Greta told me I was welcome back any time!

MAKES 8-12 SERVINGS

Prep time: 1½–2 hours | Cook time: 20–30 minutes

INGREDIENTS

BREAD:
- 2½ cups warm water
- 2 teaspoons honey
- 1 heaping tablespoon active dry yeast
- 5 cups flour (all-purpose works great but use bread flour if you have it)
- ½ tablespoon salt
- ¼–½ cup roasted or confit garlic (see pages 15 and 17), divided
- 1½ tablespoons rosemary
- ½ cup olive oil (may need more or less), divided
- 2 tablespoons softened butter

SALT BRINE:
- 1 tablespoon salt
- ½ cup hot water

INSTRUCTIONS

1. Mix together your water, honey, and yeast. The water should be warm but not burning hot or else it will kill the yeast. Let sit for 5 to 8 minutes until the mixture is foamy on the top.

2. While your yeast blooms, mix together flour, salt, half of your roasted garlic, and rosemary in a large bowl.

3. Add your yeast mixture to your dry ingredients and mix thoroughly. There should be no dry spots of flour left in the dough, but you do not need to knead this.

(Continued)

4. Once fully combined, add about ⅓ of your olive oil to the clean bowl. Make sure the bowl is completely covered in the oil and add your dough to the bowl, cover with plastic wrap, and let rise at room temperature for 1 hour or until it has doubled in size.

5. Once the dough has fully risen, start preheating your oven to 450°F.

6. You can prepare focaccia two ways, if you want thick and fluffy bread, use a 9 × 13-inch baking dish. If you want thinner, crispier bread use a large baking sheet. Either way, the next steps will be the same.

7. Prepare your pan by coating it in your room temperature butter. This will prevent your bread from sticking to the bottom of your pan. Do *not* skip this step! Add your remaining olive oil to the bottom of the pan, making sure it's fully covered on the bottom and sides. Use more olive oil if needed.

8. This is a very sticky dough, so coat your hands in oil before handling it. Transfer your dough to the prepared pan and let it rest while the oven heats up. Let the bread rise until it fills in the edges of your pan, about 15 to 30 more minutes.

9. Right before you put your bread in the oven, evenly spread the rest of your garlic over the top of your dough. Then, take your fingers and poke holes all over the surface of the bread.

10. Place on the middle rack of the oven and bake for 20 minutes or until it is a nice, golden-brown color on the top.

11. While the bread is baking, combine your hot water and salt for the brine. Immediately after the bread comes out of the oven, brush the brine onto the surface. It will sizzle a bit when you add it, so don't be scared! You will not use all the brine here, just enough to brush an even layer on your bread. I usually use about ⅓ of it.

12. Enjoy! This is perfect for sandwiches or just to enjoy on its own!

The Tavern Classic

Today I wandered into an establishment with big bold letters labeling it "The Caffeteria." And hoo boy, I think this might be the biggest building I have ever been in in my whole life. There are so many people, and tables, and drinks, and so much food! So much food! After making some conversation, I was told most of the working class gathered here for a cheap midday meal. A half a dozen different small rooms led off from the main large seating area and each place specialized in their own cuisine! My favorite was probably "The Tavern Classic."

MAKES 4 SERVINGS

Prep time: 10-15 minutes | Cook time: 30-40 minutes

Ingredients

- 12–16 red potatoes (depending on size)
- 2 kielbasa (flavor of your choice)
- 1 (32-oz) jar sauerkraut
- ½ cup water or your favorite German beer
- Salt
- Pepper
- 6 tablespoons butter

Instructions

1. Quarter your red potatoes and throw them into a large saucepan or cast iron skillet.

2. Cut your kielbasa into 4 to 5 pieces and lay them on top of your potatoes in the pan.

3. Layer all of your sauerkraut over the potatoes and kielbasa. (If you don't like so much sauerkraut, feel free to add a little less of course!)

(Continued)

4. Pour your water or beer over everything in the pan.
5. Add a generous pinch of salt and pepper to everything.
6. Cut your butter into large pads and scatter on top of your goodies.
7. Cook over medium heat until your potatoes are soft and fully cooked through, around 30–45 minutes.
8. Enjoy! I like eating mine with some crusty bread to soak up all the juices.

CHAPTER FIVE

Some Heroes Bake Chocolate Cakes

Ugh . . . Journal . . .

    The food at the Rusty Dog was bad—and I mean <u>bad</u>! I'm sure you're wondering what I ordered so you can avoid that portion of the menu, but get a load of this . . . they didn't even <u>have</u> a menu! When the barkeep shared the news with me I could barely believe my ears!

    "What kind of food do you serve then?" I asked.

    She spoke in a low, disinterested grumble.

    "If you want food, you're gonna have to get 'the meal.'"

    "The meal? What's in the meal?"

    "It's a meal, take it or leave it."

    So . . . with no other options, I took it.

    Even now I'm <u>still</u> not quite sure what it was. It was like the chef took every ingredient he could think of, diced it all up, threw it in some mashed potatoes, stirred in a tub of gravy, fried it so that just the edges were crisp, soaked it in some grease for twenty-four hours, and then slathered it all on some . . . meat? Yeah . . . I think that was meat. At least I hope so.

    Either way, whatever dwelled at the bottom of "the meal" was tasteless and overcooked to the point where it felt like I was gnawing through six pieces of leather. I looked around to see if the other customers were having a hard time, too, but nobody else even had a plate in front of them! I guess the unfortunate news about "the meal" had made its way around town. I couldn't help but wonder if the chef knew. If the food I made with love and care was this bad, I'd definitely want to know. Food is supposed to make people happy and bring everyone together, after all. So, I made it my mission right then and there to speak to the chef!

    Long story short, a tall, burly human man stomped over to my table with a wide scowl on his face. He wiped his hands on his old greasy apron, folded his arms against his chest, and glared at me, completely unblinking.

"What?"

"Hello." I smiled. "Are you the chef?"

"Of course I'm the chef."

"Great, nice to meet you! So, I had 'the meal' and I just thought I'd let you know that the meat part—if that's even what it was—was <u>preeeeetty</u> overcooked."

"<u>Overcooked?</u>" His scowl deepened.

"Yep! And quite under-seasoned, but—"

"<u>Underseasoned?!</u>"

"Yeah, but don't worry, I'm here to help!" I grinned proudly. "See, I come from a very, very, very, very long line of chefs, so I'd be more than happy to share some pointers with you!"

His face turned into a deep shade of scarlet. He clenched his fists so hard I could see his knuckles turning white.

"I don't need some random thirteen-year-old kid telling me what I can and can't do in my own kitchen!"

"Well, actually, I'm twenty, but I'm <u>very</u> knowledgeable, so you don't need to worry. I have a lot of free time today, and I'd love to help—"

"Oh, you want to help, do you?" he growled. "You can start by getting out of my sight before I smack you over the head with a frying pan!"

"But, I—"

My jaw hit the floor. Why was he so upset?! All I did was offer some help!

"<u>Get out!</u>" he roared.

"But—"

He brought his fists down on the table with enough strength to bend the wood. "<u>Now!</u>"

Before I could even react, the air was thick with the sound of heavy footsteps. A dwarven man rushed to my side, adorned in leathers and wielding a large, shiny hammer. He looked mad—<u>really mad</u>! I held my breath, bracing myself for whatever would come next.

"Shut yer mouth!" he barked in a funny little accent.

I turned to explain that I didn't mean any harm . . . but he wasn't talking to me, he was talking to the chef!

"Your food is garbage, Balador!"

Somehow, the chef's face got even redder.

"My food isn't garbage!"

"Why do you think we only order drinks, then?! Your cookin's inedible! It wouldn't kill you to grow some tastebuds n' pick up a jar of seasonin' a time or two!"

The dwarf's words seemed to hit the chef right where it hurt. He sank inwards like an embarrassed little turtle retreating into its shell.

"And that's no way tae speak to a wee lass, either! Learn some manners, you great oaf!"

The chef disappeared into the kitchen without another word. Truth be told, I did feel a little bad for him.

"Sorry!" I called.

The dwarf waved his hand in dismissal with a hearty laugh upon his breath.

"Ah, don't be sorry. We've been tellin' him he needs tae do somethin' about his temper for years. Anyway, it's very nice tae meet you, I'm Karn Irontongue."

With a wide, friendly smile he stuck out his calloused hand for me to shake.

His accent made me giggle. I couldn't help it.

"Cob CopperSpoon. Thank you for helping me, I really didn't mean to get him that worked up."

"Oh don't you worry about him, he will get over it." The dwarf looked to a table across the tavern, where three amused faces watched us with curious smiles.

"You can join us, if you'd like."

And of course I couldn't say no to the opportunity!

Karn and his friends turned out to be great—I'll get into all of that soon, don't worry—but what I'm the most excited about sharing with you right now is that both Karn and I <u>love</u> to cook. We talked about food for hours, and I soaked up all his advice like a happy little sponge! He told me about the traditional dwarven meals he'd eat back home, his favorite snacks to take on the road, and the most delicious chocolate cake he's ever tasted! He even wrote down the recipe for me. Karn's so cool!

100 Gold Chocolate Cake

Well, hello there, Cob's journal. It's a pleasure to meet ye. This 100 gold chocolate cake is a recipe me great-great-great grandmother came across. She visited a fancy eatery back in the day and had the best slice of chocolate cake she ever tasted. When she asked the chef for the recipe, the bugger said no. Well, the Irontongue family doesn't take no for an answer! She whipped out a pouch of 100 gold right then and there and the rest was history!

MAKES 8-10 SERVINGS

Prep time: 20-30 minutes | Cook time: 45-50 minutes | Decorating time: As long as you want

INGREDIENTS

CAKE:
- 2 cups all-purpose flour
- ¼ teaspoon salt
- 4 tablespoons cocoa powder
- 1 cup sugar
- 2 teaspoons baking soda
- 1 cup mayonnaise
- 1 cup cold coffee
- 1 teaspoon vanilla

BUTTERCREAM:
- 1 cup butter (room temperature)
- ½ cup cocoa powder
- 2½ cups powdered sugar
- ¼ cup heavy whipping cream

INSTRUCTIONS

CAKE:

1. Preheat your oven to 350°F.

2. Lightly coat a 9-inch round cake pan in vegetable oil or butter. To make extra sure your cake doesn't stick, you can also sprinkle some flour over the greased pan or cut out parchment paper to fit on the bottom and around the sides of your pan. Set aside until later.

3. In a large bowl, sift together your flour, salt, cocoa powder, sugar, and baking soda.

4. In a medium bowl mix your mayonnaise, coffee, and vanilla until smooth.

5. Mix your wet ingredients into your dry ingredients, until a smooth batter is formed.

6. Add your batter to the greased pan and bake for 45 minutes, or until a toothpick can be inserted into the center and come out clean.

Buttercream:

1. In a large bowl, whip your butter until it's as fluffy and light as a cloud. Use a hand mixer for the best results!

2. Add in your cocoa powder and incorporate fully.

3. Slowly add in your powdered sugar and mix until smooth.

4. Add in your heavy cream and mix until light and fluffy.

Cake Decorating Tips

1. After your cake is done baking, let cool *fully* before trying to remove from the pan.

2. After removing the cake from your pan, you can leave it whole or cut it into 2 layers. It helps if you have a guide, but the layers don't have to be perfect to still be pretty.

3. Freeze your cake layers for at least 1 hour before decorating to keep it from falling apart. This is a very moist cake, and it likes to crumble. Freezing it helps keep it together while you frost it.

4. Get a bowl of hot water and a flat metal spatula. The warm water helps give the frosting a super-smooth finish.

5. Top with anything you like! I like adding chopped pistachios or other nuts!

6. Have fun! Remember that at the end of the day it's just a cake. Who cares if it looks perfect, as long as you have fun making it?!

CHAPTER SIX
A Night at The Rusty Dog

Dear Journal,

    I spent hours at The Rusty Dog with Karn and his friends that night. Even when I started to get sleepy, I couldn't tear myself away from the conversations we were having. It didn't help that Karn's friends were every bit as interesting as he was.

    First, we have Karn (he/him), of course! We get along so well, I almost feel like we've known each other my whole life!

    Irabel (she/her)—I've never seen anyone like her before! She's from a race of cat people that originate from far, far away. Oh, and she's a sorceress, too! That means she was born with the ability to use magic on her own without the help of any aids, big inspiration, or schooling. She has a little satchel of stones and trinkets that she keeps with her, and she told me that maybe one day she'll be able to use them to read my future!

    Finheld (he/they)—I have never met an elf in person, but I always expected their ears to be longer and pointier. Finheld's are still pointy, just not as long as I thought they would be! They seem kind of grumpy, but it's in the way some of my cooler-than-life cousins are, so it's okay! Finheld used all of his incredible mechanical knowledge to replace one of his missing arms. It's really, really cool!

56

Harold (he/him)—Harold is a human. He didn't talk much, but he was very welcoming and has super kind eyes. He has a <u>buuunnchh</u> of visible battle scars; he must have been through his fair share of mayhem. I wonder what crazy stories this well-seasoned adventurer has to tell!

Cool right?! So, of course, when it was my turn to share details about myself, I couldn't help but feel . . . underwhelming? Maybe even a little boring. I grew up in a small town and I've lived there all my life—I didn't have any interesting adventures to share. But you know what I did have? Stories about my family!

I told them about the time we went on a family fishing trip where I ended up with a hook up my nose (don't worry, we got it out), and the big parties where we had pie-eating contests! My sister always won those ones, though.

However, one thing that I <u>am</u> pretty good at is illusory magic, so I decided why not use it to put on a bit of a show for my new friends? As the sun set outside of the tavern, I conjured up the image of my favorite purple dragon plush, Soapstopher, with a flick of my wrist! I showed them some of the zany adventures I'd imagine us on when I was a child—in my mind, he sneezes bubbles instead of breathing fire.

Anyway, I got a little bit carried away with the storytelling. I couldn't help myself. I changed my voice to suit each made-up character in my mind—a clumsy rat, a forgetful king, and an evil mushroom named Mr. Spitspores—bringing them to life with sparkly, glowing illusions that even caught the eyes of the other patrons in the tavern. The night was filled with laughter and joyous applause!

"You're very talented, Cob." Harold said with a kind smile.

Karn nodded in agreement, nudging him with his elbow.

"Aye. We could use some entertainment like that on the road, eh?"

"On the road?!" I asked. Was he inviting me to join their party, The Tag-Alongs?! I couldn't tell—I really tried not to get too excited, but I couldn't help it.

"I'd <u>love</u> to travel with you!"

Finheld scowled. "Okay, no need to yell—"

"What d'ya think," Karn said, waving Finheld's sassy comment away with his hand. "Do we give the lass a chance?"

Harold nodded. "I think it's a great idea,"

"It could be . . . interesting." Irabel agreed.

Finheld grimaced to himself for a silent moment before uttering, "Sure, but does she even know what kind of work we do?"

I got so wrapped up in the idea of having new traveling friends that it hadn't even crossed my mind to ask. I knew they adventured a lot, and that they'd certainly had their run-ins with some odd characters and scary monsters, but that was about it.

"What do you do?" I asked.

"We're members of The Guild of The Twelfth Knight," Harold said. "So, we take on whatever requests come the guild's way."

"Some might call it mercenary work," Finheld shrugged.

<u>Mercenary work</u>? All I'd ever heard about mercenaries was that they were shady, ruthless, and maybe even . . . criminals. Karn and his friends didn't seem like they were bad—to me, they seemed the exact opposite. "Do you guys . . . hurt people?"

Irabel flashed a fanged grin devious enough to make my blood run cold. "Yes."

"No, we don't hurt people!" Karn sighed. "And mercenary's a hefty word—"

Finheld scoffed. "But is it the wrong word?"

"Well . . . no, but we don't just go around harassin' people for the fun of it, Cob. We're just out here tae help those in need. If that means takin' down bad people, then so be it. There's all sorts of terrible things crawlin' around with only bad thoughts in their ugly little heads, we like to put an end tae 'em, one way or another."

I felt a small wave of relief wash over me. "Oh, so you fight evil."

"Exactly," Harold nodded. "We only do what's right."

I hadn't once thought of myself as a hero. All I really wanted was to share stories and recipes with people all over the world. Heading out on a big hero's journey seemed kind of scary . . . but then again, these types of adventurers <u>do</u> have the best stories to tell. I'd certainly end up meeting a lot of new people on the road, too.

"Well . . . I'm not much of a fighter."

I looked down at my hands, two parts of me that were accustomed to stirring spoons in simmering pots and digging in the garden. How could I ever picture them holding a blade?

"I've only been away from home for a short time, so I still have a lot of things to learn, but I can cook—and I can take notes of all the incredible things you do, and I'll turn it into something amazing!"

"Like a scribe?" Irabel asked.

"Yeah! And I'll share the stories with people wherever we go. I can be your . . . your resident bard!"

They all looked at each other for a moment, gauging each other's expressions as they wordlessly deliberated whether taking me on was actually a good idea. I sat on the edge of my seat, my stomach churning in anticipation. Finally, after some grunts and some nods, Karn smiled.

"Consider yourself part of the team, Cob CopperSpoon."

The warm surge of joy and belonging in my heart had me wiggling happily in my seat. "Thank you so much!"

"But first . . ." Karn's smile faded. His expression darkened, turning his face cold. "You have tae deal with . . . Hutar."

Smoked Centicore Sandwich

Well hello journal, I know what you might be thinking. <u>What</u> a cliff hanger! And now I'm just hopping into a brand new recipe?!? How dare I! But it wouldn't be a very good story if I just revealed all the good parts right away, now would it? Plus I am still hungry after that <u>awful</u> greasy goop from The Rusty Dog. The Tag-Alongs brought me to this late-night food cart and I got to try the "best sandwich in town" according to Harold. I have never tried centicore before but, I gotta say, it did not disappoint.

MAKES 4-6 SERVINGS

Prep time: 30-45 minutes | Cook time: 45-60 minutes

Ingredients

- Olive oil
- 1 (2-3 lb) centicore flank (can replace with tri-tip steak)
- 4 tablespoons steak seasoning
- 1 large onion
- 1 tablespoon butter
- Splash of whiskey or broth
- ½ cup mayonnaise
- 1-2 heads roasted garlic
- Salt and pepper
- Bread rolls of your choice (Not Your Papa's Bread Rolls on page 24)
- 1-2 cups Gruyère or any cheese of your choice

Instructions

CENTICORE:

1. Lightly drizzle some olive oil over your centicore.

2. Fully coat your meat in your seasoning. You can use any rub you like for this, or make a mix of salt, pepper, garlic, and onion powder. Just mix together about 1 tablespoon of each to make a homemade seasoning blend.

3. There are 3 ways to make this, either by smoking it, grilling it, or searing it and finishing it in the oven.

(Continued)

- **Smoker:** Turn your smoker onto its smoke setting. Place the centicore in the center of the rack and smoke for 1 hour. After the hour's up, turn your smoker to 350°F and cook for 10 minutes on each side. Probe with a meat thermometer and pull off the smoker at desired done-ness (see page 2)

- **Grill:** Prepare your grill with a medium-high heat side and a medium-low heat side. On the hotter part of the grill, cook meat for 5–10 minutes on each side, checking your internal temperature intermittently. Once cooked on both sides, move to lower heat. Cook until your desired done-ness (see page 2), making sure to keep flipping the meat every 5 minutes to cook evenly.

- **Oven:** Preheat oven to 375°F. In a large oven-safe pan or cast iron skillet, heat 2 tablespoons of oil over high heat. Once the oil is sizzling hot, place your centicore fat side down in the pan. Sear 2–3 minutes on each side until golden brown. Put the pan in the oven and bake for 30 minutes to 1 hour depending on the size of your tri-tip. At the 30-minute mark, check your meat temperature, removing from the oven at your desired done-ness (see page 2).

4. After you remove your meat from whatever you chose to cook it in, it is VERY IMPORTANT to let it rest for at least 30 minutes under some foil. This will make your steak super juicy and easier to cut for your sandwiches.

Toppings

You can add anything you please here, but I recommend the following:

Caramelized Onions:

1. Thinly slice your onion.
2. In a medium pan, add 1 tablespoon of butter and 1 tablespoon of olive oil. Heat on medium-high heat and melt your butter.
3. Add in all of your onions and a pinch of salt. Stir occasionally until they turn a deep, golden brown.
4. Once golden, add in a splash of whiskey or broth. Cook until almost fully evaporated.
5. Set aside to use as topping.

Garlic Mayonnaise:

1. Mix together your mayonnaise, garlic, a pinch of salt, and a pinch of pepper. Grind with a mortar-and-pestle or blend together in a blender.

ASSEMBLY:

1. Toast your bread in your smoker/grill/oven. Drizzle with a little olive oil for a nice, golden brown crunch.
2. Thinly slice your steak and add it to your toasted bread. Cover with cheese and place back into the oven until the cheese is just melted.
3. Top with your caramelized onions and garlic sauce.
4. Enjoy!

CHAPTER SEVEN
Trial of Might

Dear Journal,

Hutar. . . .

Karn had said his name as though it was a curse. Everybody shifted nervously in their seats as he spoke, the sheer thought of this man obviously made them apprehensive. Don't worry, I didn't let it get to me! I was actually pretty excited to meet Hutar. I've never met a guild leader before!

The next day, Karn, Harold, Irabel, and Finheld took me to the Guild of the Twelfth Knight. The colossal building made of gray stone almost looked a little castle-like, with tall pillars, defensive towers, and two large statues of a brave-looking knight.

The guild's massive main hall exuded an undeniable air of sophistication—marble floors, elegantly carved wooden tables, fixtures, and a grand chandelier hanging above—but it still somehow felt welcoming. There were several large tables where boisterous guild members of all shapes, races, and sizes sat to eat, debrief, and play card games. Bookshelves and reading nooks lined the walls on the balcony above. A bird-like man glided down from the tippy top, all the way to the bottom to eagerly show a book to the woman behind the front desk.

"You guys live here?!" I asked.

Karn laughed. "Well, some do, but we're usually on the road too often tae settle down. There's bunks 'n bedrooms fer whoever needs 'em, though."

"There's also an infirmary," Harold said. "And a non-descript church for praying, for those who are interested."

"There's workshops, too," Finheld told me, sighing as he did.

Irabel nodded. "And places to practice magic."

"Aye, and a big yard out back tae work on all types o' combat," Karn added in.

Wow, so I guess this place has a little bit of everything—but I know what you're wondering, because I was wondering the same thing. What about the <u>kitchen</u>? My mind was swirling with possibilities. <u>What if they have sixteen sinks and a hundred ovens? What if every single tool is made from gold? What if someone invented a machine that'll use the power of your mind to stir ingredients?</u>

"Can we see the kitchen?" I asked.

Fortunately, my friends were happy to oblige.

I practically held my breath in anticipation as we wandered through the guild and reached a set of huge wooden doors. These weren't just any doors, though. Carved right into the wood were huge spoons, forks, and swirling vines that signaled this was going to be the most beautiful kitchen in the world. I had to stop myself from leaping forward and barreling through like a charging bull.

I stood as still as I could as Harold pushed them open, and there it was. . . .

A kitchen—literally just a kitchen.

I've seen quite a few in my time and this one was pretty standard. Wood where wood was supposed to be, stone where it was supposed to be, too, utensils, cupboards, a pantry—you get the picture. Still, there had to be <u>something</u> interesting about this space. I trotted across the room to have a peek in their cabinets.

"Where are all the spices?" I asked.

"I've been askin' the same thing fer years, lass." Karn huffed.

"Were they stolen? The only thing here is salt and . . . a jar of old peas?"

Irabel laughed a quiet little laugh. "No. The food here's just always been . . . bleh."

"Bleh?!" I mused. "That certainly won't do."

Karn folded his thick arms against his chest. "If ye really want a decent meal 'round here, ye have tae bring yer own seasonings."

"Oh, that's no good," I frowned. "I mean I always carry my own seasonings with me but—"

"Aye, me too!" Karn huffed, giving an irritated glance at the cupboard.

"I barely have room in my pockets as is! I don't want tae carry around a whole rack's worth o' seasoning just tae have somethin' nice tae eat!"

I nodded in agreement.

"Maybe if everything goes well between me and Hutar, I can—"

"Don't get me started on the food selection here either!" Karn's gruff voice overtook mine, but I didn't mind. He'd clearly had this bottled up for a long time—I would have blown up too if I had to eat flavorless food for weeks.

"Eggs fer breakfast, sandwiches fer lunch, stew fer dinner," he continued. "Where's the variety?!"

Karn managed to find a spoon to swing around as he hollered, pointing periodically from the spice cabinet, to the door, to the pantry. He ranted of how the dwarfs would never let this happen, and if he, "didn't love this place so much he might just revolt!" I giggled at his dramatic escapade.

"The Violet Bastion's supposed tae be the biggest city on the continent. Wouldn't ye want tae show some respect by at least puttin' some salt on the eggs?! It should be a crime at this point—"

Someone with a deep, rumbling voice cleared their throat.

We turned our heads to the door in a flash. My new friends froze in fear. It was an orc. He towered over us like we were mere ants standing before a mountain, a mean look contorting his green face.

Karn laughed uncomfortably, his cheeks a slightly embarrassed shade of pink.

"Heh . . . Hutar," he greeted. "We were just showin' Cob here 'round the guild."

So _this_ was Hutar! I guess I get why they were so scared of him before, he does have _quite_ a presence.

Hutar's gaze fell on me, an expressionless look rested on his face as he eyed me from head to toe, saying nothing.

"Hi, I'm Cob!" I smiled.

Hutar simply grunted in response before looking back at Karn.

"If you are done criticizing the practices of my kitchen staff, I do believe we have a meeting to get to."

Karn nodded, his eyes flicking to the floor.

"Uh—yeah, we best get that started."

Hutar grunted again and turned away from the kitchen, wordlessly beckoning us to follow behind.

I held my head high as we followed him down the length of a very long hallway, but my friends didn't seem so sure of themselves. I couldn't help but notice the worried glances they kept exchanging with one another, or how they walked a fair distance away from the leader of the guild. It was almost like they were afraid. Wait . . . should I have been afraid?

"Are we in trouble?" I whispered.

Karn was almost white as a sheet. "We might be."

"Maybe not," Irabel whispered. "He's always a little grouchy."

Finheld scoffed. "A little?"

Karn, Harold, and Irabel hushed him—but I kept my eyes fixated on Hutar. He was always grouchy? _Why_? He had such a cool job _and_ a whole guild that looked up to him! If I were in his shoes, I'd be ecstatic every day. There's got to be an explanation for his sour attitude. I scanned his broad body with my eyes, searching for any possible reason. Maybe he had a sore back? Or maybe he was drowning in paperwork? That would make me grumpy. Ooh! Maybe his office has a grump bug infestation, and they keep biting him! I think my real theory is that he's mad about the guild's lack of spices! Either way, I made it my mission to get on his good side.

He led us up a secluded spiral staircase until we eventually found ourselves underneath a hatch in the ceiling, sealed with a large iron lock. Hutar pulled out a key, unlocked the door, and flipped it open, revealing the beautiful and unmistakable blue of the sky. A cool breeze greeted us as we followed him up and stepped out onto a flat, stone rooftop surrounded by a very short, crenellated wall. From this height, we could see almost all of The Violet Bastion!

Unmoved, Hutar made his way over to a small, elevated stone pedestal near the hatch and sat in a large throne-like chair. Bringing people up to the roof obviously wasn't a new thing for Hutar—and when my friends circled the rooftop and stood behind him, I realized that this wasn't a new experience for them, either. I felt a small burst of nerves shoot through my stomach, like I was being judged before a high-council, or something.

I discreetly peered at the city beyond. The only barrier between myself and the world was the tiny wall that only came up to my thigh—it would be so easy to fall over the edge. Or maybe even . . . be pushed? My heart dropped as I imagined myself plummeting down to the city below. What I once thought was a simple meeting now felt like a trial at the gallows. What was once a comforting breeze now prickled my skin and gently guided me towards the edge—

No. I shook my head, pushing all the bad thoughts away. I wasn't going to let my imagination get the best of me.

"So, you want to join the Twelfth Knight?" The clarity of Hutar's bellowing voice pushed me far from my terrifying fantasy.

"Yes," I nodded, swallowing all of my nerves. "I would."

"What experience do you have, girl?"

"Well . . ." I shrugged, "Admittedly, not much. But I thought I'd follow Karn, Harold, Finheld, and Irabel along on their adventures and write down all the amazing things they do. Like a scribe. Also, I'm really good at cooking!"

Hutar frowned. "Cooking?"

"Yeah! I love to write recipes, and—"

"Do you truly believe that <u>cooking</u> will save you when you come face to face with a dragon?" He asked, his eyebrows furrowing.

"Uh . . . maybe? I also tell stories, too, so—"

"<u>Stories</u>?" he scoffed. "How many hellish beasts have you quelled with a short tale and a freshly baked loaf of bread?"

"Well . . . none so far, sir," I mumbled, looking down at my feet.

Hutar pierced me with his glowering eyes.

"This guild is named after The Twelfth Knight, who has confronted full armies of demons alone."

He paused, taking a moment to size me up from head to toe.

"Let's see how you fare against just one."

Hutar reached beside his chair and pushed back a lever that I hadn't managed to notice was there.

The wall of the pedestal slid open, and out of the darkness crawled a terrifying beast.

"Huh?!" My breath hitched in my throat. "I—what—what am I supposed to do?!"

"Fight, Cob!" Karn yelled. "Fight!"

"Fight?!" My heart began to race. The scarlet-skinned, pointy-horned, dagger-fanged creature was almost my height!

Screeching, the imp leapt into the air, unfurled a set of leathery wings, and dove straight at me. My scream of terror matched the pitch of its cries as I narrowly dodged its attack. Were they trying to kill me?! No, this had to be some kind of initiation, right?

"Am I supposed to—to kill it?!"

"Look out!" Harold shouted.

The creature did a loop in the air and barrelled towards me, a wicked giggle escaping its throat. I reached for my dagger and feverishly swung it over my head.

I missed by a mile.

With lightning speed, the imp pierced my shoulder, its jagged teeth digging into my skin with ease. I yelped in pain and ripped it off, mustering what I could of my strength to push it as far away as I could. The imp snarled, tumbling to the ground, grinding the torn piece of fabric of my shirt within its gnashing jaws.

And unfortunately, that's how this battle went.

It dove—I swung—I missed—and it tore into me with its fangs.

Over, and over, and over.

By the time I figured out exactly when to time my attacks, it was far too late for me. The snarling imp had me nearly backed up against the wall that separated us from the sky. I could practically feel my back teetering over the edge. The mighty beast cackled, savoring my fear. It flapped its wings and bared its claws, readying to send me tumbling to the city below

"We have tae help her!" Karn shot to his feet.

But Hutar grabbed him by his shoulder.

"She must do this alone, Karn. Give her a chance to prove herself."

If anyone said anything further, my shriek of terror overwhelmed the sound. The beast dove again—I just barely managed to strike it out of the way, but the force sent my dagger into the air! It clattered out of reach on the stone rooftop. I staggered backwards, waving my arms wildly in an attempt to steady my wounded, quivering body.

Screeching, the creature grinned, mocking me like the monster I now knew it to be.

It dove again. . .

It pushed me with all its might. . .

I tumbled all the way down to the street below. . .

Splat!

I died a failure.

<u>Just kidding</u>! The creature did try of course, but then the sound of Hutar's voice boomed through the air like a shockwave.

"<u>Enough</u>!"

The imp froze only inches before me. Its menacing grin was exchanged for a disappointed snarl. It turned to look at the leader of the guild and shook its tiny fist in anger, and that's when I took my moment to strike—

Now, I'm sure you might be thinking, "<u>wow, Hutar was actually nice enough to spare her? Maybe he's not so bad after all!</u>"

Or maybe even, "<u>wow, Cob can't fight her own battles.</u>"

Well, you're in for a surprise. That wasn't Hutar that the imp heard at all, it was <u>me</u>! Remember I said that I liked to do character voices with my illusory magic?

While the Imp was distracted, I swallowed my fear, leapt forward, grabbed my dagger, and slayed it where it stood! So, I guess I <u>can</u> use my storytelling abilities to quell hellish beasts after all. Take <u>that</u>, Hutar!

Panting, I turned away from the painful sight of slain imp only to see my friends running to my side. "Are you okay?!" Harold asked with urgency.

"Yeah," I winced.

"Here, let me help you." His palms passed over my wounds, and a shimmering golden light radiated from his skin. A relaxing warmth spread through my body, and my wounds seemingly sealed shut.

"Oh, wow!" I gasped, "Thank you!"

Before Harold could reply, Hutar cleared his throat, the sound echoing over the stone.

"Congratulations, Cob CopperSpoon, I officially welcome you to the Guild of the Twelfth Knight."

And that's how making something of yourself in the big city's done, folks! If my family could only see me now!

Hey, speaking of family, if there's one thing us CopperSpoons are going to do, it's cook a celebration feast! It was time to put my mind, the guild's kitchen, and my family's spices to work. And it just so happens we had some fresh meat to cook up. I've never cooked Imp before but how hard could it really be?

Forager's Impy Rolls

The first step to a good feast is a nice, filling protein and what better protein to use than a freshly slain one? I crudely butchered it and cooked myself up a little piece to taste test. I was expecting something gamey, maybe even a little spicy. Imagine my surprise when the bright red meat cooked up just like pig! I think I have the perfect idea for this feast now!

MAKES 1-3 IMP ROASTS

Prep time: 25-30 minutes | Cook time: 40-60 minutes

INGREDIENTS

IMP:
2–4 Imp flank (can replace with pork tenderloin roasts)
Olive oil
Salt and pepper
Sprig of thyme
Sprig of rosemary
Garlic powder

MUSHROOM FILLING:
MAKES 1 PORK ROAST

1 (8-oz) package of mushrooms
2 tablespoons butter
1 tablespoon olive oil
1 small yellow onion
½ head fresh garlic
1 tablespoon fresh rosemary
1 tablespoon fresh thyme
½ teaspoon salt
½ teaspoon pepper
½ teaspoon paprika
½ lemon
¼ cup white wine

CHEESE FILLING:
MAKES 2 PORK ROASTS

1 (8-oz) package cream cheese
1 cup shredded Parmesan cheese
1 cup Gruyère cheese
½ head fresh garlic
1 tablespoon fresh thyme
1 tablespoon fresh rosemary
1 tablespoon chives
Salt and pepper
1 teaspoon paprika

GRAVY:
Pork drippings
¼ cup flour
1 cup broth or milk

Instructions

Mushroom Filling:

1. Dice your mushrooms and onions into small pieces. Mince your garlic, rosemary, and thyme as well.

2. Heat a large pan over medium-high heat with your butter and oil. Sauté your onions and garlic until caramelized, about 5 to 8 minutes.

3. Add your mushrooms, rosemary, thyme, salt, pepper, and paprika to your pan and combine everything.

4. Add in the juice of your lemon and your white wine. Cook until wine has reduced by half, then remove from heat and let cool before stuffing your pork.

Cheese Filling:

1. Combine all of your ingredients in a large bowl and thoroughly mix.

Imp:

1. Preheat your oven to 400°F.

2. At this point you're going to butterfly the imp flank. You can ask your butcher to do this ahead of time or see page 18 for in-depth instructions.

3. Spread whichever filling you're using, or even a mix of both, across the full length of your imp. Roll the imp back onto itself, creating a spiral log of meat and filling. Use toothpicks or some roasting twine to hold the seam closed. Place your imp roasts in a large cast iron or roasting pan.

4. Drizzle your imp with your olive oil. Coat everything in a generous amount of salt and pepper and top with your thyme and rosemary.

5. Bake for 25 to 30 minutes or until your pork is fully cooked through. Once finished, remove imp from the pan and cover with foil. Let the roast sit while you make your gravy.

6. Pour all of your pan drippings into a medium saucepan with flour. Cook for 2 to 3 minutes on a medium-high heat.

7. Slowly add in your milk or broth, whisking constantly until a thick gravy has formed. Enjoy!

Crispy Roasted Spuds

Karn told me that the Dwarven stronghold he was raised in grew the very best potatoes in the world. He was even willing to put money on it! And while there are probably a quadrillion ways to cook potatoes, this is one of my favorites. The best thing about making it for a bunch of people is that you can ask them to help chop stuff up! Yay, teamwork!

MAKES 6-8 SERVINGS

Prep time: 25-30 minutes | Cook time: 25-40 minutes

INGREDIENTS

- 7-8 large yukon gold potatoes
- Salt
- 2-3 tablespoons olive oil
- 2 tablespoons butter
- 1 tablespoon fresh minced thyme
- 1 tablespoon fresh minced rosemary
- 2 tablespoons minced garlic
- Pepper
- ½ cup grated Parmesan cheese

INSTRUCTIONS

1. Wash and cut your potatoes into bite-sized pieces or wedges.

2. In a large pot, bring 4 to 5 cups of water to a boil with a big pinch of salt. Once boiling, add your potatoes and cook until tender, about 10 to 12 minutes.

3. Pour your olive oil into a large cast iron or oven-safe pan. Place the pan in your oven and preheat to 400°F while your potatoes boil.

4. Strain your potatoes then throw them back in their pot. Toss them with the butter, fresh herbs, garlic, a big pinch of salt and pepper, and Parmesan cheese. You want to try and keep these as whole as possible so mix them gently.

5. Take the pan and oil carefully out of the oven. It will be very *very* hot, so make sure you move slowly and pay attention at this step.

6. Carefully pour your potatoes into the hot oil. Place the pan back in the oven and bake for 10 to 15 minutes. You want the bottoms of the potatoes to turn golden brown.

7. Pull your potatoes out of the oven and carefully flip them over. Bake another 10 to 15 minutes until your potatoes have fully started to turn golden brown. Repeat this process until your potatoes are your desired crispiness.

8. Serve with some flaky salt and enjoy!

Cheesy Garlic Swirls

Have you ever had a cinnamon roll and just thought to yourself . . . what if this was made of cheese and garlic instead? Well I have! Technically Mama Copper has . . . but she's not here right now so I will happily take the credit. This is a very versatile recipe that can be easily amended. Try adding caramelized onions, shredded chicken, pizza sauce, and toppings, anything you can think of!

MAKES 12 ROLLS

Prep time: 1½ hours | Cook time: 25–30 minutes

INGREDIENTS

DOUGH:
- 1 cup warm milk
- ¼ cup warm water
- 1 tablespoon honey
- 2¼ teaspoons yeast
- 3 cups all purpose flour (+extra for kneading the dough, need about ¼–½ cup)
- 2 teaspoons salt
- ¼ cup olive oil

GARLIC SPREAD:
- ½ cup butter
- ½ cup roasted garlic (see page 15)
- Salt and pepper, to taste
- 1 teaspoon Italian seasoning

CHEESES:
- 2 cups of your preferred cheeses (I recommend 1 cup each of mozzarella and Gruyère)

INSTRUCTIONS

1. In a small bowl, mix together your warm milk, water, honey, and yeast. Mix until combined and set aside for 5 minutes to bloom. Your liquids should be warm to the touch but not hot.

2. While your yeast is blooming, measure and mix together your flour and salt in a large bowl.

3. Once your yeast is ready, combine your flour mix, olive oil, and yeast mix until it just starts to come together. The dough should be very sticky.

4. Dump your dough out onto a well-floured surface; you'll want a lot of flour on your board for this part.

5. Knead your dough for 5 to 7 minutes, adding a sprinkle of flour every once

in a while when the dough starts to stick to the board again. In this case, you're not just using the flour so the dough doesn't stick to anything, but also incorporating it into the dough! The goal is to have a nice smooth dough ball that isn't sticking to the cutting board or your fingers.

6. Place your dough ball into a lightly greased bowl and cover with a clean rag. Let this sit at room temperature for 1 hour or until it has doubled in size.

7. While your dough is rising, mix together your garlic spread. The key to this is to make sure your butter is very soft, and your garlic has fully cooled. I roast my garlic the night before and leave it in the fridge overnight.

8. Shred your cheese and set aside.

9. Once your dough has doubled in size, start to preheat your oven to 350°F.

10. Pour your dough out onto a lightly oiled, clean surface. Gently stretch your dough into a rectangular shape before rolling it into a large rectangle that is about 1 cm thick.

11. Evenly spread half of your garlic butter over the top of your dough, making sure it coats all the way to the edges.

12. Add your cheese in a thin layer over the garlic spread, making sure to reserve a little bit for the top.

13. Once your dough has been topped, gently roll it into a long log. Slice the log into 12 even pieces. To easily evenly slice, start by cutting your log in half. Cut those halves into halves and then cut those halves into thirds.

14. Place your rolls into a well-oiled cast iron or baking dish (it's okay if they're touching).

15. Top the rolls with your remaining cheese and bake for 25 to 30 minutes or until golden brown on top.

16. Serve with remaining garlic spread and enjoy!

Fudgy Brownies (Gluten-Free)

What's a feast without a dessert? I heard that a member of the guild had an intolerance to a thing called Gluten. That basically means they can't eat anything with wheat in it, which also means they have never eaten cake! Or bread, or brownies, or cookies, or anything else with wheat in it! I count myself lucky to have a Nana who specializes in no-wheat desserts! Now everybody can enjoy!

MAKES 6-9 SERVINGS

Prep time: 10-15 minutes | Cook time: 30 minutes

Ingredients

- ⅓ cup cocoa powder (or 4 ounces unsweetened chocolate squares)
- ¾ cup butter
- 1¼ cups sugar
- 2 eggs
- 1½ teaspoons gluten-free vanilla
- ⅔ cup Gluten-Free Flour Blend (see page 19)
- ⅜ teaspoon baking soda
- ½ cup gluten-free chocolate chips
- ½ cup chopped nuts (optional)

Instructions

1. Preheat your oven to 350°F.
2. Add your cocoa powder/chocolate squares and butter to a saucepan. Cook over low heat, stirring constantly until it's melted and smooth.
3. Remove your chocolate and butter mix from the heat and set aside in a large mixing bowl. Allow your chocolate butter to cool for 5 to 10 minutes or else it will cook your eggs!
4. Add your sugar to your cocoa and butter mix and stir well.
5. Crack your eggs into the mixture one at a time, combining between each egg.
6. Add in your vanilla and mix well.
7. In a different bowl, combine your flour and baking soda. Once fully combined, add to your chocolate mix and combine until there are no more dry spots.
8. Mix in your chocolate chips and any nuts if you are adding them.

9. Grease an 8 × 8 baking dish with butter/oil and a light dusting of gluten-free flour. Pour in your batter then bake for 30 minutes.

10. Let cool for 15 minutes and enjoy!

Dwarven Float

Alright, Journal! Cob asked me tae scribble down this here recipe fer ye! Now, <u>this is an adult beverage</u>, but I added in some options if ye want tae make it fer the kiddos, too! Cheers! Karn

Makes 1 serving

Prep time: 5 minutes

Ingredients

Ice
1 ounce Dwarven whiskey or your favorite dark liquor (optional)
Root beer
1–3 ounces Irish cream or vanilla coffee creamer

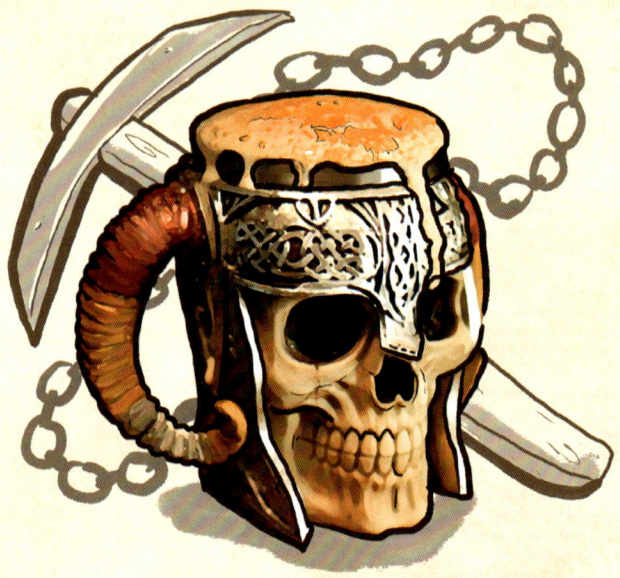

Instructions

1. Fill your glass with lots of ice. You want to keep this drink as cold as possible, so use lots!
2. If you want a stronger drink, add your whiskey now.
3. Pour your root beer into your glass until it is about ⅔ of the way full.
4. Top your float off the rest of the way with your cream.
5. Enjoy!

CHAPTER EIGHT
Feeding the Grumpy

Hey Journal,

    Guess what? The meal was a hit! Everybody, from a lady with a bat-nose to a guy with a weird pet koala, absolutely loved it! I couldn't be more proud of myself! All in one day I slayed my first creature, and cooked it into a delicious new recipe, too! But I wasn't entirely satisfied. There was one person in particular who I wanted to be sure was <u>especially</u> enjoying my food: cranky, old Hutar.

    With a steaming plate in my hands, I searched the guild from top to bottom, but he was nowhere to be found. I eventually ended up heading to the front desk. Sitting there in her wheelchair was a short-statured half-elf lady with a fork in her hand and a smile on her face.

    "Hi," I greeted. "I'm looking for Hutar. I want him to try my food."

    The woman smiled pleasantly.

    "Oh, that's very sweet of you. Leave it with me and I'll pass it along when I see him."

    I pulled the plate close to my chest.

    "I'd like to give it to him myself."

    The woman's kind expression quickly turned into something almost cautious.

    "And why's that?"

    "Because there's nothing better than seeing everyone's happy faces as they enjoy a big delicious meal. I think it would be nice for Hutar to—well . . . smile. No offense to him."

    Her look of caution faded instantly, and she hid a small chuckle behind her lips.

    "You know what?"

    "What?"

    "I think you're absolutely right," she told me. "His office is this way."

    The woman, whose name I learned was Telfina, led me through the gigantic guild until we came to a large, dark wooden door. She knocked, and once we heard Hutar grunt in acknowledgment from within, she gave me a quick wink and pushed the door open.

    "There you are, darling" Telfina smiled at Hutar, beholding him as he sat hunched over his desk.

<u>Darling</u>? I looked at Telfina, and then at Hutar, and then at Telfina, and then at Hutar, until I saw a small framed painting of them kissing in formal wear on Hutar's desk. They were married!

"Hutar, our new friend Cob, here, has brought you a little something." Telfina said.

Hutar watched in skeptical silence as I stepped into his dark office, food in hand.

"Thank you for letting me join your guild, mister Hutar, sir." I smiled.

Hutar sighed.

"Just call me Hutar, like everybody else."

"Okay," I smiled. "I made a big meal for everybody, and I didn't want to leave you out. Here you go."

Telfina nodded as I placed the plate before Hutar.

"It's actually quite good."

Hutar examined it with his eyes, a look of complete disinterest plastered across his big, grumpy face. You think it would be easier to smile with those big tusks justing out of his mouth but he had mastered the art of permanantly frowning.

"Thank you," he grumbled.

"You're welcome." I took a step back and stood there with a smile, waiting patiently for him to give the food a try.

A few silent moments passed before Hutar grumbled, "Is there anything else I can help you with?"

"Nope!"

Silence blanketed the room once more. Hutar looked at me, then at Telfina, and then back at me again. Maybe he and I weren't so different after all!

"Well, if you'll excuse me," He uttered, nodding towards the door. "I have quite a lot of work to do."

Was he joking?

"Don't you wanna try the food first?"

"I'm not very hungry."

My smile fell in an instant.

"Oh, okay. I'll get out of your hair then, I guess."

My pout turned to an embarrassed grimace when I looked atop his head to see not a single hair in sight.

"I mean—uh—sorry!"

Hutar heaved a heavy sigh over Telfina's muffled giggle and waved me off. I didn't need to be told twice, so I scampered out of the room and pulled the door shut.

But, all was not lost! As I left, I overheard a tiny whisper—Telfina was quietly urging Hutar to eat!

I couldn't help but take a peek just before the door shut, and I caught a quick glance of Hutar trying out "Cob CopperSpoon's Big Day at The Guild of the Twelfth Knight Special!" As the door came to a close, I could have sworn I saw his lips curl in a teeny, crooked smile.

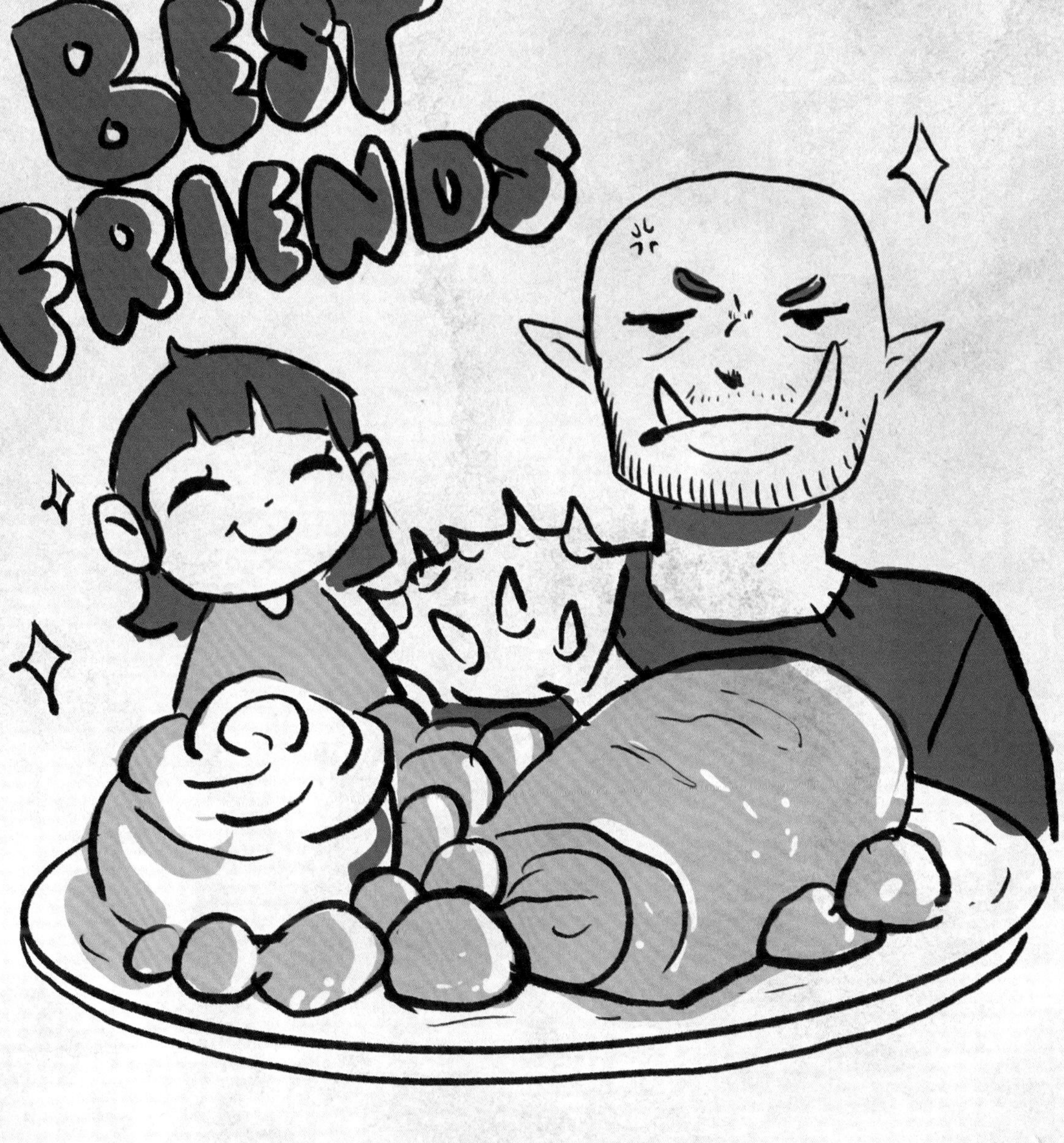
BEST FRIENDS

CHAPTER NINE
Misfits of the Bastion

Good evening journal!

I spent most of my time with Karn today! He told me that many of the places I've visited in the city so far are all <u>waaaaay</u> too touristy, and that there's so much more to the Violet Bastion than meets the eye. So, naturally, he took me on a tour.

I got to see all the nitty, gritty, secret, and delicious corners of the city, and believe me when I tell you I <u>love</u> this place. It's <u>alive</u> with the hum of vendors and chatter. Witnessing the vibrant tapestry of cultures, people, and stories right before my eyes was incredible!

We journeyed to a part of the city with a market called The Old Manor Bazaar. According to Karn, the bazaar's the city's best-kept secret. It was built in an old, previously abandoned estate that I guess was once owned by a near-ancient family of nobles. They ended up fleeing the country for one reason or another (drama!), and eventually someone had the creative idea to turn the dilapidated carcass of the house into a market. They fixed it up enough so that it's safe, but kept the old, run-down exterior, leaving behind a mystical, well-lit, but dangerous-looking environment.

There were all sorts of neat things at the market, too! One place sold only seashells from distant lands; another sold little needle-work portraits of rare flowers! There were vendors selling food, too, of course, but one vendor in particular caught my eye; a rickety blue cart run by a blue-skinned gnome. He sold pastries in all sorts of shapes and sizes, many of them featuring berries and other fruits I had never seen before.

"Karn!" I gasped, stopping us in our tracks. "We <u>have</u> to stop by that cart."

Karn, who was in the middle of chewing the last bit of a banana muffin, didn't pause to speak.

"Aye, I could go for . . . what's that?" He glanced at the cart's painted sign, squinting his eyes narrowly to make out the words.

"A bramblebloom berry éclair tower drizzled in caramel and primple jam," I read, wondering if we needed to buy him a pair of glasses on our way out.

"No, not that, look!" Karn nodded to one of the patrons who had just begun to browse the cart. They were dressed in oversized, colorful rags that hung loosely over their hands. They walked—no—<u>wobbled</u> quite awkwardly, and swung each leg wide with every step they took.

"Reminds me of a clown on stilts."

I giggled, he wasn't wrong. "Yeah, or—wait . . . look at <u>that guy</u>!"

A very short, red-nosed noble dressed in purple and furs of all different patterns rounded the corner, adjusting what I could have sworn was a paper crown on his head.

"You, sir!" he said, pointing to the gnome. "How much for the primple jam tower?"

The gnome straightened up in an instant.

"Well, it depends on how many tiers you'd like," he said, his voice gravelly and tired. "The tower starts with three tiers—"

"I'll take thirty!" the noble barked. "At once!"

The gnome raised an eyebrow. "Thirty?"

"Yes!"

"Well . . . I suppose that's doable. This would require me to put quite a long dowel down the center of the tower, however, and—"

"I don't care what it requires, you'll do it, and you'll do it now!"

I couldn't help but grimace. This guy might be rich, but he sure was rude.

"Well, I'd have to find a tall enough dowel first, Sir . . ." the gnome's sentence trailed off expectantly.

"Rubenport," The noble replied, his glance ever so quickly meeting the eyes of the person in rags. "Sir Rubenport."

"Sir Rubenport of . . . ?"

The noble sniffled, wiping his red nose with the back of his velvety purple sleeve.

"Does it matter?"

"Well yes, I see you have a . . . crown, of sorts, and if you're perhaps from one of the local noble houses I'd be more than happy to offer you a discounted price."

Sir Rubenport glanced around, his eyes flicking from the gnome to the dilapidated shell of the Old Manor Bazaar to the person in rags.

<u>Wham!</u>

A loud crash boomed through the baazar as the person in rags collapsed to the ground, wailing in such a way that I was almost positive they were laughing.

"Help!" they cried, "I can't get up!" they kicked their legs wildly in the air, revealing that they had a few bricks tied to their shoes. Maybe in an attempt to seem a little taller? I guess that explains the awkward gait.

The gnome sprung to life, shoving the noble aside in attempts to bring the person in rags to their feet. Sir Rubenport was having none of this! He gasped and loudly began to rant about the gnome's lack of manners.

"Karn, should we help?"

I watched the gnome struggle to help the person in rags, who rolled around on the ground, flailing around like a fish out of water.

"I don't think they need help, Cob."

Karn grunted, nodding to the cart.

81

Amid the commotion, my eyes caught a pair of tiny hands reaching from what I once mistook as a completely normal wooden crate. Whoever was inside snatched not one, not two, but <u>eighteen</u> pastries from the blue cart before they stood up, crate and all, and scurried off into the market! That's right, Journal, Karn and I were key witnesses to a <u>robbery</u>!

I covered my mouth in shock.

"They stole!"

Once the crate disappeared into the distance, the person in rags was suddenly able to stand on their own. Sir Rubenport entirely lost his interest in the pastry tower, too! Both ended up wandering off in similar directions while the poor gnome yelped in surprise to see that a third of his stock had disappeared.

Karn grimaced, his eyebrows furrowing deeply in resolve.

"We have to follow them."

Well, I've never had a chance to fight crime before, but I knew that this was it! That's right, Violet Bastion, Karn and Cob are here to protect you!

Karn was determined, and I mean <u>determined</u>. He had a steely gaze in his eyes like none I had ever seen, and every muscle of his seemed tense as we crept stealthily through the market. We kept our eyes on the person in rags and the now crown-less Sir Rubenport as they wove through the crowds and reunited deep within the Old Manor Bazaar, shedding small layers of their outfits as they walked. We kept to the shadows, blending in seamlessly with our surroundings. Those thieves had no idea we were hot on their trail.

"What do we do when we catch them?" I asked.

"We'll make sure they answer fer what they've done," Karn uttered as we followed the delinquents into a quiet alley. "And then we'll give 'em what they deserve."

I imagined us, the bravest duo in the world, kicking down the door to their secret, evil lair with a loud bang! We'd scrap for a bit, but easily come out on top, and then the city guards would file in just in time and arrest the criminals for years of pastry-related crimes and tomfoolery.

Well, we finally had them cornered when they crawled into a nearly hidden hole in the wall.

"That must be their secret lair," I whispered.

Karn uttered a stern grunt and, without another word, slithered in after them. I bravely followed suit, but the heroic grin on my face soured once the scent of stale-clothes and dirt began to tickle my nose.

I immediately realized why.

This tiny hole in the wall led to a cramped, hidden, candlelit crawlspace, where seven dirty, sooty, people had managed to comfortably tuck themselves away to nibble on pastries amongst ramshackle furniture and bedrolls. They looked at us with wide, horrified eyes and rosy cheeks, their dirt-stained faces betraying their youthful innocence. That's right, these sugar loving criminals were just kids! Kids who screeched upon our arrival.

Most of them clung to each other for dear life, but the tallest child, the one I recognized as Sir Rubenport, scowled and brandished a rusty sword, pointing it right in Karn's direction. The blade was only inches from his face, but Karn didn't move a muscle.

"What are you doing here?!" The boy growled, his hands trembling in fear. "Get out!"

"We caught you, Sir Rubenport!" I couldn't help but flash a devious little grin.

The boy raised an eyebrow, "What? That's not my name—"

"We saw what you did to that gnome," Karn's voice was low and gruff. "Stealin' is a very serious matter."

He swallowed hard, a bead of sweat trickling down his forehead, smearing the dirt on his skin.

"We're just trying to get by."

"We work for the Guild of the Twelfth Knight, we don't take kindly tae those who think they can just take whatever they want without consequences. Now, it's time for you—*all* of you—tae pay for yer crimes."

Fear crept into the boy's widened eyes, the other children whimpered, and I felt a pang of guilt in the pit of my stomach.

"Wha—what are you gonna do to us?" he asked, limbs shaking.

"First, we'll make sure you understand that what you've done is wrong—"

"We know it's bad, but we have no choice! We're orphans!"

Karn shook his head, dismissing his words with a stern exhale.

"So, you'd think in that case you'd have some sympathy instead of decidin' taw rob someone else of their livelihood. Did you see the state of that gnome's cart? He was obviously just tryin' tae get by like the rest of you!"

The children hung their heads in shame. Karn was right, after all, but I couldn't help but wonder where else all these young kids were supposed to get food and clothes if it wasn't by stealing from people who had what they needed.

"Karn, we—"

"It's important you feel the weight of yer actions," Karn continued. "We'll teach you all a lesson that ye'll not soon forget, one that'll stick with you fer a lifetime."

The boy, who still kept his trembling sword pointed at Karn, took an unnerved step back. His face paled, and his eyes began to shine with tears.

"If you think I'll let you arrest us, you—you got another thing coming!"

"We've seen all sorts in this city—pickpockets, murderers—some end up with a slap on the wrist, others are turned over to the guards and a few . . . well, lets just say they wish they'd never crossed our paths at all. As for you, we're takin' you tae the guild, and we're takin' you now."

"No!"

Karn let silence hang in the air for a moment, the hefty weight of the circumstance blanketing the entire space.

"<u>But</u> . . ." his voice softened and his hardened gaze lifted entirely. "Then we'll give you somethin' you've been missing—a chance tae do things the <u>right</u> way, and tae get the help you need. My friend here, the rest o' the guild, and myself can help you find a better path, one where you don't have to steal to get by. We'll start by at least makin' sure your bellies are full tonight, and then we'll figure out the rest together. How does that sound?"

The children all exchanged a sceptical look, some cautiously hopeful, others still untrusting. I felt myself exhale in relief, though. Helping the kids felt so much better than turning them in to the guards or even letting mean old Hutar yell at them.

"Really?" The boy asked, "All of us?"

"All of you. You have my word." Karn said, reaching out his hand for him to shake.

The boy hesitated, perhaps questioning if it was true that their reality could change so drastically.

"You have <u>my</u> word, too!" I told him.

He looked at his friends for reassurance, and he was met with freshly eager nods and faces plastered with wide grins.

"Fine," he shook Karn's hand, a smile soon breaking free from his frown. "Thank you very much. We really appreciate it"

The rest of the children thanked us, shaking our hands, too, and giving us happy hugs. Helping these down-on-their-luck kids filled my heart with a warmth I hadn't felt before. Not once have I ever had the opportunity to change someone's life like this! Was this what working at the guild is all about? If so, it's definitely something I'm interested in doing way more often!

One by one we ushered the kids out of their hiding hole. Our first stop was the gnomes pastry stand. Each of the kids apologized and Karn handed over a small sack of coins. I don't know how much was in there but I know one of the kid's eyes lit up with joy as he peered inside. I already knew Karn was a good person but this mission really proved it!

As we traveled we talked for some time about their hobbies and interests. One little girl in particular loved to cook. Ember excitedly told me some of the things she liked to eat (besides pastries), and I have to say, she's pretty creative! I even showed her you, Journal. All the recipes we have come across, and even the family spoon and my spice pouch. To express their gratitude, the kids offered to cook us something special—Surprise Fries! Karn and I watched as they scrambled around the guild kitchen scraping together random ingredients that were laying around. Upon request I even let Ember borrow my Copper Spoon and she waved it around the kitchen, barking orders at her peers.

We all shared stories as we ate, and I learned each of the children's names. Mindy, Tophius, Ember, Jack, Kieran, Tommy—who was the one with bricks on his feet—and their brave leader, Sir Rubenport. Just kidding, his name's Nielson.

Karn waved his fork in the air as we wrapped up our meal.

"Now kids, remember: if you're gonna steal, don't steal from small businesses. Big corporations only!"
"Karn!" I gasped, "They shouldn't steal at all!"
He laughed one of his soulful, hearty laughs.
"Aye, I know. I'm just kidding."
What a rascal!

Surprise Fries

Tophius explained to us that the "surprise" in surprise fries is just whatever leftovers they could find discarded in the streets. In this instance they scoured the guild kitchen to find some leftover cooked beef, peanuts, and some partially moldy cheese that was hidden in the back of the root cellar. Don't worry, we used the non-moldy parts. They put together a pretty good base and with some help from the good ole spice pouch we made a delicious new recipe!

MAKES 4-6 SERVINGS

Prep time: 30-60 minutes | Cook time: 30-60 minutes

INGREDIENTS

FRIES:
- 4-6 large russet potatoes
- 2 tablespoons cornstarch
- 1 tablespoon seasoning salt
- 2-4 cups of frying oil (vegetable, canola, peanut, etc.)
- Salt

BULGOGI BEEF:
- 1 pound ground beef
- 3 tablespoons soy sauce
- 1½ tablespoons brown sugar
- 2 teaspoons toasted sesame oil
- 1 teaspoon mirin
- 1-3 cloves garlic, minced
- Red pepper flakes and/or ground ginger (optional)
- 1 teaspoon cornstarch

TOPPINGS:
- Mozzarella cheese
- Lettuce
- Peanuts
- Sweet chili sauce
- Hoisin sauce
- Sriracha mayo
- Green onions

INSTRUCTIONS

FRIES:

1. Peel your potatoes and chop them into your desired fry shape! The bigger your fry, the longer it will take to cook in the end, so keep that in mind while chopping.

2. Add your fries to a large bowl and fully submerge in water. Let your

potatoes soak for at least an hour before straining and patting dry with a clean paper towel.

3. Mix together your cornstarch and seasoning salt. Then, pour the mix over your potatoes. Toss until each fry has an even coating of the cornstarch/seasoning mix.

4. In a medium to large pot, start heating your oil over medium-high heat. If you have a thermometer, heat until it reaches 350°F. If you don't, you can still test the heat of your oil with a wooden spoon. If you place the end of a wooden spoon in your oil and it begins to bubble, that means it's ready to go.

5. Working in small batches, begin to fry your potatoes. Gently drop a handful of fries into the oil with a slotted spoon or spider strainer. Give it a gentle stir so the fries don't all stick to each other, then let it be for 5 to 6 minutes. The fries will begin to get some color but won't be fully crispy yet. Right now, just focus on cooking the potatoes through. We'll fry them again later to make them crispy.

6. Transfer your fries to a paper towel–lined baking sheet to drain while you finish cooking the rest of your fries.

7. Once all of your potatoes have gone through their first fry, we're going to start frying them again! This time you can work in bigger batches, and it will only take 2 to 3 minutes per batch to get them nice and crispy!

8. Once your potatoes have turned a beautiful golden brown, transfer them to another paper towel–lined baking sheet.

BULGOGI BEEF:

1. Heat a large pan over medium-high heat. Add in your ground beef and cook until fully cooked and golden brown, about 5 to 10 minutes.

2. While your beef is cooking, mix together your soy sauce, brown sugar, sesame oil, mirin, garlic, and cornstarch. Make sure to whisk this well to try and avoid any large clumps of cornstarch.

3. Once your beef has finished cooking, add in your soy sauce mix. Cook for an additional 5 minutes to help thicken the sauce and cook out any cornstarch flavor.

(Continued)

ASSEMBLY:

1. Preheat your oven to broil.
2. Add your fries to the bottom of a cast iron or parchment-lined baking sheet.
3. Top your fries with your bulgogi beef, then add on as much mozzarella cheese as you want.
4. Place under your broiler just until the cheese becomes ooey and gooey, about 5 to 7 minutes.
5. Remove from the oven and serve with all the toppings you want! This dish is fun because everybody can make it with whatever they like the best.

CHAPTER TEN
Mysteries of the Deep

Journal!

Oh my goodness, I'm so nervous but so, so, <u>so</u> excited! We were assigned a quest, which will mark my very first adventure with my new friends. We even get to go on a boat!

Apparently, this type of mission wouldn't even normally be given to our guild because of the great distance we have to travel, but Telfina and Hutar are old friends with the tribe that needs assistance. Yep, we get to help out a whole group of people! I'm so excited I could dance for six hours straight. But I shouldn't. Not just to conserve my energy, but because I have to stay composed. Things could get very dangerous, and I'll need to focus as hard as I can.

Telfina told us that we have to travel west, far along the coast. There's a village called Nautinara, which is home to water-faring people who live on islands off the mainland. It's said that there's a great coral reef there that's alive with aquatic life and has very important resources for the people who live nearby. However, something evil lurking in the deep has begun to torment the waters. While the tribe members are safe from the creature on land, they're completely unable to reach the reef to harvest the resources they need to sustain themselves. How horrible!

It gets worse, too. Telfina said that everyone who's gone out to help either hasn't returned, or they've made it back to the island just barely clinging to life. The survivors all told the same terrifying story: the creature in the water moves and strikes with lightning speed.

I'm not quite sure what we can do to stop it. Like I told my friends before, I'm no fighter. Harold told me that sometimes in situations like these it's not skill that's important, not even strength—but it's all about one's desire to do what's right. He said that in the end, light will prevail over darkness, and sometimes all it takes is one single flame to light up an entire room. And boy, I'm so full of the desire to help the water tribe that I feel like I might burst like a firecracker!

With the reassurance from Harold, I decided to dig deeper into how Hutar and Telfina knew these remote villagers. I learned from Telfina that she and Hutar used to be in an adventuring party together, and they once got into a big, horrifying shipwreck! The vessel was torn apart, supplies and crew members alike were flung into the ocean's turbulent waves. Telfina in particular was in horrible shape; her head was wounded from the wreck, and she could barely manage to keep herself above water. Disorientated, the waves relentlessly tossed her from side to side. Just when she thought she'd never make it out alive, <u>splash!</u> Hutar to the rescue. (What a hero!)

    They eventually washed up along Nautinara's shores, and the people of the island nursed them back to health with a soup their medicine woman concocted. Scouting parties were sent out to sea to check for survivors—or anything they could salvage from the trip, really—but they only found two other people curled up in refuge on a shallow part of the reef bed. The others were never found. The people from the island, all members of the Adva'lora tribe, eventually helped Hutar, Telfina, and the two survivors find their way back home. They even showed them the safest route to return if they ever wanted to visit the island. We're using that very same route on our trip!

    I've never been at sea before, and I really, really, really hope that everything goes swimmingly and nothing like that wreck happens to us. As beautiful as people say it is, the ocean's no joke.

Ocean's Embrace

Telfina is a <u>great</u> story teller. She doesn't do voices or throw illusions but her soft, calming voice reminds me of when my mother used to read me to sleep. She is also a great payer-attentioner. She instantly clocked my excited expression at the mention of a "healing sea soup." At the end of her story, she led me to a small bed chamber and removed a small chest from a set of drawers.

"You're not allowed to keep this," she told me, placing an un-labeled piece of parchment softly in my hands. "But you can copy the recipe. Our secret, ok?"

MAKES 4-6 SERVINGS

Prep time: 10-15 minutes | Cook time: 30 minutes

INGREDIENTS

- 1 pound bacon
- 1 large onion
- 2 –3 large russet potatoes
- 1 tablespoon butter
- 1 head garlic
- 1 tablespoon chopped rosemary
- 1 tablespoon chopped thyme
- 2 (6-oz) cans clams
- 1 teaspoon salt
- 1 teaspoon pepper
- 1 teaspoon paprika
- 1 teaspoon coriander
- 2 bay leaves
- 3 –4 cups chicken broth
- ½ cup flour
- 2 cups heavy cream

INSTRUCTIONS

1. Prep all of your ingredients. Chunk your bacon into bite-sized bits, dice your onion and potatoes, and mince your garlic, rosemary, and thyme. Also strain your clams through a fine mesh strainer, making sure to save the juice from the can.

2. Heat a large pot or Dutch oven over medium-high heat. Add in all of your bacon and cook until nice and crispy, about 5 to 10 minutes. Once fully cooked, remove from the pan into a paper towel–lined bowl. Drain most of the bacon grease from your pan, leaving about 1 tablespoon worth inside.

(Continued)

3. Add in your butter, onions, garlic, rosemary, and thyme. Sauté until the onions are nice and translucent.

4. Once your onions are fully cooked add in all of your potatoes, salt, pepper, paprika, and coriander. Mix until potatoes are fully coated in seasonings.

5. Add in all of your clam juice and then chicken broth until your potatoes are fully covered, putting in your bay leaves last.

6. Bring your broth to a boil and then reduce heat to a medium-low. Cover with a lid and simmer until potatoes are fully cooked, about 15 to 20 minutes.

7. In a small bowl, mix together your flour and ½ cup of your heavy cream until a thick paste is formed. Slowly mix in the rest of your cream until there are no large chunks of flour left.

8. Once your potatoes are fully cooked, remove both bay leaves and add in your cream-and-flour mix. Increase heat and bring to a boil. It should start to really thicken at this point.

9. Once your chowder starts to thicken, add in all your clams and cook for an additional 2 to 3 minutes, just enough for them to warm up.

10. Enjoy! Serve in bread bowls and top with your bacon bits!

CHAPTER ELEVEN
A Taste of the Tropics

Dear Journal,

    I'm feeling kind of icky so this one might not be very long, but I have a few interesting things to share!

    Firstly, since the Adva'loran's needs us to arrive A.S.A.P., Hutar let us travel to the coast via teleportation circle. It was so cool! We stepped into a big fancy circle, he cast the spell, and then <u>poof</u>! Next thing we all knew, we were in Marlin's Shore, a beautiful town right near the endless, sparkling ocean.

    Secondly, I'm sure you've probably already assumed, but I've never seen the ocean before! It was amazing! There were big calm waves rolling to the shoreline all at once, carrying a cool, refreshing breeze on their backs. And that breeze? It was salty. How is that even possible? I so badly wished I could just take a jar, swing it around to collect the air, and bring it back home to share with everybody. Unfortunately, it's not quite that easy. I guess I'll just have to bring my family on vacation next time. I was completely unprepared for what was waiting for me in town. Street vendors. Everywhere! If you turned a corner, walked into an alley, or even lifted up a rug there was a street vendor right there, ready and happy to serve you. I had to pinch myself to make sure I wasn't dreaming. It was like my birthday and every single holiday that's ever existed had been wrapped into one beautiful, life-altering delicious moment!

    While the rest of the group went off to find an inn to stay at, I dragged my fellow foodie, Karn, along to try everything we could get our teeth on before we had to leave in the morning. We only had <u>one</u> night to make it count.

    We spent hours running from cart to cart, ordering the very best and most interesting things off of what felt like hundreds of menus. The further into the markets we roamed, the more the scent of roasting meats and exotic spices mixed with the refreshing scent of the ocean. It was invigorating! I took notes the whole time, recreating and sometimes finding ways to improve every dish that I tried.

There's an indescribable bliss that comes along with taste-testing new foods. I could have stayed there for months, but my tummy can only hold so much. I'm not very tall, you see. By the time night rolled around, I was stuffed to the brim, groggy, and a little bit nauseated. Karn and I were so full that we had to practically crawl back to the inn. I wished we thought ahead and tied a rope to the front door, that way could have just dragged ourselves limply along with our arms instead of standing upright.

Sorry, I said this one wasn't going to be long, but I guess I got carried away. Here's a few recipes inspired by the amazing foods we ate today—some were even shared with me out of the kindness of the vendor's hearts. Isn't that sweet?

Ugh . . . <u>sweet</u>.

That word reminds me of candy. And I still feel pretty sick.

Colossal Crab Cheese Dip

We walked up to this one stand in the market that had a <u>huge</u> tank of crabs that were as tall as me! Karn too! They were varying shades of purple and they all had pieces of what looked like coral growing on their backs—the half-orc lady who ran the stand let me have a teeny piece of coral for free. I think I'm gonna turn it into a necklace!

Karn said that, usually, when animals are brightly colored that means they're poisonous, but the old man claiming to be the owner said that wasn't a problem, so here's hoping!

MAKES 4 SERVINGS

Prep time: 10–15 minutes | Cook time: 25–35 minutes

INGREDIENTS

WONTON CHIPS:
1 cup vegetable oil
Wonton wrappers
Salt

CRAB DIP:
4–5 cloves garlic
6 green onions
1 (12-oz) package crab meat (imitation works great)
1 tablespoon olive oil
½ teaspoon black pepper
1 (8-oz) package cream cheese
1 tablespoon soy sauce
1 tablespoon lemon juice
1 tablespoon Worcestershire sauce
¼ cup mozzarella cheese
¼ cup Parmesan cheese
Sweet chili sauce (optional)

INSTRUCTIONS

WONTON CHIPS:

1. In a large pan, heat your oil until sizzling hot over high heat (about 350°F).
2. Cut your wonton wrappers diagonally into triangles, making 48 even pieces.
3. Fry your wonton wrappers, a few at a time, making sure not to overcrowd your pan. Fry until golden brown, it should only take a minute to perfectly fry.
4. Remove your chips from the oil and let drain on a paper towel–lined baking sheet. Sprinkle with a pinch of salt immediately after you remove from oil.
5. Repeat until all of your wontons are cooked.

(Continued)

CRAB DIP:

1. Preheat your oven to broil.
2. Mince your cloves of garlic, slice your green onions, and chop your crab into rough chunks.
3. In a medium oven-safe or cast-iron pan, heat your oil over medium heat.
4. Add your green onion, garlic, and pepper and sauté until fragrant, about 2 to 3 minutes.
5. Once fragrant, add in your cream cheese, soy sauce, lemon juice, Worcestershire sauce, and crab meat. Stir constantly until cream cheese is melted and everything is incorporated.
6. Top the dip with your mozzarella and Parmesan cheese, then place under your broiler just until the cheese melts and gets bubbly.
7. Serve the dip warm with your wonton chips and enjoy! For an extra kick, serve with some sweet chili sauce!

Cheesy Harvest Wands

Hey Journal, it's nice to <u>sea</u> you. I would <u>wave</u> to you, but you don't have any hands to <u>wave</u> back! I'm sorry, is this too <u>corny</u>?

This recipe has to be one of my favorites of the night! The cheese is super salty, and the corn is super juicy and fresh! I could eat a dozen of these easily.

Makes 4 cobs (corn cobs, not cob-cobs!)

Prep time: 5-10 minutes | Cook time: 15 minutes

Ingredients

- ¼ cup mayonnaise
- ¼ cup sour cream or Mexican crema
- 1 lime
- Bundle of cilantro
- 1 cup queso fresco
- 4 cobs of corn
- Tajin

Instructions

1. Prep your ingredients! In a small bowl, mix together your mayonnaise and sour cream. Slice your lime into wedges, roughly chop your cilantro, and crumble up your queso fresco.
2. Grill your corn. Heat your grill to high or use a grill pan on your stovetop. Cook until there are some nice char marks all around your corn. If you have neither a grill or grill pan, you can either boil or bake your corn until heated, about 12 minutes in a 350°F oven or boiling pot.
3. Once your corn is fully cooked, brush with your mayonnaise and sour cream mixture.
4. Roll your corn in the queso fresco until the whole thing is covered.
5. Top with a squeeze of lime, your cilantro, and your tajin. You can also add some cayenne or paprika for a little kick.
6. Enjoy!

Bayberry Taffy

One really cool thing Karn and I learned about today is the bayberry. It's really unique because it can only be found growing under the sea, and only next to where eels live! Unfortunately, the bayberry can't survive above water for very long, so if you pick one you better eat or cook with it fast.

Makes 24-30 candies

Prep time: 5 minutes | Cook time: 1-2 hours

Ingredients

- 1 cup white sugar
- 1 tablespoon cornstarch
- ½ teaspoon sea salt
- 1½ tablespoons butter plus extra for greasing your pan
- ½ cup honey
- ¼ cup light corn syrup
- ⅔ cup water
- 1 teaspoon bayberry juice (can substitute strawberry extract instead)
- ½ teaspoon vanilla extract
- Food coloring

Note: You will also need a candy thermometer for this recipe!

Instructions

1. Add your sugar, cornstarch, sea salt, butter, honey, corn syrup, and water to a medium-small saucepan. You will need a bigger pan than you think, but you still want your candy thermometer to be able to reach the mixture without touching the bottom of the pan.

2. Place your pan over a medium heat. Stir your mixture constantly until it comes to a boil.

3. Once your mixture is boiling, stop stirring it. Add your candy thermometer to the pot and leave it alone until it reaches 250 to 253°F. This should take about 15 to 30 minutes depending on how hot your stovetop gets.

4. While your mixture is coming to temperature, grease a baking dish with a little bit of butter.

5. Once your mixture reaches 250°F remove it from the heat and immediately stir in your bayberry flavoring and vanilla. Make sure if you're using any plastic utensils, they are candy-proof because this heat will melt certain plastics.

6. Transfer your candy mix to your buttered baking dish to begin cooling. You want to let the mixture cool enough so that you can easily touch

it without hurting yourself. This will take 15 to 30 minutes depending on the temperature you are working in. You will know it's ready to check once the candy has started sticking to itself instead of pooling together like a liquid. Use a butter-coated spatula or scissors to cut a line down the middle of your candy, and if it doesn't immediately form back together it should be safe to softly touch to test the temperature.

7. Now, the fun part: pulling the taffy. This is going to be very sticky, so make sure to put on some gloves if you want, and cover your hands in butter so the taffy doesn't stick. You can make your taffy all one color or get fancy and do 2 or 3 different colors of your choice. Before starting to pull, section off your taffy into however many colors you want, then add in your food coloring.

8. Begin by stretching the taffy out then folding it over itself. At first, it's going to be very sticky and it's not going to want to come together. Just trust the process and keep pulling. Make sure you re-grease your hands if it starts to get sticky, though. Your candy is going to turn from clear and glossy to an opaque creamy color. This process can take anywhere from 15–45 minutes, depending on how long your arms can last. It's okay if the taffy comes out a little goopy, it's still going to taste delicious. (P.S. This step is the most fun when friends and family are involved.)

9. Once your taffy thickens and turns creamy colored, you're ready to roll it into a log and start cutting it. You can use a buttered surface, but I do this step on a large piece of parchment paper to prevent it from sticking to anything. Using a sharp knife or scissors, cut your taffy into bite-sized pieces then individually wrap in wax paper.

10. Enjoy! Truthfully, you can add any flavor you like, but this way's my favorite.

Chewy Gnome Bread and Cheese Sauce

This was one of my favourite treats. The version I made on my own didn't look nearly as pretty as the one from the stand, but is it really the shape that makes it a gnome bread? Don't know, don't care. I just know I love gnome bread!

MAKES 8 SERVINGS

Prep time: 1½ hours | Cook time: 20-30 minutes

INGREDIENTS

GNOME BREAD:
1⅓ cups warm water
1 tablespoon active dry yeast
4 cups flour
2 teaspoons salt
3 tablespoons softened butter
4 cups water
¼ cup baking soda
1 egg
Coarse sea salt

CHEESE SAUCE:
2 tablespoons butter
2 tablespoons flour
1 cup milk
1 cup sharp cheddar
Pinch paprika
Salt and pepper, to taste

INSTRUCTIONS

GNOME BREAD:

1. Mix together your warm water and yeast. Let sit for 5 minutes until it has bloomed. Your water should be warm but not hot, or else your yeast will die.

2. Mix your flour and salt in a large bowl.

3. Add your yeast mix and butter to your flour and mix until everything is fully incorporated.

4. On a dry, un-floured surface, knead your dough for 5 to 10 minutes until it holds a nice smooth consistency.

5. Once fully kneaded, add to a lightly greased bowl and cover. Let rise for 1 hour until it has doubled in size.

6. Once fully risen, pour your dough out onto a dry, un-floured surface. Split your dough into 8 even(ish) pieces.

7. Roll each piece into about 20- to 22-inch ropes. If you are having a hard time rolling them out, spray a small amount of water onto your work surface and then roll your dough.

8. Shape the logs into your gnome bread by making a loop in the middle of your rope. Twist the dough once around each other and then fold the two ends

over the top of the loop. Place your gnome bread on a parchment-lined baking sheet.

9. Preheat your oven to 400°F.
10. In a large pot bring your water and baking soda to a simmer. You just want your water warm, but it should not be boiling.
11. Drop your gnome bread 2 or 3 at a time (depending on how large your pot is) into your baking soda water. Let soak for 1 to 2 minutes and then flip. After each side has been simmered for 1 to 2 minutes, remove from the pot and place back onto your baking sheet. Repeat for all of your gnome bread.
12. Right before you put your gnome bread in the oven, whisk your egg in a small bowl and brush the surface of each gnome bread with it. Top with your coarse sea salt then place in the oven.
13. Bake for 15 to 20 minutes or until golden brown.

CHEESE SAUCE:
1. Add your butter and flour to a small saucepan. Heat over medium-high heat while stirring constantly until your roux starts to bubble.
2. Let your roux cook for 2 to 3 minutes, and then slowly start adding in your milk. It will be chunky at first, and that's okay! Just keep slowly adding your milk and mixing constantly.
3. Keep stirring your milk until it thickens and starts to bubble. Then fully remove from the heat.
4. Once you remove the milk from the heat, immediately add your cheese. Whisk constantly until the cheese is fully melted.
5. Add in a pinch of paprika, stir in, and then give your cheese a taste. Add any salt and pepper as needed.
6. Serve with your soft gnome bread and enjoy!

Huntsman's Hoagie

Karn and I stopped at a stand with a cute little old lady working at it. The stand has been in her family's care for five generations! Her son is a huntsman providing the meats for the stand and apparently this is his favorite recipe. The family-wide dedication to food really reminded me of home. I just wanted to give her a big old hug!

MAKES 4-6 SANDWICHES

Prep time: 30-40 minutes | Cook time: 2-2½ hours

INGREDIENTS

PORK:
- ⅓ cup soy sauce
- 1 tablespoon sambal chili paste
- 1 teaspoon white pepper
- 1 teaspoon coriander
- 1 tablespoon paprika
- 1 tablespoon sesame oil
- 1 tablespoon brown sugar
- 5 cloves fresh garlic
- 1 medium onion
- 2 small or 1 large pork roast (3-4 pounds) (Can use pork belly if it's available to you)

PICKLES:
- 2 cucumbers
- 3-5 whole carrots
- 5 cloves fresh garlic
- 1 teaspoon whole peppercorn
- 1 cup white vinegar
- ¼-½ cup white sugar

CONDIMENTS:
- 1-3 jalapeños
- Cilantro
- Vietnamese baguettes (can substitute with normal baguette or French bread)
- Kewpie mayonnaise
- Paté

INSTRUCTIONS

PORK:

1. In a small bowl, mix together everything besides your garlic, onion, and pork. Make sure everything is well combined and there are no seasoning clumps.

2. Peel and quarter your onion. Make sure your garlic is peeled as well.

3. Place your pork in an airtight container with your seasoning mix,

(Continued)

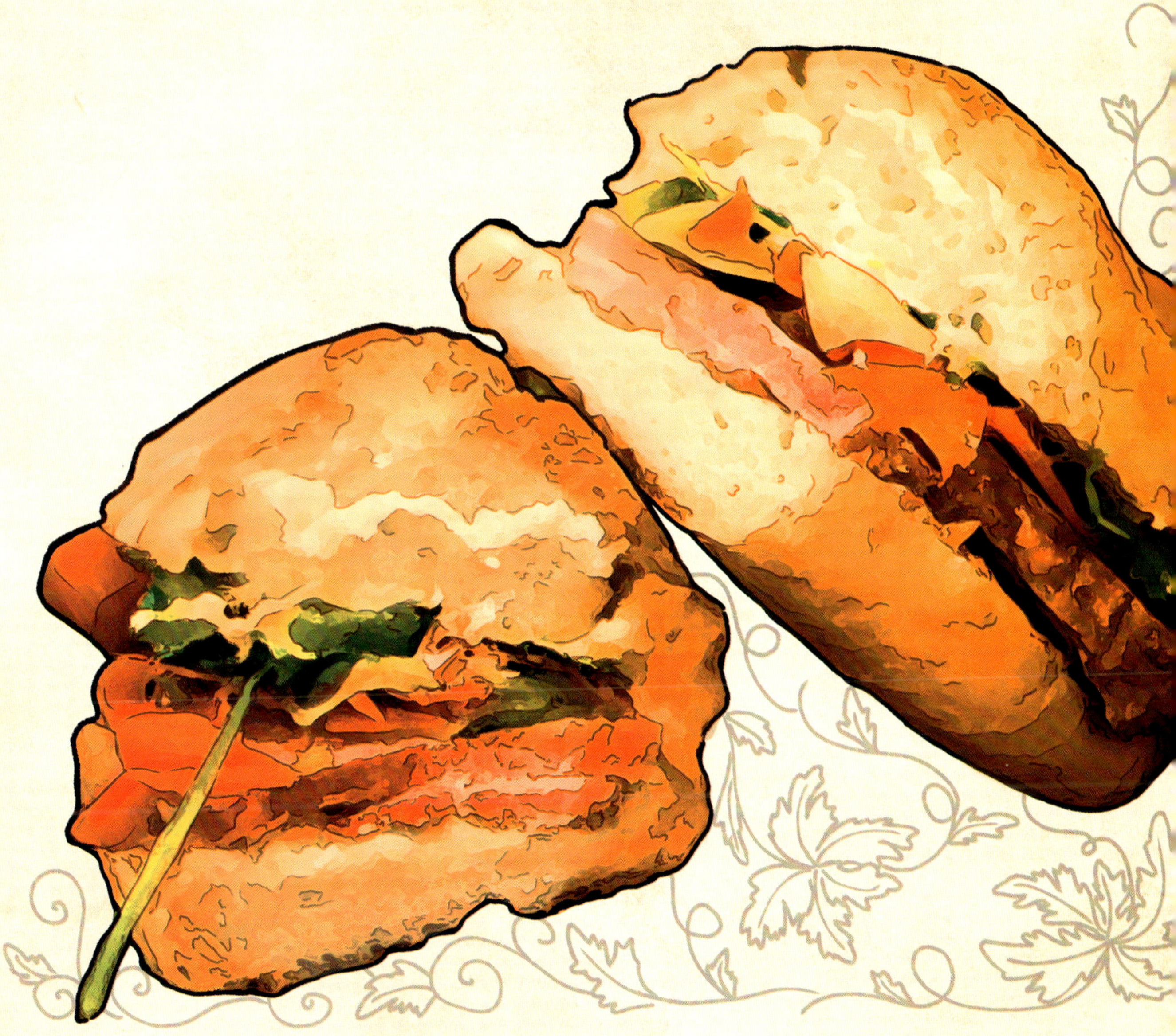

garlic, and onion. Place in the fridge and let sit for at least 1 hour, if not overnight.

4. When you are ready to cook, bring a steam pot to a boil over medium-high heat. If you don't have a steam pot, you can just bake your roast in a 350°F oven.

5. Once heated, carefully place your pork, onion, and garlic into the steam pot. Cover and leave for 2 hours. If you go with the oven route, bake for 1 hour or until it has reached an internal temperature of 145°F.

6. After it has cooked fully, remove from the pot and let it cool completely. Once cooled, thinly slice.

PICKLES:

1. Thinly slice your cucumbers and carrots after washing them. The best and easiest way to do this without any fancy tools is to use a potato peeler. Run your potato peeler down the length of your veggies. You should be left with long thin strips of cucumber and carrot. You will be left with scraps from the center part of the carrot and cucumber, but you can use that in salads or as a nice snack.

2. Put all of your shredded vegetables, garlic, and white peppercorns into a large jar layering each ingredient as you go to make sure it all gets evenly mixed. If you don't have a jar, you can also use a tupperware or glass bowl that can fit in your fridge.

3. In a small saucepan, mix your white vinegar and white sugar. Use more sugar if you like a little bit sweeter pickle; if you like a tarter pickle, stick with ¼ cup.

4. Bring your vinegar mix to a simmer over medium heat. You want all of the sugar to be dissolved and small bubbles to appear on the bottom of the pan, but you want to pull it off the heat before it starts to boil.

5. Pour your hot vinegar mix over your vegetables and into the jar. The vinegar will not cover all of your veggies so top with water until everything is fully submerged.

6. Cover tightly with lid or plastic wrap and let sit for at least 30 minutes. This will keep in the fridge for weeks and get better over time!

ASSEMBLY:

1. Slice your jalapeños and roughly chop your cilantro.

2. Cut open your bread and spread a thin layer of your mayonnaise and paté on each side. Add as much pickles, pork, and toppings as you want and enjoy!

Tropical Cream

A colorful toucan stopped Karn and I in the middle of the street. I found it very odd that it wore a small bow-tie as if in uniform! I guess it was handing out samples or something because it led us to a drink stand not too far away. It was squawking the words "Tropical Cream" at us as we grabbed our sample, so that's what I have dubbed this drink!

Karn added a little alcohol to his, but I prefer mine with none.

MAKES 1 SERVING

Prep time: 5 minutes

Ingredients

- Crushed ice
- 1 ounce coconut rum (optional)
- Orange soda
- 1–2 ounces Irish cream or coconut cream
- Whipped cream and/or orange and pineapple slices for garnish

Instructions

1. Fill your desired drinking vessel with crushed ice. The larger the glass, the less strong your drink will be.
2. Pour your coconut rum into the bottom of your glass then top with the orange soda, making sure to leave some space for your cream.
3. Top off your drink with your cream and stir well. For the best results, you want to keep your drink as cold as possible.
4. Garnish your glass with some whipped cream and fruit and enjoy! This tastes just like an orange dreamsicle, so be careful and drink responsibly!

Siren Fry

As Karn and I wandered, we came across a man with a peg leg and eyepatch. A colorful bird sat on his shoulder, he wore a captain's hat, and behind him was a half sunken pirate ship. He gestured to a rickety ramp leading to a makeshift door.

"There are two kinds of sirens in this world." He growled at us. "The first ones lure pirates and sailors to their deaths, and they have fish bodies but women's legs. The second kind serves fried food on a pier! Step inside and see which one ye find!"

Spoiler alert, it was the latter!

Makes 4-6 Servings

Prep time: 30-45 minutes | Cook time: 15-20 minutes

Ingredients

Pineapple Salsa:
- ½ pineapple
- ½ small red onion
- 1–2 jalapeño
- ½ cup cilantro
- 1 tablespoon honey
- 1–2 limes
- 1 teaspoon salt
- 1 teaspoon pepper

Chipotle Sauce:
- ½ (7-oz) can chipotle peppers in adobo
- ½ cup mayonnaise
- Salt and pepper, to taste
- Drizzle of honey

Fish:
- 8–12 pieces cod or halibut
- 1½ cups flour
- 4 eggs
- 1½ cups panko
- 3 teaspoons salt, divided
- 3 teaspoons pepper, divided
- 3 teaspoons paprika, divided
- ½ cup vegetable oil

Tacos:
- Corn tortillas

Instructions

Pineapple Salsa:

1. Dice your pineapple, red onion, and jalapeño into small pieces, making your red onion and jalapeno slightly smaller than your pineapple chunks.
2. Roughly chop your cilantro.

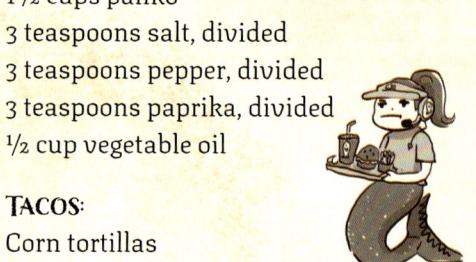

3. In a large bowl, combine all your chopped ingredients, as well as your honey, the juice of your limes, and a pinch of salt and pepper. Taste and adjust measurements to your liking, and feel free to add more honey for a sweeter salsa and some red chili flakes for a spicier salsa.

Chipotle Sauce:

1. In a mortar-and-pestle, crush your chiles in adobo into a paste. This can also be done with a blender or food processor.
2. Once your chipotles have been thoroughly smashed, add in your mayonnaise, salt, pepper, and honey. Taste as you go until you get the perfect flavor.

Fish:

1. Slice your fish into thin strips that can easily fit into your tacos and pat dry with a paper towel. Set aside while you prepare your bread crumb coating.
2. Get 3 bowls big enough to fit your fish strips. In one, add your flour, the next, your egg, and finally to the last, add your panko bread crumbs. Season each with 1 teaspoon salt, 1 teaspoon pepper, and 1 teaspoon paprika.
3. Dredge your fish starting with the flour, making sure the piece is fully coated. Then fully coat it in the egg mix, making sure to let any excess drip off before coating it in your panko bread crumb mix. Place coated fish aside while you repeat this process for each piece of fish.
4. Heat a large cast iron or non-stick skillet over high heat with your oil. Once it's sizzling hot, add in your fish, making sure not to overcrowd the pan. You want there to be a bit of space between each piece of fish.
5. Cook for 3 to 5 minutes on each side until golden brown. Set on a paper towel–lined plate to let excess oil be absorbed. Sprinkle it with a bit of salt immediately after it comes out of the pan.
6. Heat your tortillas, assemble, and enjoy!

CHAPTER TWELVE
Sick at Sea

Hello Journal,

    I'm convinced that society should just stick to land travel. I think I said something about the sea not being a joke the other day, but I don't think I was prepared for this. The waves are relentless, the ship is constantly teetering from left to right, and when it's not doing that, it's tipping forwards and then backwards again. I feel like I'm stuck inside a spinning cheese wheel that someone threw down a mountainside.
    <u>Why did I eat so much food before we left?</u>
    "Euuughhhhhhh."
    I leaned over the side of the ship. The wood creaked as the ocean rocked us, then cool salty mist landed on my skin as waves crashed against the stern.
    "It's not that bad, Cob," Finheld sighed.
    They were leaning on the side of the ship about ten feet from where I was, completely unaffected by the sea.
    "The water's pretty calm."
    "It's <u>so</u> bad,"
    I gurgled. The pinkish glow of the sun setting over the horizon didn't do anything to calm my nausea.
    I heard Irabel's voice coming from somewhere behind me, but I didn't have the strength to turn around.
    "I'm trying to meditate, can you two keep it down, please?"
    "It's not me!" Finheld uttered over another one of my nauseated groans. "It's her."
    "Sorry," I managed to blurt just before stifling something rising in my guts.
    "You shouldn't be so loud if you can help it, Cob," Irabel told me. "Or you'll . . . make the ghost mad."
    I stiffened in surprise.
    "The ghost?"
    "The ghost," she confirmed, her footsteps growing ever closer. "A woman died on this ship many years ago."
    She leaned next to me, smiling so widely that I could see her pointy fangs.
    "She comes out at night, looking for . . . uh, her fiancé."
    "Her fiancé? Why?"
    "Oh, because he . . . he abandoned her on their wedding day. For another woman. Right, Finheld?"

"Yeah," Finheld said with a smile. "She jumped in the sea to chase them and get her revenge—"

"And then she was <u>never</u> seen again. Except for when she comes out at night, of course . . . as a ghost."

I couldn't believe it. A ghost?! I felt like I had just bitten into the zestiest, most mind, body, and soul-clarifying lemon. I <u>had</u> to see the ghost with my own two eyes!

"Where?!" I asked.

Irabel's eyes widened, but she laughed a small little laugh.

"Cob, I was just trying to—"

"The hold," Finheld interjected, pointing at the opposite end of the ship, right to the cabins.

"The hold? What's that?"

"It's like the ship's basement, I guess—below deck. The hatch is over there."

I chirped a quick "thanks!" and scurried across the rocking deck.

I knew what Finheld and Irabel were doing. The distraction from my seasickness was only half of the reason I didn't turn back. Earlier I'd heard odd footsteps and creaking around the place long before Irabel's story. There <u>had</u> to be a ghost creeping around, and I was gonna be the one to find her!

I swung open the hatch and a ray of sun illuminated the ladder leading down, so I scurried my way below deck. As soon as my feet hit the floor, I heard a loud <u>bang</u>! I let out a small yelp as darkness surrounded me. The door to the hold had slammed shut . . . was it the ghost? I steeled myself against my fear and the churning of my stomach. The creaking of the wood was relentless and the roar of the ocean felt like it was surrounding me down here.

"Hello?" I whispered, squinting through the dark. "Miss ghost?"

A faint orange glow sparked in the distance for a fraction of a moment, illuminating the jumbled silhouettes of the crates and supplies. Sacks of rice and wheat that had been fastened down cast long shadows across the hold. A shiver crept down my spine—I only saw the space for a moment, but I was certain that I was the only one down there.

"Hello?" I whispered.

I heard no response.

"Hello?"

The light flickered again. Shorter—duller.

"Are you, uh—" <u>Dang, I wish I knew the ghost's name.</u> "Are you the woman that haunts this ship?"

The light, hidden by crates, swelled tenfold, bathing the room in burning orange. It was her! She was beckoning me forward!

Gritting my teeth, I stiffly headed through the maze of crates and supplies before me. My mind raced—what was I even going to do when I found her? Was she nice? Finheld said that she wanted revenge, so what if she was mean? What if she tried to throw me to the ocean the same way she threw herself? But I reminded myself I wasn't the one who broke her heart. She wouldn't do that to <u>me</u>, right?

"Hello?" I called.

There was a thud. And then a clattering crash—the light went out in an instant, blanketing us in nothing but darkness again.

"Agh! Ma'am?" I called. "I'm not here to hurt you—"

"<u>Ma'am</u>?" The voice that replied was unexpectedly deep.

"Uh—oh, sorry. I don't know your name—"

"Who's that I hear?"

"Cob," I said, feeling my way through the dark. "Who are <u>you</u>?"

"It's me," the voice hissed slightly in pain. "Harold."

"<u>Harold</u>?" I asked, disappointed but relieved. What a bittersweet discovery. "What are <u>you</u> doing down here?"

The orange light sparked into existence, fizzled, and soon swelled back up to its previous strength. Sure enough, there was the top of Harold's head peeking over a particularly large stack of burlap sacks.

"I'm looking for something, but my matches wouldn't light."

"Are you okay?" I asked, finally rounding my way over to him. Harold was standing next to an open crate that was filled with several small compartments of what looked to be assorted herbs. His lantern—the glowing light—sat on a neighboring crate and happily lit up the space for us.

"I'm okay. I didn't hear you coming and when you called out, it surprised me," he laughed. "I hit my elbow."

"I'm sorry! I thought you were a ghost."

"No ghost here," Harold smiled, beginning to dig through the open crate. "At least, I hope not."

"What are you looking for?"

"Well, I couldn't help but notice how sick you looked, and I wanted to make you something to help." With a shy smile, he pulled a small ginger root from the crate and gently stuffed it in his pocket. "But only if that's okay with you, of course."

His kindness made my heart swell with joy.

"Of course that's okay! Thank you so much!"

But just then I started to realize just how nauseated I still was. Suddenly, all I could focus on was the ship rocking back and forth again.

"You're turning green," Harold said.

I clapped my hands on my cheeks. "Seriously?!"

"No, but you do look like you're gonna hurl," he said with a kind laugh. "We should probably get you to the cabin so you can rest."

I nodded. "I think you're right."

Harold escorted me to The Tag-Alongs' shared room and I climbed into my bunk. He quietly brought one of his traveling bags to a small writing desk and pulled out a teeny wooden mortar and pestle. I watched as he emptied out what he gathered from his pockets and relished in the faint scent of fresh herbs.

For a long time, Harold didn't say a single word. This wasn't surprising, though; he was always quite quiet.

<u>Why</u>, though?

"Are you okay?" I asked. "You're pretty quiet."

Harold nearly seemed to wince at the sound of my voice, almost as though he either forgot I was here, or was discretely dreading this exact moment. That only made me more curious.

"I'm okay," he nodded, keeping his eye on his work. "Are <u>you</u> okay, though?"

"I'm not great, but I think whatever you're making will help."

Harold's usual kind smile spread across his cheeks, but his eyes never left his hands. "Well, let's hope it does."

Another silence fell between us.

"How do you like working with the group? I'm really having fun so far."

Using the mortar and pestle, he began to grind up the various herbs he found and a minty aroma filled the air in an instant.

"I love it."

I was a little surprised to hear him say this. I hadn't once thought badly of Harold, but when I really looked back at all the silence, it made me wonder if he thought we were all super annoying.

"Really?"

"Yeah," Harold nodded, his eyes meeting mine for just a moment. "There's a lot of groups out there that don't really get along, but they stick together anyway because there can be quite a bit of money in the work we do, if you're good enough. This group feels . . . different."

"Have you ever been in one of those other groups?"

Harold frowned ever so slightly.

"A few."

"What was that like?"

He shrugged, continuing his work.

"Well, teamwork's important, so I never stayed very long in the ones where everyone's constantly at each other's throats. The group I was in most recently was okay in the beginning, though."

"What were they called?" I asked.

"The Jade Titans."

"I've never heard of them."

"They were local heroes in a few farming towns," he told me. "But they weren't big-time famous or anything."

I nodded, easily imagining Harold and the members of his old party sitting at the head of a great feast, decorated as the most noble of heroes.

"And you left because they were arguing with each other a lot?"

Harold shook his head, an uncomfortable little frown on his face. "Well, sort of . . . they were arguing with me. <u>A lot</u>."

"You?" I asked, surprised that anyone could find enough issues with Harold to feel the need to yell at him about it. "How come?"

Shrugging, Harold leaned back in his seat.

"I don't . . ."

He hesitated, his eyes flickering around the room as he organized his thoughts.

"Things started off great. They wanted to do good—and I wanted to do good too, so I fit right in. We traveled together for a long time, and almost every night we'd gather as a group and sit around the fire."

He paused, idly tapping his finger on the desk as he collected his thoughts once more.

"They were a loud bunch; they'd stay up all night telling stories and singing songs, which sometimes drew in the attention of bandits, wild animals, you name it. It was frustrating because I'd occasionally remind them that we'd be better off if they kept the volume down—especially when we were traveling in dangerous areas—but they didn't want to hear it. I eventually stopped trying."

"That sounds bad. Is that why you left?"

"I put up with it for a while, actually. But one day they, uh . . . I don't really know. Lucan, their leader, came up to me and told me that they didn't appreciate my attitude."

"Attitude?"

"Just because my power comes from a god, they thought that I consider myself better than everyone. I don't."

I had no idea that Harold got his powers from a god, how interesting!

"Which god?"

"Helirion," He said, "The god of the sun."

"So, they kicked you out because you were hand-picked by a god to do magic and stuff? Sounds like they were jealous."

"I think they mostly just hated how I was always quietly sitting on the side and apparently leering at them while they were trying to have fun," He muttered. "I never once judged them. I was just . . . watching."

"Watching what?"

"Watching them sing, and dance, and have fun," Harold said, the memories causing him to smile ever so slightly. "I never meant any harm by it. I've just always been a quiet person."

"Why?" I asked. "I come from a big, loud family, so I've never, ever been a quiet person. I don't think I've ever been quiet. Period."

Harold laughed, but I noticed his eyes never met mine. In fact, his gaze was on the floor.

"Growing up I always shied out of the spotlight. I was worried that I might say the wrong thing, I guess. Or maybe that I'd freeze up and ruin everything, I don't know."

He sighed.

"So, as I grew, I became accustomed to keeping to myself. It's just part of my personality at this point. I didn't think that it was an issue until that moment, though. I thought that everyone could just tell that I didn't mean anything by it."

After this conversation, I felt like I finally understood Harold. I had no reason to question the silence anymore. He didn't think we were annoying at all; he was just shy!

"Oh! I'm so sorry. Did they kick you out afterwards?

"No. It snowballed into argument after argument, and that wasn't an environment I wanted to stay in, so I left. Good thing I did though, because then I found The Tag-Alongs."

I grinned from ear to ear.

"It wouldn't be the same without you."

Harold turned away from me, but I caught just a hint of redness on his cheeks. "Thanks."

"I really mean it. You can be as quiet as you'd like, and we'd all enjoy your presence just the same," I told him, pulling my blankets up to my ears. "Don't be afraid of saying the wrong thing either."

Harold quickly began fiddling with his herbs, surrounding us in his special kind of silence. It wasn't long before he excused himself for a few moments and returned with a teacup and a kettle of hot water. He poured the water into the cup, added the herbs, and after a little bit more fussing he handed it off.

"Thank you, Cob," he said, his embarrassed smile spread under a pair of rosy cheeks. "You're very kind."

"No, thank you!" I took the cup and inhaled. The scent of peppermint and ginger almost immediately quelled some of my nausea. "This smells great."

"Sometimes even the steam from something like this can make you feel a little better."

I couldn't wait a moment longer, I had to taste the concoction Harold had whipped up for me. It was time to drink!

"Oh—be careful, Cob, it's hot."

But I didn't listen. Hot or not, after the first sip, my senses were awash with a delightful balance of the tingly coolness of mint and the bold impact of ginger. An odd warmth spread through my body, and it wasn't just because of the drink's temperature. Just like magic, I immediately started to feel better. It was perfect!

"Wow," I gasped. "You're really good at this."

Harold smiled and began to clean up the desk. He didn't say a word, but he really didn't need to. I found comfort in his silence, and even more comfort in knowing that he trusted me enough to share a piece of his story with me.

Harold's Ginger Peppermint Tea

In typical Cob Copperspoon fashion, I simply had to ask for the recipe the moment I was cured of my nausea. Yes, Harold has a particular kind of magic that really makes this tea pack a punch, but magic or not, this one's sure to be a little pick-me-up when you're feeling under the weather!

MAKES 1–2 SERVINGS

Prep time: 5 minutes | Brew time: 5–7 minutes

Ingredients

- A small nub of ginger (about ½ inch)
- Lemon peel
- ½ tablespoon lemongrass
- 1 tablespoon dried chamomile
- 2 teaspoons dried peppermint
- Honey and lemon juice, to taste

Instructions

1. Roughly chop your nub of ginger into small pieces.
2. Carefully peel a couple pieces of your lemon peel, trying to avoid as much of the white pith as possible.
3. Mix your ginger, lemon peel, lemongrass, chamomile, and peppermint and add to a tea steeper. (If you don't have a tea steeper you can just add these to a pot of boiling water and strain later.)
4. Boil 2–3 cups of water. Carefully pour your hot water in a mug and add in your tea steeper.
5. Steep for 5–7 minutes before adding honey and lemon to your taste preference. Enjoy!

CHAPTER THIRTEEN
Discourse on Ivory Shores

Journal,

    Finally, after days at sea, we saw an island in the distance: Nautinara. A beautiful paradise, the island was replete with tall, twisting palm trees, flowers with petals shaped like flame in every color imaginable, and a village full of carefully crafted huts made of wood, mud, stone, and foliage.

    The moment we stepped off the ship, we were greeted by the many smiling faces of the people of the Adva'lora tribe. They were unlike any I have ever seen before. The tribe is a conglomeration of all sorts of races, but each of them have somehow managed to evolve over time and develop some sort of physical trait that makes it easy to swim and live near water—gills, fins, powerful tails, sometimes all three.

    We were immediately introduced to Advina Tidewater, the chief's daughter and successor. She was beautiful—and I mean it! I can't even capture it in words, I simply have to draw her for you!

    See? So elegant!

    As she shook our hands, Advina spoke to us in a soft, soothing voice.

    "Thank you so much for making the trip here, especially on such short notice."

    "Of course!" I smiled. "We'll do whatever we can to help—"

    Finheld practically reeled back.

    "Whoa, wait," his voice host to an unsure laugh. "We won't be doing <u>whatever</u> we can . . . but we <u>will</u> try. I'll risk my life, but I won't give it entirely for some people that I just met," He looked at Advina. "No offense."

    I looked to Advina, expecting to see a look of hurt or even anger on her face, but to my surprise she just gave him a gracious, understanding nod.

    "We appreciate your efforts all the same," she said. "This way."

Advina walked ahead of us, leading the way down the beach. We followed along, but kept our distance, quietly bickering amongst ourselves. I wasn't just going to let Finheld's impoliteness go.

"You should apologize," I whispered, crossing my arms against my chest. "She's basically a princess."

"Barely," Finheld murmured, walking backwards as we talked. "She's a chief's daughter."

"Aye, but in a place like this, that's considered royalty, isn't it?" Karn injected.

"Probably not, there's probably a king-fish guy or something out there."

Harold frowned. "I don't know, Finheld. I think they're right."

I scowled, crossing my arms against my chest.

"Yeah, but even if we were wrong, it was rude either way!"

"Very rude." Irabel agreed.

"I stand by what I said," Finheld said, cooly turning away from us. "Cob could have put the expectation in their heads that we'll do <u>anything</u> to solve their problem. None of this is about saving the world at any cost for me, and you all know that. I'm just in it for the money."

I couldn't help but scowl. What a grump!

Harold heaved a heavy sigh.

"Fin, just try not to be so abrasive next time, please."

"Yeah, <u>Fin</u>," Irabel snickered, "Cool it."

"Don't call me Fin!"

I couldn't see Finheld's face, but I could have sworn I heard just a hint of embarrassment in their voice.

Irabel gestured to Harold. "But <u>he</u> can?—"

The bickering went back and forth as we headed through the village. I was worried that Advina could overhear us, but if she did, she graciously kept it to herself. Thank goodness for that. She's a princess in my books!

When we reached the village, I noticed a deep, water-filled trench spiraled elegantly through the sandy pathways, probably to give the people nearly instant access to the water that was so beloved to them. One particular path of the trench branched off from the rest and led straight into a trident-shaped hut, slipping right underneath the short cloth doorway that separated the inside from the rest of the world.

Advina pulled the cloth curtain across and gracefully beckoned for us to enter. As we passed through the doorway, I kept my eyes on the water's path, which circled around the room like a ring, leaving just a tiny bit of dry walking space between it and the wall. At the very center of the stone floor was a large, circular pool that glowed a serene bright blue, which illuminated the room enough to remind me of being underwater. I couldn't believe that I had declared all water to be my enemy not long before this!

Beside the pool sat an elderly Adva'loran woman with long ears, and a head of white, sea-weedy hair messily braided to the side; several beads and oceanic trinkets were weaved into it. There was a simple gold circlet atop her head, featuring a tiny blue crystal that hung right between her eyes. The woman was accessorised from head to toe with a mishmash of wooden and coral beads, which brought out the rich blue and golds in her robe. I knew immediately that this was the chief—she looked so much like Advina. So much like a queen.

"See?" I whispered to Finheld. "They're royalty here."

Finheld shushed me in an instant.

"Have a seat," the woman said, gesturing at the room around her. As the candlelight flickered, I noticed that her eyes were extremely unusual. They look like someone had inlaid glittering opalescent marbles into her skull—it was like looking at the vastness of an oceanic universe.

Advina stepped into the trench that circled the room and made her way around it, sinking deeper the further she headed. By the time she circled around to the back of the hut, she was submerged up to her stomach.

I plopped myself down on the edge of the trench and dipped my toes in while Karn and Harold sat next to me. I had a quick look back to see where Irabel and Finheld had gone, but they were standing behind us, leaning against the hut's wall. Irabel probably didn't want to get her fur wet, which I'm certain would have taken hours to dry. But Finheld? He was just being rude again!

Soon enough, Adva (that's the chief's name!) gently cleared her throat and began to wave her hand over the strange, glowing pool of water, beckoning it to glow brighter. The blue light bounced off her face, deepening the appearance of her wrinkles.

"Let me share with you the horror that plagues our reef."

Adva dipped her hand into the pool, scooped up a big handful of water, and closed her eyes.

"A-tul, le mar de sha." Adva spoke in an ancient-sounding language. As she did, Advina softly translated beneath her breath for the rest of us to understand.

"Great web, lend me your aid so I may share with our guests what stalks our home."

Then she flicked her hand and threw the water in our direction.

As though time itself had stopped, the water suspended in the air before her in the shape of a wavy, vertical wall. On that wall was an image—a moving image! It looked like we were looking through the eyes of someone swimming in the ocean with the utmost ease past a great, colorful coral reef.

"Whoa!" I gasped. "Cool!"

The swimmer dove deep, until the vibrancy of the reef began to slowly fade, and the sparkling sunlight lost much of its radiance. Somehow, still perfectly able to see, the swimmer pressed on. They reached the bottom of the ocean and shifted their fingers through the rolling sands, sending it upwards into the water like a cloud. Mesmerized, we watched in silence as they collected oysters and put them into a small sack. They unearthed shells, pieces of discarded coral, and somehow knew which oysters weren't worth collecting.

"Ah, see the amethyst jewelry around her wrist?" Adva asked. "This must be the perspective of Kania, one of the women whose lives were claimed by the beast."

Wow, I never thought I'd be able to look through the memories of someone who passed on. But all she was doing was gathering.

Just when I was about to ask why we were watching this, the swimmer looked up from the sandy floor, only to reveal that pure darkness had swiftly surrounded her. And I don't just mean that the sun had set. This felt <u>wrong</u>. So wrong that it sent a chill down my spine.

The darkness shifted, and I held my breath as a faceless shadow revealed itself, slowly eclipsing the swimmer's vision. Even though it must have been looking at the swimmer . . . it almost felt like it was peering right into the room. Peering at <u>us</u>!

The wall of water fell to the floor. I yelped in surprise as it splashed on my face, torso, and arms.

Adva looked at us with a solemn, haunted expression.

"No one's been able to get a better glimpse of it than that," Advina said. "But we do know that it's extremely dangerous. It seems to be an opportunistic creature. It doesn't go for groups of people; it'll wait until someone has fallen behind. Sometimes it'll even try to separate everybody or lure people away."

Advina's eyes met the floor.

"It's ruthless, truly. I wish it weren't so, but I won't do you the discourtesy of making it seem less of a threat than it is."

Adva peered over at Irabel and I with her vast stare.

"It seems to prefer targeting women."

Finheld scoffed.

A slight snarl escaped from Irabel's maw, and I heard the unmistakable sound of a boot kicking a leg.

"Shut up," she hissed.

"Ow!"

Karn cleared his throat.

"We'll do our best. We might not have gills, but we got a few tricks up our sleeves."

The chief and her daughter offered their most sincere thanks and went over the finer details of the mission, but I have to admit that I missed quite a bit of it. All I could focus on was the memory of the shadowy creature slowly lurking through the water. What if it separated us from each other? What if it only targeted . . . me? I had enough trouble fighting that demon imp in my initiation, how could I possibly defeat something like <u>that</u>?

Once the elderly Adva dismissed us, Advina led us to the moss-covered hut that they had given us to stay in. I looked at my friends' faces, and their unease mirrored that of my own.

Harold sat down on his bed and let out a defeated sigh. He looked down at a small stone in his hands—one of five that Adva had given us. The stones were enchanted to allow us to breathe underwater for up to six hours.

"What are we going to do?" he asked, flipping the stone over in his hand. "I knew that we were supposed to fight something in the ocean, but I didn't quite expect this."

Irabel nodded in agreement.

"I thought it would just be a big fish that we could . . . harpoon, or something."

Finheld's face creased with irritation.

"Did you even bring a harpoon?"

"I thought they'd have one," Irabel grumbled. "It's a water village."

"Surprise, surprise, Irabel's not prepared—"

"No one is! I don't know why you're singling _me_ out. What have _you_ done since we got here other than complain?"

"_Complain_?! I'm trying to—"

Karn raised his hands in the air.

"Okay, okay. Let's not get tae arguin' when we have work tae do."

Irabel rolled her eyes and leaned back in her cot, grumbling something to herself under her breath.

Finheld, however, didn't seem to be finished.

"So, you actually want to go through with this?"

"Of course I do." Karn nodded. "We came tae help."

"Yeah, help—not _die_!"

Harold sighed once again and shoved the stone into his pocket.

"I _am_ a little worried about dying."

"Exactly!" Finheld waved his hands in the air in exasperation. "This whole thing was a bad idea! We're not getting paid nearly enough for this."

"You didn't let me finish," Harold said. "I'm a little worried about dying, _but_ these people need help, and I think we should at least . . . try."

"Seriously?"

Irabel's grimace grew wide, and what she said next surprised even me.

"I'm actually kind of with Finny on this one. I do want to help, of course . . . but how do we outswim something like that?"

"My point exactly," Finheld nodded. "And cats don't even like water."

Irabel snarled. "Don't call me a cat."

"Don't call me Finny—"

Karn slammed his boots on the floor, silencing their argument with three loud thuds. "Enough, the two of you!"

Harold sighed. "There's gotta be a way we can do this that'll make everyone comfortable."

"Aye . . . Well, what if we barely do any swimmin' at all?" Karn said, "What if we . . . lure it in somehow? Give it a taste of its own medicine."

The defeated frown on Harold's face almost disappeared. "That might work."

"Here's an idea for ya'; we get a dummy of sorts prepared tae look like one of these water folk—a female one, perhaps, tae make it more enticin'. Once we're sure it's around us somewhere, we swim off and leave the dummy behind. That thing will think it's one of the villagers and it'll attack! That's when—"

"We <u>harpoon</u> it," Irabel grinned.

"Or somethin' like that, aye."

That sounded like a good plan—a <u>great</u> one even! But I had an idea to make it even better.

"Remember how I—"

But Finheld's groan of displeasure stopped my words in their tracks.

"Can we think logically here, people? What if it doesn't take the bait and comes after us? That thing has us outmatched in the water. We don't even have fins!"

Irabel snickered quietly to herself. "You have a <u>fin</u> . . . in your name."

"Shut up," Finheld grunted. "All I'm saying is that you don't bring a fish onto land and ask it to hunt a lion, right? So, what business do we have going into the water to hunt this thing?"

Karn crossed his arms against his chest.

"Do you have a better idea?"

"<u>Yes</u>!" Finheld snapped and raised their arms in the air. "We leave!"

I wanted to convince him that our plan would work—but a strange look on his face kept me out of the argument. It took me a while to understand, but I realized it wasn't just a look of anger. He was <u>terrified</u>.

"Finheld!" I chirped. The sudden sound of my voice ceasing theirs. "I know you're scared, I am too, but—"

"I'm not scared!"

"We can do this together, I know we can," I said, gesturing my arms wide to my friends. "We just have to believe in ourselves!"

"<u>And</u> the harpoon," Irabel nodded.

Harold shrugged. "Maybe not a harpoon exactly, but <u>something</u>," he said. "I think Cob's right, Fin, we can do this."

I nodded, emboldened by the belief of my friends.

"Whatever."

He huffed and let himself fall backwards on his cot, allowing a more than welcome silence to fill the hut for just a few moments. "Do what you want, just count me out."

Karn, Irabel, and I all exchanged worried glances, but Harold, in particular, looked the most rattled, maybe even hurt.

"We could die out at sea without you there tae help, lad," Karn said.

Finheld dragged his hands down his face.

"And we'll all die out at sea even if I _do_ go, so what's the point?"

I felt defeated but refused to give up. There was no use trying to convince Finheld right now even though the others tried. I listened for as long as I could but eventually slipped out of the hut when nobody was paying attention. I could still hear their soft bickering from outside but after a few paces I was met with a peaceful silence. I took a deep breath, and set off to find something, anything else to do.

As I wandered the village, I was met warm smiles and curious glances. I decided to follow the water trench and see where it would take me. One path in particular led deeper into the island so I decided to follow it. It wasn't long before the path led into a large patch of what looked like bright green grass growing out of a shallow pool of water.

I found watching the grass sway in the breeze while basking in the sun was extremely calming. That is until all of the sudden a face popped out of the water right in front of me!

"Ahhhh!" We screamed in unison! I was half expecting to see a terrible face with gnarled teeth and glowing eyes, but I soon realized it was not the monster. In front of me was a young girl, no older than fifteen with round halfling features just like me. Except she had no hair. That and her ears poked out like fins with rows of gills hiding behind them. We both sat in silence for a moment until she broke the tension.

"I . . . am . . . Ajarta." She spoke slowly and in very broken common. "You . . . are?"

"Oh! I am Cob." I spoke slowly, gesturing to myself.

"Co-ob." She mimicked. "Cob, help?"

I was confused at first. Help with the monster? Of course that's why I was here. But then I noticed her holding up a small basket. She placed the basket on the ground in front of me and revealed that she had been gathering the tall grass from this valley. I hadn't even noticed her swimming between the stalks.

She crawled out of the water and placed the basket between her feet to brace it. Then she gathered up a bundle of harvested grass and started beating it against the side of the basket. To my surprise, little grains of rice began to fall from the bundle of grasses. I had never once thought about how rice was harvested but it looks like I know now.

"You help?" She repeated, holding a bundle of grass out to me.

"Oh! Yes!"

I grabbed the bundle from her hands and placed my feet on either side of the basket. As I began to repeat her motions, she dove back underwater.

<u>Thwack! Thwack! Thwack!</u>

I whipped the grass over and over but found this was a lot harder than I thought. I found my arms getting very sore very fast, but never-the-less I <u>thwacked</u> on!

I harvested pile after pile of the grass, Ajarta popping up every once in a while to drop off a new stack. She began trying to trick me, popping up in new places, splashing me with her webbed hands. I joined in, moving the basket far away from the original spot, lying in wait. Every time I thought I had the drop on her though she somehow seemed to thwart me.

We laughed, we played, we worked. So this is what it was like growing up on this island? I knew then and there that no matter what, we had to save these people.

Sea Bullet Rice

Adjarta and her mother taught me how to make this dish when we eventually returned to the village. Apparently it is a generational specialty of the Adva'lorans. It is a culmination of their entire society's hardships! The divers trap the shrimp, foragers gather the wild honey and herbs from the island, the farmers tend a rice paddy as well as a small vegetable garden, and their alchemists ferment/process the sauces used! Its truly a team effort around here.

MAKES 4-6 SERVINGS

Prep time: 15-20 minutes | Cook time: 15-25 minutes

INGREDIENTS

SHRIMP:
- 16–20 large shrimp
- 1-inch nub fresh ginger
- 2 cloves garlic
- ½ teaspoon red pepper flakes
- 1 tablespoon honey
- 2 tablespoons soy sauce
- 1 tablespoon lemon juice

RICE:
- 4–5 cloves garlic
- ½ cup diced shallots
- ½ cup diced carrots
- 2–3 large eggs
- Salt and pepper
- 1 tablespoon sesame oil
- 1 tablespoon olive oil
- 3½ cups cooked, day old rice
- 3 tablespoons soy sauce
- Bundle of fresh chives, chopped (Garnish)

INSTRUCTIONS

SHRIMP:

1. De-vein and remove the shells from your shrimp if necessary. Pat your shrimp dry of any excess liquid and set aside in a large bowl.

2. Peel and grate your ginger and garlic into a small bowl using a zester. If you do not have a fine grater, you can mince instead.

3. Add your red pepper flakes, honey, soy sauce, and lemon juice to your grated aromatics. Mix thoroughly.

4. Pour your soy mix over your shrimp and toss it in the marinade, making sure all the shrimp are coated. Set aside while you prepare your other ingredients.

(Continued)

RICE:
1. Peel and thinly slice your garlic.
2. Dice your shallot and carrot. You can add as little or as many vegetables as you like. This is my preferred amount, but feel free to add more!
3. In a small bowl, beat your eggs with a pinch of salt and pepper.
4. Heat a large non-stick pan, cast iron, or wok over medium-high heat with your sesame and olive oil.
5. Once your oil is nice and heated, add in your shrimp. Make sure you evenly scatter them throughout the pan, so no pieces are overlapping. Cook about 2 to 3 minutes per side until fully cooked. Once finished, remove from the pan and set aside.
6. Immediately after removing the shrimp, add your garlic. Fry just until it starts to turn golden brown. You want it to get a little crispy, but not so much that it burns, so make sure to move it around a lot and don't leave it alone, about 1 minute.
7. Right as your garlic is starting to turn golden brown, add in your carrots and shallots. Sauté until they are your desired softness; cook time will vary depending on the size of your pieces.
8. If you are using a pan, you can push your veggies off to one side to cook your eggs. If you are using a wok, remove your veggies entirely and set aside while you cook your eggs. Add in your eggs and scramble, making sure not to mix with your vegetables until the eggs are fully cooked. Should only take 2 to 3 minutes in a hot pan.
9. Once your eggs are cooked, mix in with the veggies. At this point, you'll add your rice.
10. Mix your rice with your eggs and vegetables, making sure everything is evenly distributed. Your pan will probably be a little dry at this point, so feel free to add a pat of butter or a little extra olive oil, making sure to mix it in with the rice.
11. Fry your rice. Spread it evenly through the pan and forget about it for a few minutes before stirring to avoid burning. Repeat this process 2 to 3 times. For crispier rice, fry for 5 minutes without stirring it. When you stir it again it should start to turn a golden brown. If it's not, leave it for a bit longer to fry. Stir up your rice and repeat 2 to 3 times until you reach your desired crispness.

12. Add in your soy sauce, making sure all of your rice is coated. Fry for an additional 2 to 3 minutes.

13. Add your shrimp on top, making sure to add juices from the plate over your rice.

14. Enjoy! Garnish with fresh chives and dig in.

CHAPTER FOURTEEN
Plans on Plans

Dear Journal,

    Brainstorming is so fun, but it can be super hard sometimes. There are so many tribe-saving possibilities out there, it's hard choosing the right one! I scribbled down some of our musings as fast as I could while we devised the best plan of action. Some of our ideas were a bit wild, but those ended up being my absolute favorites! Here are my top three:

1. Step one: make a gigantic underwater tuba. We sneak down into the ocean, hide amongst the reef, and throw out a mannequin made to look like an Adva'loran. Then, when the creature is close enough, we blow on the tuba with all our might, creating a loud noise. And I mean <u>loud</u>. So loud that it causes the entire reef and the ocean floor to quake. This will cause thousands upon thousands of angry crabs to come out of hiding and they'll pinch the creature into submission.
2. We create a giant puppet made to look just like the creature in the water. The twist? We give it long eyelashes and some hair, so it looks like a super attractive version of the creature in the ocean. Seeking the bliss of an epic, sweeping romance, the creature will come in close to get a better look—and then we catch it with a net and lug it to shore!
3. We each spend the next few days sewing up costumes to make us look like baby versions of the creature. We pathetically drift down to the ocean floor and cry out to it. The creature sympathetically scoops us up and takes us to its lair, where it'll tuck us into bed for the night. We wait for it to fall asleep in its bed after a long night of terrorizing the sea, and then we strike!

None of these ideas ended up being what we decided to go with, but I can admit it was nice to have something to laugh about during such tense planning. After many hours of deliberation, I could see nothing but clear exhaustion on everybody's faces. Finheld's extreme reluctance to help certainly wasn't making it any easier. I didn't want my friends to get burnt out, so I thought up this quick recipe to help put a little pep in their step!

Sea Moon Charcuterie

OK, I might have lied. It may be less of a recipe and more of just a how-to on how to arrange cheese and dried meats. But my Papa always said you eat with your eyes first, so making it pretty counts! Plus it was some much needed play time between planning.

MAKES 2-8 SERVINGS, DEPENDING ON HOW MANY EXTRA GOODIES YOU WANT

Prep time: 15-20 minutes | Cook time: 15-20 minutes

Ingredients

- 1 (8-oz) wheel of Brie
- 1–2 apples
- Red grapes
- Blackberries
- Baguette
- Thin sliced salami
- Your favorite nuts and berries (optional)
- Assortment of your favorite cheeses and cured meats (optional)
- Jam of your choice (optional)
- Pickled vegetables (optional)

Before you start building, choose the appropriate board for displaying your charcuterie. If it's a smaller board, you won't need as many ingredients. For a larger board, however, make sure you have plenty of your favorite meats, cheeses, fruits, nuts, and pickles to fill the space.

Instructions

1. Start by placing your Brie in the center of your board. You can either place it here cold, or optionally bake it in a 350°F oven for 15 to 20 minutes until it gets nice and melty.

2. Thinly slice your apple. Arrange your apples in a crescent moon shape curving halfway around your brie, leaving about an inch between the apples and the cheese.

3. Fill in the space between the apples and brie with your red grapes, forming a full circle around the brie.

4. Surround your apple moon with your blackberries.

5. Thinly slice your baguette. You can either scatter your bread around the board or put it in a bowl on the side.

6. To make a salami rose, you need thinly sliced salami. Using a glass or jar, start folding the salami over the rim of the cup. Keep doing this, scattering the salami around the full cup rim until it is nice and full. Flip the cup over and you should have a beautiful and delicious rose.

7. Play with your food! Slice more fruit and cheese, make some more roses,

put things in cute little bowls. Play around with where you want to place things until you find the perfect spot for everything on your board.

8. Grab some friends and enjoy!

CHAPTER FIFTEEN
Destined for Doom

Well Journal,

    We headed out on our mission in the morning—and by "we" I mean the four of us. Finheld stayed behind. No one wanted to attempt the mission without him, but the people of the water tribe were counting on us.

    Of course, it would have been much better with Finheld at our side, but the plan was airtight and I was absolutely certain we could do it without him.

    When we reached the ocean, we were greeted by the sparkling cerulean waves. The skirts of the tide ebbed and flowed while tropical birds chirped overhead, almost as though they were harmonizing with the sweet sound of the sea. If I didn't know what lurked in the deep, dark blue, I would have considered the beach a haven of tranquility.

    We waded into the warm water, and once we were far enough, we touched our stones to our lips and dove down into the ocean. With their aid, breathing was just as simple as it was on land. I couldn't help but wonder if Adva and Advina would let us bring them home.

    It wasn't long until we saw a brilliantly colored coral maze in the distance. Pink, yellow, blue, green—it was like someone had trapped a rainbow under the tide. I had only heard tales about the kinds of cute little creatures that lived their lives amongst coral, but the closer we swam the more I realized that the sweeping visuals of those tales would remain locked in my imagination. The reef looked alive, but no one was home. No fish, no snails, no starfish, not even a cranky little lobster. My heart sank right then and there. The creature must have scared everything away.

    We descended alongside the reef, swimming further and further from the warmth and light of the sun's rays. The chill seemed to perfectly accompany the odd, eerie energy that surrounded this once-happy place. I could imagine the shadowy thing bursting from all the darkened nooks and crannies of the reef, like a patient spider in wait for a silly little fly to touch its web. Still, we pushed on.

    Once we found ourselves in a suitable position, we enacted our plan. In one swift movement, I touched Irabel's hand and we cast our spells simultaneously, hoping that our timing was seamless enough to fool whatever creature lurked around the reef. What spells? Well, Irabel's rendered us completely invisible, so my friends and I allowed ourselves to sink down through the water entirely unseen. Meanwhile, I created an illusion of our party, and as we sank, we watched them swim onward in the direction we were once heading. If we were lucky, the creature would have no idea that it wasn't really us heading deeper into the reef.

I grinned and waved my invisible arm goodbye as the fake, slightly understaffed Tag-Alongs headed off, keeping an extra close eye on the illusory me. Soon, she started to hunch forward, her arms dangling tiredly before her. The fake group members didn't pay her any mind as she started to slow down, and soon enough, poor, exhausted fake-Cob was stranded on her own, right near a hidden trap we had invisibly set—the perfect bait.

Meanwhile, the real us landed softly on a large coral-covered rock. I kept my eyes peeled for a glimpse of the creature that haunted these depths. Fortunately, it didn't leave us waiting for long. The gigantic creature slowly slunk out of the darkest corners of the reef. Its lower body consisted of an oily, tar-black tail covered in scales—but its torso and head resembled something humanoid . . . just not quite. The spiny sets of fins, which stretched from its head, down its spine, along its elongated arms, to a set of webbed, rotting claws, shifted as it guided itself to its target. Its almost-human face was set with eyes that were so dark it looked like two hollow holes bore into its skull. Underneath a slit-like nose was a smile adorned with jagged, yellowed teeth.

It grinned as it stalked its prey, unknowingly creeping closer to where we hid in wait.

But one thing that I wasn't quite sure of was whether its black eyes were fixated on fake-Cob or if it somehow knew we were there.

As it passed us, nearly close enough to touch, it grinned even wider.

<u>Wham!</u>

The trap sprung to life, covering the creature in nets fitted with jagged stones and seashells. The beast screeched, thrashing wildly as its voice sent violent ripples through the water that hit us with enough force to break Irabel's invisibility spell! We were sent somersaulting back through the water.

I grit my teeth and steadied myself—we had no time to lose!

The four of us sprung to action, landing as many hits on the beast as we could.

But its strength was immense and an unsettling darkness began to surround us as the slowly shredding trap began to burst.

"It's breaking free!" I called, the water nearly deadening my voice.

"We're running out of time!" Karn yelled. "Finish it off!"

The creature screeched again, and its hollow call reverberated across the ocean floor for what could have been miles. I clamped my hands over my ears—but that was a mistake! With my focus lost, the creature knocked me back with its powerful tail.

But something strange happened when its scales met my torso. Something that had never happened to me before. For an instant, I wasn't in the ocean anymore. The world around me changed. I saw things . . . a forest? Twisted trees . . . women wandering through the thick underbrush.

The women became one . . . and then the woman became . . . me?

I looked down and at my feet was a dark black pit.

I wanted nothing more than to jump—

"Cob!" Harold's voice somehow cut through my mind.

Reality swept back in as my side collided hard with the sharp coral reef. I grunted painfully and turned to the group—but I didn't see them. No, I saw the beast, tangled up in ropes, its inky eyes glinting in what remained of the light as it rushed towards me faster than I could comprehend.

It grinned and raised its claw high above it's head, ready to strike. And then it screeched in pain.

The beast whipped around, revealing to me a large, silver harpoon through its tail. I didn't have much time to react because it lunged for something in the shadows. A human figure skirted out of the way just in time—Finheld!

"You came!" I called, but my voice didn't travel far.

"We don't have time for this right now, Cob," I heard Harold's voice say. "Fight! Quickly!"

Together, as the brave group of five I knew we were, we furiously fought the wounded beast while its blanket of darkness slowly enveloped us. Finheld's surprise attack slowed it down immensely. And, just when the waters were so dark that we couldn't see our own hands in front of our faces, Karn laid the final blow on the creature's head with his hammer.

The darkness lifted, and we knew then and there that the oozing, terrifying beast was slain. The people of the water tribe were free at last.

When we arrived back on the shore a big celebration was waiting for us. And I mean <u>big</u>. There was dancing and singing and so much delicious food! A few of their divers even decided to catch us some fresh fish now that the threat was gone. I offered to dive with them but they refused, insisting we rest after the hard won battle. For that, I was grateful.

After we ate, I shared the tale of our triumph. I even got to use my powers of illusion to act it out for everyone! I had the whole water tribe sitting on the edge of their seats all night long!

I'm not much for sailing, but if I ever get the chance to come back for a visit, I'd absolutely make the trip!

Honey-Glazed Pink Lance

As we sat to enjoy our meal, there was an old man telling a story of the time a bear wandered into the village, lured by the scent of honey and fish. He waved a long walking stick in the air as he exclaimed, "Every festival we make this recipe I stand ready, waiting for the beast to return! He wont steal our meal again if I can help it!"

MAKES 1 SERVING

Prep time: 5-10 minutes | Cook time: 15-25 minutes

Ingredients

- 1 fillet pink lance (can use salmon)
- Pinch salt
- Pinch pepper
- Pinch paprika
- Drizzle olive oil
- Drizzle honey
- 1–2 pats butter
- 2 whole cloves garlic
- 2 slices lemon

Instructions

1. Preheat your oven to 350°F.
2. In a small piece of tin foil, start by adding your piece of pink lance to the bottom. Top with a pinch each of salt, pepper, and paprika. Top with a small drizzle of olive oil, honey, and 1 to 2 pats of butter. Add in your garlic cloves and lemon slices before wrapping fully in the foil.
3. Repeat the above step for each piece of pink lance you are cooking.
4. Bake for 15 to 20 minutes until fully cooked.
5. Enjoy! You can use this same method on one large piece of salmon, just make sure the fish is fully covered in all the ingredients and bake for an additional 15 to 20 minutes, as the larger pieces take longer to cook.

Roasted Coral Bulbs

Served with our fish were these delicous little green balls. I asked the villagers what it was and they explained to me that there is a special typle of coral that grows in the reef. Sometimes its blue, other times orange or purple, and this time its green! Each have their own unique flavor and texture, the green being slightly bitter with many layers just like cabbage!

Makes 4-6 servings

Prep time: 20-30 minutes | Cook time: 40-60 minutes

Ingredients

- 1½ pounds green coral bulbs (can replace with Brussels sprouts)
- ½ cup melted butter
- 1½ tablespoons all-purpose seasoning/ seasoning salt of your choice
- 1 tablespoon minced or 1 teaspoon granulated garlic
- 1 tablespoon honey
- ¼ cup shredded Parmesan cheese
- 8–10 slices bacon

Instructions

1. Preheat oven to 350°F.
2. Clean your coral bulbs. They may have some dark-brown spots left on them in the end, but don't worry about it, it's completely fine.
3. Trim the rough end of the coral bulbs and then cut in half lengthwise. Do this with all of your coral bulbs and put in a large bowl.
4. Melt your butter. Once melted, mix in seasoning salt, garlic, and honey.
5. Pour your butter mix and shredded Parmesan over your coral bulbs and toss until everything is coated.
6. Slice your bacon into bite-sized pieces.
7. On a parchment-lined baking sheet, evenly spread out your coral bulbs. Sprinkle your uncooked bacon over the top, making sure to spread it out as much as possible.
8. Bake for 40 minutes to 1 hour or until bacon is fully cooked and coral bulbs are starting to turn golden brown. Enjoy!

Kelpie Cookies (Gluten-Free)

It's really hard for the people of the water tribe to get flour on Nautinara, so they blend up what grows naturally on their island to make something that's pretty close! It's a very similar process that my Nana uses with a few special island exclusive ingredients. I can't wait to go home and tell her all about their techniques!

Makes 12 cookies

Prep time: 10-15 minutes | Cook time: 12 minutes

Ingredients

- ¾ cup softened butter
- 1½ cups sugar
- 1 large egg
- 1 teaspoon vanilla extract
- 1 teaspoon lemon extract
- 2 cups Gluten-Free Flour Blend (see page 19)
- ½ teaspoon gluten-free baking powder
- ¼ teaspoon salt
- Colored sugar sprinkles (optional)

Instructions

1. Preheat your oven to 375°F.
2. Combine your butter and sugar until light and fluffy.
3. Add your egg, vanilla extract, and lemon extract. Mix until fully combined.
4. In a separate bowl combine your gluten-free flour, gluten-free baking powder, and salt.
5. Add your dry ingredients to your wet and mix until fully combined.
6. Get about 4 tablespoons' worth of dough and roll it into a ball. Optionally, you can roll your balls into colored sugar to decorate them.
7. Place 6 balls spread evenly onto a baking sheet. Bake for 12 minutes.
8. Let your sugar cookies cool and enjoy! This is also a great recipe to use for gluten-free tart shells!

Sea Dandelion Lemonade

They call it "Sea Dandelion" because of its bright yellow color! It's a little bitter raw, but creates a sweet syrup when cooked. According to Advina, the Adva'lora tribe's best kept secret is their underground lemon tree grove, and they say the syrup goes great mixed with its juice. The trees get light from some nearby volcanic activity. Maybe that's why the island's so hot?

Anyway, Adva and Advina gave me and Finheld permission to pick some of the lemons, so I'm not in trouble, don't worry!

Makes 8–12 servings

Prep time: 25–30 minutes

Ingredients

Sea Dandelion Syrup:
- 1 cup sea dandelion (can replace with regular dandelion petals)
- 2 cups water
- 2 cups sugar

Lemonade:
- 2–3 cups ice
- 4–6 lemons
- 10–12 cups water
- ½–1 cup Sea Dandelion Syrup

Instructions

Sea Dandelion Syrup:

1. Mix together your sea dandelion and water. Set in the fridge overnight (at a minimum) until a nice yellow tea is formed. If you forage for your dandelion, make sure you only grab in areas that are safe from poison or pollutants.

2. Strain the liquid from your sea dandelion. You should be left with just sea dandelion tea now.

3. In a medium saucepan, mix your dandelion tea with your sugar. If you have a little less than 2 cups of tea, just add a bit of water to make it 2 full cups of liquid.

4. Heat your sugar mix over medium-high until the mix just begins to boil. Stir constantly until the sugar is fully dissolved and the syrup starts to thicken a bit, about 10 to 15 minutes.

5. Remove from heat and store in an airtight container. This will last up to a month in the fridge.

Lemonade:

1. Fill up a large pitcher with your ice.
2. Juice your lemons into your pitcher.
3. Start by adding half of your water and half of your dandelion syrup. Everybody likes their lemonade a little bit different, so taste as you go. It's going to start off very tart, so just keep slowly adding water and syrup until you reach the perfect flavor.
4. Grab a glass to share with some friends and enjoy!

CHAPTER SIXTEEN
Revenge of the Gnomes

Dear Journal,

    The journey back to The Violet Bastion went much smoother than the initial trip. Armed with Harold's tea and a new knowledge of sea life, I was much more prepared this time! You still won't find me traveling by boat if at all possible, but at least now I can say for certain the pirate life is not for me.

    Luckily, the long boat ride gave me plenty of time to scheme. I'm not sure if you noticed, but Finheld has a liiiiiittle bit of an attitude problem. Or maybe it's just grumpiness, I don't know. Either way, after all that water tribe stuff, I decided that I'm going to see if I can fix them! Or at least help them get a little bit more in tune with their soft, squishy, caring side.

    So, imagine my surprise when I passed the job board and saw an open quest to help two elderly gnomes, Granny Fran and Aunt Jo, solve the mystery of their disappearing baked goods way out in the swamp. The suspected thief? An evil creature! I was hoping that "evil creature" was just an exaggeration, but either way, who doesn't love helping out their elders?

    Well . . . Finheld, clearly. When I showed them the posting, they all but hissed at me like some kind of vampire! I couldn't believe it at first, but, just like my aunt would say, "a persistent pepper always prevails!"

    "Please?" I insisted. I basically had to drag him to the job board. "They're just two sweet old ladies! They can't do these things alone. They need our help."

    Finheld leaned back on the board, covering the posting and crossing their arms. "No way."

    "Please!"

    "Cob, I'm not wasting my time helping some wrinkly old ladies for basically no pay. Let's at least do something that's worth our time."

    "Come on! What if it was your grandma that needed help? You'd go then, right?"

    He scoffed. "Nope."

    "Liar," I pouted. I know he's not that heartless!

    But Finheld didn't look like they were going to change their mind.

    "I'll bake you a whole pie," I said with a smirk, switching tactics. "Apple with extra . . . apples!"

Something other than aggravation and anger almost flickered across Finheld's face.

"Really?"

"Yep! Maybe even triple if I can make them fit!"

He paused for a moment to think. The suspense almost ate me alive!

"Maybe quadruple?" I suggested.

"Fine, Cob, whatever," he groaned, purposefully knocking the back of his head on the board. "But only because of the pie, and because Harold told me to come hang out with you. If this 'evil creature' turns out to be anything like that monster in the ocean, I'm leaving."

He snatched the poster as he stood up and shoved it in his pocket.

"Understood, boss!" I smiled, wasting absolutely no time leading us to the doors.

"Tell me the details." Finheld grumbled.

"Well, for starters, they own an alligator ranch."

"A what?"

"Yeah, I think they raise alligators and stuff."

"Why would anyone do that?" he said with a raised eyebrow. "It's probably one of the alligators stealing their stuff. This is so stupid."

I grinned wide. "Stupidly . . . fun?"

The sound of Finheld's tired groan made me giggle. I was certain we were going to have a great time!

We left The Violet Bastion and made our way towards the swamp, which was about a three-hour horse ride south of the city. Using the directions on the poster, we found our way to Little Jo's Gator Getaway, "the best dang gator ranch this side of the city." A thick-wired fence surrounded what consisted of the main house—a cozy white and pastel-colored bungalow nestled happily in the swamp, what I assumed to be some sort of huge stable, and a big yard full of topiaries trimmed perfectly into the shape of alligators playing various sports. In the distance, there was a big watery pen that comfortably housed what seemed to be over fifty alligators.

Finheld huffed in irritation as we thwacked mosquitos off our arms and walked the narrow wooden-planked path to the bungalow's front door. When we knocked, though, there was no answer. In fact, there was no sign of the sweet old ladies at all!

"Hello?" I called, peeking through the door's frosted windows. Nothing!

"Great. Total waste of time," Finheld complained.

"They have to be around here somewhere," I said as I continued peering into the house. "Granny Fran? Aunt Jo?!" I called out. All that came in response were several hisses from the alligators in the distance.

"Let's just go," Finheld muttered. "They're not here."

"What if something happened to them?!" I frowned, looking around for any indication as to where they may have gone. I wasn't sure what I was even looking for, though.

"Maybe the evil creature kidnapped them, too."

"That's not funny!"

<u>But what if he was right?</u>

Finheld took a step off the pastel pink wooden porch.

"I'm going back before we get turned into gator food."

Just as I was about to follow him, Finheld stopped near the crooked planked path in the mud. I watched him crouch and stare intensely at something, and when he turned his head and gazed deeper into the murky swamps, I walked towards him.

"What?" I asked.

He stood up and pointed down at what he'd been staring at. A torn piece of pink, quilted fabric. Maybe a dress?

Fear gripped me like a gator on a leg.

"Oh, no!" I gasped. "We need to find them! They could be in danger!"

Finheld suddenly sprung into action. "I think they went this way," he said, pointing to the tiny footprints in the mud heading towards the trees.

We trekked through thick mud, narrowly avoiding the lurking wildlife and whatever else hid inside the swamp. I could barely focus with all the bugs that kept clinging to our skin. The mud was so thick and sludgy and the plants were so dense and untamed. What if Granny Fran and Aunt Jo got tangled up in some vines or something?!

Finheld was doing just fine, though. Maybe because he's taller than me? He chopped our way through trees, leading us through the earthy murk, and when I was finally able to divert my attention from the bugs and overwhelming mud, I saw a trail of breadcrumbs. Yup, actual breadcrumbs! I swear I could even almost smell fresh bread and sugary treats. We were definitely close to something. The thief? Granny Fran and Aunt Jo? Or a bakery out in the middle of the swamp (if I had a bakery out here, I think I'd call it "Swamp Cakes").

We emerged into a small clearing in the trees where an old, decrepit hut stood, barely holding on by its last wonky nails. And there, hanging from one of the protruding planks was a ripped pink shawl.

"Look!" I gasped, racing over to grab it. It looked <u>just</u> like the piece of fabric we found. "I think they were here at some point!"

When I examined the hut, I saw half-eaten cakes, pies, and pastries inside. But . . . ew, they were old, hairy, and rotting. Whatever had stolen them had moved on long ago. But where?

Then we heard a grumble in the distance.

Finheld stormed past me and into the trees.

"Come on!"

Finheld was on the case! He <u>did</u> care! Or was he just doing all of this for pie? I wanted to ask, but I didn't want to distract him.

I hurried along, wrapping the shawl around my shoulders for safe keeping. As I followed, I noticed more of the small boot prints in the mud. They took us deeper and deeper into the swamp. The earthy, musty smell in the air got thicker—so thick that I could almost taste it. Finheld was totally unbothered—either that, or they were really good at hiding their disgust?

The deadpan look on Finheld's face faded when something echoed through the eerie chatter of chirping insects and hissing alligators.

Voices.

"Get it off me!" someone shrieked.

Someone else screamed—a woman.

<u>Two women</u>!

Finheld wordlessly burst into action, looking more determined than I'd ever seen—and worried!

We chased after the voices—Finheld was so much faster than me, but I did my best, dragging my shins through the icky, sticky mud.

"It's right there!" one woman screamed.

"Get it!" the other exclaimed, her voice getting louder. I heard a dull <u>thunk</u>.

"Ha!"

"There's another one, Jo!"

It <u>was</u> them! Two, dirty, teeny elderly gnomes, one dressed in a blue muumuu with white flowers, and the other dressed in a yellow frock. Both of them had neon blue visors that said Little Jo's Gator Getaway.

"Hurry! They're in trouble!" I called to Finheld.

But they were already on it.

I stumbled to a halt by a tree, setting my eyes on what I knew in my heart was Granny Fran and Aunt Jo. With a rolling pin, Jo was thwacking at a swarm of . . . <u>snapping turtles</u>?! Fran was holding a steaming pie above her head with a large bite taken out of it—and the tin had a bite in it, too! Let me tell you, these snapping turtles had a pep in their step. They were practically jumping up in the air, desperate for a taste of that pie.

"Stand back!" Finheld called, as they rushed over to Jo and Fran and pulled out their crossbow.

"Who the heck are you?" Fran asked.

I smiled, "Cob and Finheld, we came to rescue you!"

"Rescue?!" She laughed. "Look at us, we're in the prime of our lives! We don't need rescuing!"

We disagreed and got to work. Truth be told, it was Finheld who did most of the rescuing, they even clocked one or two angry snapping turtles over the head with their boot as they desperately tried to snatch Fran's pie.

"Evil creatures, begone!" Jo shouted, whacking one with her rolling pin. "Ha!"

"Get lost!" Finheld yelled, flailing their arms around as the turtles began backing off.

"Yeah, that's right!" Jo laughed, "Get out of here before I sick my gators on you!"

Huh, who would have known the evil creature was just a bunch of thieving snapping turtles!

"Are you okay?" Finheld asked the old gnome women, wiping mud splatters from their forehead.

"Oh, aren't you just so handsome?" Fran brimmed and wrapped her small arms around Finheld. "Take a look at him Jo!"

Jo nodded, "About as handsome as a dragonfly with a bowtie."

"Ooh!" Fran laughed. "She likes you!"

Surprisingly, Finheld didn't shove the old woman away. "Oh . . . thank you?"

"I'm glad you two are okay," I said and chuckled a bit. "I was really worried."

"These darned things have been stealing from us for months! We didn't think anybody was coming, so we took matters into our own hands."

Finheld exhaled deeply and put their crossbow away. "Snapping turtles are no joke. You should be more careful."

See? They did care. I knew it! I felt like I was bursting with excitement, but I didn't want to embarrass them, so I decided I would just point it out to them a million times on the way home.

Before we journeyed back, Grandma Fran and Aunt Jo treated us to the Terrolecki Swamp Special: Chimera Roast and Homemade Biscuits. It took some convincing, but 15 gold pieces bought me the recipe for both, and one of those bright blue visors from the giftshop.

Aunt Jo's Alligator Ranch Biscuits

Not only is this recipe great for the largest of goliaths to the tiniest of fairies, but Aunt Jo says that the alligators at the Gator Getaway also <u>love</u> these biscuits, too! I tried to convince Finheld to hand-feed one like Aunt Jo does, but he didn't seem too interested.

MAKES 8 LARGE ROLLS

Prep time: 1½ hours | Cook time: 15-20 minutes

Ingredients

- ⅓ cup warm water
- 1 tablespoon active dry yeast
- 3 cups all-purpose flour
- 1 teaspoon salt
- 2 tablespoons sugar
- 2 teaspoons baking powder
- 4 tablespoons oil
- 1 cup milk

Instructions

1. In a small bowl, mix your warm water and yeast. You want your water to be warm, but not hot. Let this sit for 5 minutes until it's bloomed and foamy.
2. In a large bowl, mix together your flour, salt, sugar, and baking powder.
3. Once your dry ingredients are mixed, add in all of your wet ingredients, including your yeast mix. Mix until fully combined.
4. On a large, floured surface, roll out your dough until its roughly ¼ inch thick. Cut out your biscuits and place them close together on a lightly oiled baking dish.
5. Let biscuits rise for 1 hour at room temperature, covered with a clean towel.
6. Heat your oven to 425°F.
7. Bake your biscuits for 15 to 20 minutes until golden brown.
8. Enjoy! You can also brush with melted butter as soon as they come out of the oven.

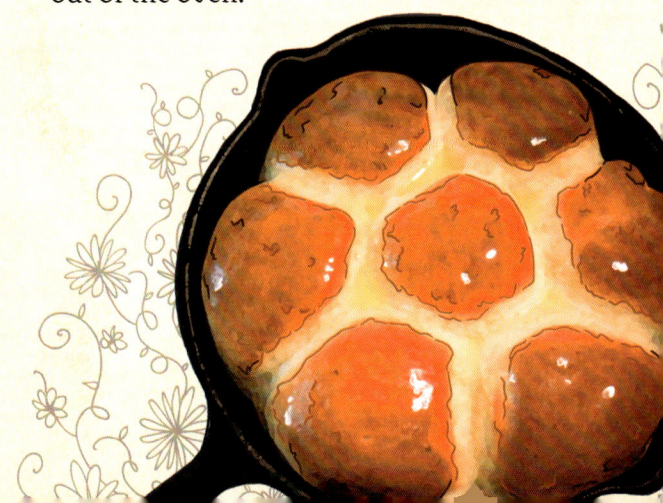

Chimera Roast and Root Veggies

Grandma Fran has been trapping chimeras in the swamp since she was a little girl. She doesn't let being small get in the way of being feisty—those nasty chimeras never did and never <u>will</u> stand a chance. (I'm starting to wonder why they put out that job in the first place?)

MAKES 6-8 SERVINGS

Prep time: 15-20 minutes | Cook time: 1½-3 hours

INGREDIENTS

ROAST:
2 tablespoons olive oil
5-6 pound chimera roast (substitute with prime rib)
2-3 tablespoons mustard
3 tablespoons salt
1½ tablespoons pepper
1 tablespoon dried rosemary
1 tablespoon dried thyme
1 tablespoon dried basil
1 tablespoon fresh oregano

VEGGIES:
6-7 large yukon gold potatoes
5-6 large carrots
2 small yellow onions
1 tablespoon pepper
1 tablespoon basil
1 tablespoon paprika
1 tablespoon rosemary
Salt and pepper, to taste

EXTRAS:
3-4 heads garlic, divided
Olive oil
¾ cup beef broth
1 stick butter
Bundle fresh rosemary

GRAVY:
Pan drippings
¼-½ cup flour
2-4 cups beef broth

INSTRUCTIONS

1. Preheat your oven to 350°F.
2. Heat a large cast-iron or oven-safe pan over high heat with your oil. Heat this until spitting hot.
3. Add in your roast, fat-side down to start. You want to sear this prime rib on every side for about 2 to 3 minutes

each, or until golden brown. Get as much of your roast seared as you can, the sides, top, and bottom. Once fully seared, remove from your pan.

4. Brush your mustard all over your roast. I promise, this will not make your roast taste like mustard, it just helps the seasoning stick to the outside.

5. Mix your salt, pepper, rosemary, thyme, basil, and oregano. Coat your entire roast evenly in this mixture.

6. Chop all of your veggies into large chunks. They don't have to be perfectly even, just 2- to 3-inch wedges or pieces.

7. Place all of your vegetables into the pan you seared your meat in. Using the oil from the pan, coat your veggies in all their seasonings.

8. Add all of your veggies to the bottom of a large roasting pan. If the pan you seared your roast in is oven safe and big enough, you can use that instead!

9. Snip or slice the tip of your garlic and nestle them on the edges of your baking dish or skillet, making sure to reserve 4 to 6 cloves for later. Add a small amount of olive oil on each one to prevent it from burning.

10. Place the seasoned roast in the middle of your baking dish, resting on top of the veggies.

11. Add your beef broth to the bottom of the pan, making sure not to pour over the meat, just around the veggies.

12. Place your roast in the oven. While your meat begins to roast, melt your butter on the stovetop.

13. Every 30 minutes, use the rosemary bundle to baste your roast in melted butter. After about 1 hour and 30 minutes of doing this, begin to check the internal temperature of your meat with a meat thermometer. Pull out your meat once it reaches your desired doneness (see page 2).

14. Once you pull out the roast, remove it and the veggies from your pan. Cover it in foil and let it rest for at least 20 to 30 minutes. While your meat rests, you can make your gravy.

15. Add ¼ cup of your flour to your pan drippings and mix it well. You want about equal parts fat and flour, so add extra flour as needed to make a smooth mixture. It's ok if it gets a little lumpy at this step.

(Continued)

16. Slowly add in your beef broth, whisking constantly. Start with half of your broth, then let it cook for a few minutes and thicken. Just keep stirring until it comes to a boil. Keep adding beef broth and letting it thicken until you reach your desired consistency.

17. Carve up your roast and enjoy!

CHAPTER SEVENTEEN
Menagerie of Monsters

Hey Journal,

    So sorry I haven't been writing much lately! We've been really, <u>really</u> busy fighting monsters, helping people from across the nation, and beating up bad guys! I have been absolutely tuckered from all of our traveling, but don't you worry! I have been collecting recipes the whole way just for you, journal. We visited a witch that could tell the future with tea (my future says that I will be a business owner! Oh, and that I'm in grave danger too . . . wonder what that's about?), we saved a bunch of baby dragons, and we met some pretty snooty elves!

    I think my favorite story from the past few weeks has to be this one, though! A village by the name of Twinebrush reached out to the guild. Barely anyone had heard of them before, but they needed help with a big problem they were having with a nasty unicorn. <u>A unicorn!</u> I never thought I'd come face to face with something so rare and majestic. Don't worry, we didn't intend on hurting it, but the villagers <u>did</u> need our help.

    Long story short, we chased the mean old unicorn deep into the forest, and it was around then that we realized it was . . . corrupted? I'm not too sure, it had a weird inky, goopy, pitch-black blob growing out of its side. Nothing we tried to dispel the corruption worked, until Harold asked his god to intervene. With a bright golden light, and a creepy hissing sound from the blob, the unicorn was cured!

Blob Thing
- citrus scent
- mean
- tastes wierd
- might be what soap is made from

    The unicorn completely chilled out after that (thank goodness, getting kicked by a horse hurts). As a gesture of thanks, the creature conjured some of its shimmery magic on a plain bramble bush. It turned it into the most beautiful, shiny, aesthetically pleasing tree I've ever seen! The tree bore only one single fruit, and of course, we had to make a recipe, but I will share that with you later.

    I know these stories are shorter than normal, but I promise I will get back to the good stuff soon! I just need a nap first.

Stuffed Dragon Scale

We just so happened to stumble upon three—that's right, THREE—abandoned dragon's eggs during one of our quests in the Scovterra Desert. With some clever thinking and skillful tracking, we were able to find the mother. Instead of eating us, as a thank you she gave us some of her scales! They're <u>so</u> cool, and so delicious!

Makes 4-6 servings

Prep time: 35-45 minutes | Cook time: 30-40 minutes

Ingredients

Pickled Red Onions:
- ½ cup red wine vinegar
- 3 tablespoons sugar
- 1 tablespoon salt
- 1 teaspoon whole black peppercorns
- 1 medium red onion
- 2 cloves garlic
- ¼–½ cup water

Pico de Gallo:
- 4 Roma tomatoes
- 2 medium jalapeños
- ¼ medium red onion
- ¼ cup cilantro
- 1 tablespoon honey
- Salt and pepper
- 2–3 limes

Black Bean Hummus:
- 1 (20-oz) can black beans
- 1 tablespoon lime juice
- ¼ cup cilantro
- 2 cloves garlic
- Salt and pepper
- 2 tablespoons sesame oil
- ¼ cup olive oil

Chicken:
- 2–3 chicken breasts
- Salt and pepper
- Galic powder
- Onion powder
- Paprika
- Cumin
- Chili powder

Tostadas:
- ¼ cup corn or vegetable oil
- 4–8 corn tortillas
- 4 dragon scales (you can replace with flour tortillas)

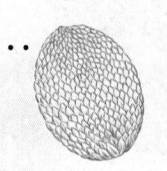

Instructions

Pickled Red Onions:

1. Mix your vinegar, sugar, salt and whole black peppercorns in a small saucepan. Heat over a low heat until the sugar and salt have fully dissolved, about 2–3 minutes. You do not want to bring this mix to a boil, just warm it enough for your ingredients to dissolve.
2. Thinly slice your red onion and peel your garlic.
3. Put your onions and garlic into a 10-ounce mason jar or medium container with a lid.
4. Pour your vinegar mix over your onions.
5. Fill your container with water until the onions are fully submerged in liquid.
6. Tighten your lid, give your onions a good shake, and then leave them in the fridge for 20 to 30 minutes.

Pico de Gallo:

1. Dice your tomatoes into small pieces.
2. Dice your jalapeño and red onion into even smaller pieces.
3. Roughly chop your cilantro.
4. Put all your chopped ingredients into a large bowl.
5. Add in your honey, some salt and pepper, and juice your limes over top.
6. Make sure to give it a taste test and see if it needs a little extra of anything.

Black Bean Hummus:

1. To a food processor or blender, add in your beans, lime juice, cilantro, garlic, salt, pepper, and sesame oil.
2. Pulse or grind the mix until it becomes thick and chunky.
3. Keeping your food processor or blender on high, slowly pour in your olive oil. Blend until the mix is smooth and creamy.
4. Taste test to make sure you don't need to add anything extra.

> Don't worry if you don't have a blender or food processor! You can easily do this with a mortar and pestle or even just a potato masher. Just follow the steps above but instead of blending get to mashing by hand!

(Continued)

Grilled Chicken:

1. Heat a grill plate or large skillet over medium-high heat.
2. Season your chicken breast with your salt, pepper, garlic, onion, paprika, and cumin (leave out if you don't have any). For spicier chicken, add a light dusting of cayenne or chili powder, too.
3. Grill your chicken until it reaches an internal temp of 165°F, being sure to flip it every few minutes to help cook evenly and keep it from burning. Should take 10 to 20 minutes, depending on how thick your chicken pieces are.
4. Once your chicken is fully cooked, chop into bite-sized chunks to go in your dragon scale.

Tostadas:

1. In a small frying pan, heat your oil over high heat.
2. Once your oil is spitting hot, add in a corn tortilla. Fry until golden brown, flipping about every 30 seconds. This should take 2 to 3 minutes per tortilla.
3. Once nice and golden, remove from the oil and drain on a paper towel–lined plate. Immediately sprinkle with a touch of salt.

Building your Stuffed Dragon Scale:

1. Heat a large skillet or griddle over medium-high heat with a light amount of oil.
2. Spread some of the black bean hummus on one half of a flour tortilla.
3. Sprinkle cheese and chicken pieces over the black beans.
4. Break a tostada in half and layer that over the beans, meat, and cheese.
5. Fold in half and place gently on your griddle.
6. Fry each side until a golden-brown crust is formed, about 2 minutes per side.
7. Open up your scale and add any lettuce, pico, pickled onions, avocado, sour cream, or salsas on top of your tostada.
8. Enjoy with your friends and family.

The Tea Witch Soup

I got this recipe from a really cool witch who did all their spells using tea leaves. They even used them to predict my future! It turns out that I'm in grave danger . . . but <u>then</u> they told me that I'll also be a business owner pretty soon. Weird, right?

Harold and Karn say if the danger's <u>that</u> grave then I wouldn't even live long enough to run a business at all, so I'm not too worried about it.

MAKES 4–6 SERVINGS

Prep time: 15–20 minutes | Cook time: 45–60 minutes

INGREDIENTS

- 3 heads roasted garlic (see page 15)
- 1 large onion
- 1 tablespoon rosemary
- 1 tablespoon thyme
- 1 (8-oz) package mushrooms
- 2 large russet potatoes
- 1 tablespoon olive oil
- 1 pound chicken sausage
- 1 teaspoon salt
- 1 teaspoon pepper
- 1 teaspoon ground mustard
- 2 teaspoons paprika
- 1 teaspoon coriander
- 1 teaspoon red pepper flakes
- 5 cups chicken broth
- 2 bay leaves
- 1 can coconut cream
- 2 cups baby spinach
- ⅔ cup Parmesan cheese
- Chili oil to garnish (optional)

INSTRUCTIONS

1. Start by getting your garlic in the oven to roast and then prepping all of your vegetables. Dice your onion, mince your herbs, slice your mushrooms, and quarter and slice your potatoes. To do this, cut your potato in half lengthwise and then cut those 2 pieces lengthwise again. Slice those wedges as thinly as possible to prepare for the soup.

2. Heat a five-quart-or-larger Dutch oven/pot over medium-high heat. Add 1 tablespoon of olive oil and your sausage. Cook until the sausage is fully done.

3. Add your onions and cook until fragrant and translucent.

(Continued)

4. Next, add your rosemary, thyme, and mushrooms. Cook for 2 to 3 minutes until mushrooms are warmed through.

5. Mix in salt, pepper, ground mustard, paprika, coriander, red pepper flakes, and potatoes. Stir until everything is thoroughly coated in all of the seasonings.

6. Pour in your chicken broth and bring to a boil. Once boiling, sprinkle in your bay leaves, reduce your heat to medium-low, and cover for 25 minutes or until your potatoes are fully cooked. Remove bay leaves.

7. Finally, add in your roasted garlic, Parmesan and coconut cream. Stir until combined then you are ready to enjoy! I added chili oil to top it off and add a little more spice, but it is completely optional.

Gold Coins

My friends and I had to venture to the very bottom of a freaky, spooky, cobwebby dungeon to find a lady's missing amulet. She said that we could help ourselves to anything else we found down there, and lo-and-behold we discovered a <u>huge</u> treasure chest! Crazy thing is, though, it wasn't actually a chest. The second I reached out to unlock it, the chest sprung to life, bearing rows of razor-sharp teeth, a bunch of drool, and eight sets of eyes. It almost bit my hand off! Thank goodness Karn was there to push me out of the way.

Anyway, I came up with the idea to cook up some teeny, little pancakes to see if the weird chest-creature would let us swap them with the gold. It worked! I guess money isn't everything—food is!

MAKES 4-6 SERVINGS

Prep time: 20-30 minutes | Cook time: 15-20 minutes

Ingredients

- 3 cups flour
- 1 teaspoon salt
- 2 tablespoons baking powder
- 3 egg yolks
- 2 cups milk
- 3 egg whites
- ¼ cup sugar

Instructions

1. Sift together your flour, salt, and baking powder.
2. Add your egg yolks and milk to your dry mixture and mix until thoroughly combined.
3. In a separate bowl, you are going to whip your egg whites. This is easiest with a hand mixer but will just take a little extra time if you are doing it without. Your egg whites will start to get a little frothy and start turning white.
4. At this stage, stop mixing and add half of your sugar. Beat again until the egg whites are fully white and just starting to hold their shape in soft peaks.

(Continued)

5. Once again, stop stirring and add your remaining sugar. Whip this until the egg whites are thick, glossy, and can hold their shape in stiff peaks.

6. Add about a third of your batter mix to your egg whites. You are going to fold the egg whites into the rest of your batter. You want to mix this gently to keep the mixture as fluffy as possible. Add the rest of your batter and keep mixing this way until everything is combined.

7. Heat a large pan or griddle over medium heat. Lightly coat with non-stick spray or a small amount of butter.

8. Once your pan is nice and heated, add 1 tablespoon of batter in small circles around the pan.

9. You will know your pancakes are ready to flip because you'll start seeing small bubbles form on the batter. Once those start to pop, it's time to flip. This should take about 2 to 3 minutes.

10. Adjust the heat of the pan as needed. If it's cooking your pancakes too fast, reduce the heat to low; if your pancakes are cooking too slow or aren't turning golden brown, turn your heat up a little. Every stove is different, so play around and see what works best for you.

11. Add your favorite toppings and enjoy!

High Elven Garden Tacos

The High Elven Court invited us to dinner to discuss a problem they were having with a very serious basilisk infestation. As a thank you for ridding the basilisks from their city's sewers, the highest high elven healer prepared us one of their best dishes with a really cool blend of spices, herbs, and magic stuff.

    I asked for a little bit more information on the spice-blend (the tacos were <u>so</u> good), but the healer snubbed me! He told me, "ancient recipes like this aren't for children like you." Rude right?! So, I did a little bit of CopperSpoon kitchen magic and came up with my closest rendition of the flavors we experienced that day. It might be even better than the stupid healer's version, too. Take that, elven healer!

Makes 2–4 servings

Prep time: 20-30 minutes | Cook time: 30-40 minutes

Ingredients

Cauliflower-Chickpea Mix:
- 1 head cauliflower
- 1 (16-oz) can chickpeas
- 1 poblano pepper
- 2–3 tablespoons olive oil, divided
- Salt and pepper
- 1 teaspoon garlic powder
- 2 teaspoons paprika
- ½ teaspoon coriander
- ½ teaspoon white pepper
- ½ teaspoon red pepper flakes
- ½ teaspoon cumin
- 1 teaspoon oregano
- Cayenne pepper (optional)
- ¼ cup tomato paste
- ½ cup vegetable broth

Slaw:
- 1 green cabbage
- ½ red onion
- 2 large carrots
- Bundle of cilantro
- 1 avocado
- ½ cup vegan Greek yogurt
- 2 limes
- Salt and pepper
- 1 teaspoon paprika
- ½ teaspoon garlic powder
- 1 tablespoon honey
- ¼–½ cup olive oil

Other:
- Corn or flour tortillas

(Continued)

Instructions

Cauliflower-Chickpea Mix:

1. Preheat your oven to 425°F.
2. Chop up your cauliflower into bite-sized pieces and drain/rinse your chickpeas. Also, cut your poblano pepper in half and deseed it.
3. Scatter your cauliflower and chickpeas onto a parchment lined baking sheet. Make room for your poblano pepper on the baking sheet as well. Drizzle with half your olive oil and toss with your seasonings.
4. Roast your veggies for 20–25 minutes until everything starts to get a little brown around the edges. While this is baking, it's a perfect time to make your slaw (see instructions on right).
5. Once your vegetables are done roasting, chop up your pepper into bite-sized pieces.
6. Heat a large pan or cast iron over medium-high heat with your remaining oil. Add in your tomato paste and sauté for 2 to 3 minutes.
7. Add your cauliflower, chickpeas, and peppers to your tomato paste as well as your vegetable broth.
8. Simmer for 5 to 10 minutes until a thick sauce forms. Taste and add any extra salt and pepper as needed.

Slaw:

1. First, thinly slice your cabbage and red onion, grate your carrots, and chop up your cilantro. Mix all your vegetables in a large bowl.
2. Scoop your avocado into a molcajete, if you have one, or a medium bowl if you don't. Alternatively, you can make the dressing all at once in a blender.
3. Smash up your avocado. Add in your Greek yogurt, the juice of half a lime, all of your seasoning, and your honey. Mix well.
4. Slowly add in your olive oil until you reach your desired consistency.
5. Taste your dressing and add any seasoning or lime juice as needed.
6. Add your dressing to your vegetables and toss well.

Assembly:

Now all that's left is assembly! Toast up your tortillas, add in your filling and slaw, and enjoy!

Uni-Fruit Cheesecake

Remember that unicorn story I told you about earlier? Well, this recipe is the <u>fruit</u> of our labor! I wasn't just going to let the legendary unicorn fruit rot away in my backpack. Anyway, I called it the "uni-fruit." The <u>one</u> fruit. Get it, like a unicorn has <u>one</u> horn? You get it, right?!

Makes 6–8 servings

Prep time: 45–60 minutes | Cook time: 20–30 minutes | Cool time: 30–60 minutes

Ingredients

Shortbread Crust:
- ½ cup butter (room temperature)
- ½ cup sugar
- 1 teaspoon vanilla
- 1 cup flour
- 1 teaspoon salt

Cheesecake:
- 1 pound cream cheese (room temperature)
- ½ cup sugar
- 1 teaspoon vanilla
- 3 eggs

Uni-Fruit Curd:
- 6 egg yolks
- ½ cup uni-fruit juice (can replace with lemons)
- ½ cup sugar
- ½ cup butter (cold)
- 2 tablespoons uni-fruit zest (can replace with lemon zest)

Instructions

Shortbread Crust:

1. Preheat your oven to 350°F.

2. In a large bowl, whip together your butter and sugar with a hand mixer. You want to mix it until the butter lightens in color and gets very fluffy. You can do this by hand. The butter won't get as fluffy this way, but it will still come out just fine.

3. Once whipped, add in your vanilla and mix until incorporated.

4. Add in your flour and salt. Mix at a low speed. You want the dough to be crumbly. **Important note:** Do not over-mix. The dough should look like a bunch of little beads and there might be some un-mixed flour pieces. That is exactly how you want it.

(Continued)

5. Lightly oil an 8-inch cast iron or pie pan. Spread your shortbread mix evenly throughout the bottom of the pan, gently pressing down to make an even surface.
6. Bake for 6 minutes then remove from the oven.

CHEESECAKE:
1. In a large bowl, mix your cream cheese and sugar until smooth and fluffy.
2. Add your vanilla to the cream cheese mixture and combine.
3. Crack in your eggs one at a time, making sure each is fully incorporated before you add the next. This will help keep the mixture smooth and silky.
4. Pour your cheesecake batter over the partially baked crust. Place the pan back in the oven for 20 to 30 minutes until the top has become firm. It will still be a little jiggly, but it will look a lot less shiny and move a lot less than it did before baking.
5. Let cool for 30 minutes then place in the fridge to cool completely before cutting.

UNI-FRUIT CURD:
1. Heat a medium saucepan filled with water until it comes to a boil.
2. In a large glass or heat-safe bowl, combine your egg yolks, uni-fruit juice, and sugar.
3. Prepare your cold butter and uni-fruit zest. Cube the cold butter and set aside.
4. Once your water has come to a boil, place your bowl of egg mix over the pan, resting above the water. Whisk constantly until the egg mix becomes thick, nearing a pudding-like consistency. This will take anywhere between 20 to 40 minutes, depending on the heat of your double boiler. Make sure to keep whisking, or you'll end up with fruity scrambled eggs.
5. Once it's starting to thicken, remove from heat and immediately add in your butter and uni-fruit zest. For extra-smooth consistency, push egg mix through a fine-mesh sieve before adding the butter and uni-fruit zest.
6. Cover your curd and let cool completely until it is nice and thick.
7. Top your cheesecake with your uni-fruit curd and enjoy!

CHAPTER EIGHTEEN
Dongle the Troll

Dear Journal,

<u>Oh my gosh</u>! I have the <u>craziest</u> story for you today! Are you ready to hear it? What am I saying? Of course you are. You're a journal, you love stories!

As you know, we have been very busy lately. Well, we finally got done with our last guild quest and began the long trek back to the good ol' Bastion. When it started getting dark, we thought it would be best to set up camp for the night. We didn't know the area, but Harold and Finheld are both really good with nature stuff, so they scouted out a nice little spot for us to set up camp in the woods. Not too close to the road, but not too far either.

While Karn and Harold set up some tents, Finheld built a fire-pit and Irabel and I got to work gathering firewood. Of course while we were gathering, I kept my eyes peeled for any goodies we could forage for dinner. What kind of party-chef would I be if I didn't?

As we wandered a bit away from the camp, all of a sudden . . . it hit me. I smelled a smell . . . a delicious smell. The aroma of spices toasting in butter.

"Hey Irabel, do you smell that?" My feet had already started floating me in its direction. It was enticing, I just had to see what was cooking!

I had wandered a bit away and Irabel seemed to just now be noticing. "What?"

"I think somebody's cooking! We should really go check it—<u>aaaaaah</u>!"

My words trailed off into a loud scream as the earth below gave way. I found myself barreling straight down a perfectly Cob-sized hole that had been covered by small twigs and leaves. It was a trap!

It felt like I was sliding down the tunnel faster than the speed of light, and at some point it even began to widen and curve, sending my whole body into disorienting summersaults. Next thing I knew, I was airborne, shot right out of the earthen tube until my body smacked into a hard surface. I laid on the ground for a solid minute, the wind knocked out of me, the world spinning around, and around, and around.

Where was I?

"Cob!" The voice was distant, but I recognized it. Irabel! With a quick glance, it looked like I was in a small stone room. It was dark aside from a fire-like light that was coming from the barred window on a cell-like door on the wall. It was made from thick sticks and looked to be secured tightly with a large, horizontal, wooden post.

"Irabel! I'm down here!" I tried to whisper-scream.

Luckily, I have my illusion magic, so I was able to throw my voice a little bit.

"Ok, just hang tight! I'm gonna get the boys and we can come pull you out!"

"Hurry please, I think it's a trap!"

You know that feeling you get when you're absolutely certain that someone is staring at you? Well, consider me a popsicle because I was shivering. I looked over my shoulder to see a hulking, dark shadow in the firelight outside the cell door.

"I thinks we caughts one, I do!"

Its voice was deep and menacing. I pressed myself against the back wall, trying to make myself small and—for some reason—that's when I noticed it. The smell! It was coming from here.

Suddenly, a massive hand slammed down on the cell door. I let out a squeal of terror as a giant, seven—maybe eight—foot tall humanoid came into view. He had greyish blue skin and piercing green eyes, but the most prominent feature was the massive boar-like tusks protruding from his lower jaw.

"I've caughts one!" He spoke to himself excitedly, standing only feet from me.

"Now I can finish me Gnomebalaya!"

He waddled away from the cell, shut the door behind him, and began rummaging through something in the other room.

Gnomebalaya?

I slowly peeled myself from the wall and made my way to the door with a curious frown. Near a fire with a huge simmering pot, the man stood over what looked like a bunch of stones stacked carefully enough to form a table. He held a gigantic kitchen knife in his hand, and was now wearing an old, stained apron.

He began humming to himself as he hunched over a bundle of carrots on the table. Skillfully—honestly, way more skillfully than I had seen anyone do—he chopped them all up into little pieces. Then he moved onto onions, then peppers, humming the same part of a song over and over, but slightly different every time. Maybe he forgot how it went? Doesn't matter, I had bigger fish to fry.

"Uhm, excuse me sir?" I gently asked. "Whatcha makin?"

"Oh this?"

He seemed to get excited at the mention of food. He stomped over to his large pot and started adding in the vegetables he chopped, making sure to give them a nice stir.

"This is Dongle's Homemade Gnomebalaya! You wanna know the secret ingredient?" he asked, as his face contorted into a menacing look.

<u>Does this guy think I'm a gnome?</u>

"Lots of love?" I nervously croaked out.

A look of confusion crossed his face for a moment, then he let out a big guttural laugh.

"No little one, it's gnome!"

"And I'm the gnome? Me? Cob?"

He nodded with malice, and in two gigantic strides he quickly closed the distance between us. He swung the door open with his massive hand and I, screeching, zipped to the darkest corner of the room—but he quickly captured me in his colossal grip.

"Wait—mister! Mister! What's your name?! We haven't even introduced ourselves yet!"

Maybe if I stalled for long enough, my friends would burst through the door and save me! But how could they find me? There's no way they could fit down that hole I fell through. It's perfectly halfling-sized . . . and gnome-sized! This guy was smart.

"My name is Dongle. Dongle the Trolls," he said, carrying me into the room. Turning the corner revealed a large birdcage on the floor. Perfectly my size.

I was NOT going in that thing! I spoke so quickly it felt like my words blended together.

"Hi mister Dongle, my name is Cob, and I think there has been a huge misunderstanding! You see, I'm not actually a gnome at all. I'm a halfling!"

He threw me into the cage, regardless, tying a long rope to the top of it.

"I thinks Dongle knows a gnome when I sees one."

"Actually, sir, it's true! I understand the confusion because we're both small races—"

"I'm not small," he grumbled, throwing the rope over a makeshift beam above the large pot.

"No, not you! Halflings and gnomes! They're—we're—both small, so I guess it's easy to mix us up. There are quite a few differences between us, though, for starters—"

The cage lurched, swinging wildly in the air as he began hoisting it directly over the fire. I could feel the heat coming from the searing vegetables below me.

"Wait!"

"No, no, no, no, no . . . Yous just don't wanna get eaten by Dongle's customers."

He fastened the rope to a large rock on the ground then returned to his table, where he chopped up some more vegetables I didn't recognize.

I began to sweat, if not from the heat, from the stress! Where were my friends?!

"You—you have customers? So, you sell food! That's so cool, I've always wanted a tavern of my own."

My heart was pounding, and my feet were getting warmer and warmer.

"Maybe I could help you with your recipe?!"

Dongle's knife slammed into the stone table. He slowly turned his head towards me, a menacing expression painting his face. He slowly began walking towards the cage, knife still gripped tightly in his hand. He stopped inches away from where I helplessly hung. I backed up as far as I could, which made the cage swing back and forth.

"You? Help Dongle? Now why woulds Dongle need that?"

If I said the wrong thing this could be the end. No more Cob CopperSpoon, no more recipes, no more Journals. Doneso, bunso, kaput—ow, my foot!

"Well," I took a nervous gulp. "You see, as a halfling family tradition, I've kinda been on this journey to fill up my cookbook. I've gone to a lot of places and tried a lot of things. And you know what I found out?"

Dongle tilted his head in curiosity. "What'd you find out?"

"Gnome tastes just like . . . like . . ." I looked around the room trying to find something—anything—to say and that's when I noticed it! There was a crude henhouse next to the cell where I was held captive. Those chickens were awfully quiet, though.

"Chicken! We taste just like chicken, but chicken meat is actually much more tender than gnome!"

I crossed my fingers in hopes he would buy it.

"Chickens?" He looked over at the terrified hens with a confused expression. "But they is Dongle's snacks. They're juicy and crunchy."

I almost gagged at the thought of this troll eating whole live chickens as snacks but kept it together to try to convince him.

"Have you ever eaten one cooked before? It's a delicacy! Waaaaayyyy better than gnome!"

Dongle grunted and began to pace the room for a moment, a look of contemplation on his face. This was it, I had him right where I wanted him!

"I don't know. . . ."

"How about this? You let me out of this cage, I'll show you how to properly cook chicken, and if you don't end up liking it better the . . . gnome . . . way, you can chop me up and cook me instead. Sound like a good deal?"

I was frantic.

"Also, casual reminder that if you cook me, it will taste different than gnome, because I am, again, a halfling!"

Dongle kept pacing. He mumbled to himself for several moments of contemplation before striding back to the cage. He snarled a bit as he looked in at me and for a moment, I was worried. Then, surprisingly, he opened the cage, gently grabbed me, then set me on the ground.

"Ok, gnome. Show me how to make chicken."

"Halfling!" I corrected as politely as I could. "Let's go!"

For what felt like a millennium, I taught Dongle how to properly butcher a chicken. Then, together, we finished making his recipe. It was actually a really interesting dish! I even gave him some of our cured sausages to add.

Of course, it wasn't long before Irabel returned to the hole with the rest of the group. While Dongle cooked, I yelled up to them explaining what was going on—with his permission, of course. They all seemed worried and wanted me to come back up, but I told them I made a deal. I asked Dongle if it would be okay for my friends to join us so they could try out our meal too, and he said it was alright as long as they paid—otherwise, he would cook them. Sure, buddy, whatever's gonna get my friends down here so we can all get out as fast as possible! Dongle gave them directions to his secret cave, and before long, everybody was hanging out in the underground kitchen!

My friends seemed a bit tense when they got there, but by then Dongle and I were kind of . . . having a nice time? We were laughing and joking, sharing old stories of different recipes. You know, behind the big dead eyes and <u>murdery</u> tendencies, Dongle was a pretty cool guy!

Finally, the moment of truth came: The taste test. Dongle grabbed a large wooden spoon and scooped some out for himself, making sure to get a big piece of chicken. First, he took a big sniff.

"Smells pretty good."

After a moment of pause, he shoved the spoon in his mouth and started chewing. I watched his face intently, hoping that chicken really did taste like gnome, because I had absolutely no idea what gnome tasted like.

Dongle looked down at me with a stone face. My heart dropped.

"Good?" I asked, giving him two cautious thumbs up.

"Better than gnome!"

Dongle let out a hearty laugh before plunging the spoon back into the massive pot, grabbing another bite.

"Dongle doesn't have to cooks you or your tiny gnome friend, there!" he said, pointing his dripping spoon at Karn.

"Wait, what?" Karn gasped.

"So, who's hungry?!" I yelped. As I turned and looked at my friends, I noticed each of them reaching for their weapons. The last thing we needed was them leading Dongle to suspect something.

"Come on, guys. Food!"

Dongle dished up a bowl for each of us, and we all, a little tensely, enjoyed our meal at his side. I made sure to give him a piece of gold for each of us. He deserved it for doing such a great job at showing mercy and a willingness to learn! And of course, I made sure to copy the recipe down for myself, too.

Gnomebalaya

Don't worry! No gnomes, halflings, or dwarves were harmed in the making of this dish!

MAKES 6–8 SERVINGS

Prep time: 20–30 minutes | Cook time: 1–1½ hours

Ingredients

- 1 yellow pepper
- 1 red pepper
- 3 celery stalks
- 1 medium onion
- 4 medium okra
- 7–8 cloves garlic
- 1 (14-oz) package andouille sausage
- 1 pound shrimp
- 1 pound boneless, skinless chicken thighs
- 1–2 tablespoons olive oil
- 3 tablespoons Cajun seasoning, divided
- Pinch salt
- 1 tablespoon paprika
- 1 teaspoon coriander
- 1 tablespoon Italian seasoning
- ½–1 teaspoon red pepper flakes
- 1 teaspoon black pepper
- Cayenne pepper (optional)
- 1 (14-oz) can crushed tomatoes
- 1½ cups white rice
- 3 cups chicken broth
- 2 bay leaves
- Chives

Instructions

1. Start by prepping all of your ingredients. Dice your peppers, celery, and onion, thinly slice your okra, and mince your garlic. Set those aside in a large bowl. Slice your andouille sausages, peel, and devein the shrimp, if needed, and chop your chicken thighs into bite-sized chunks. Make sure to prep your ingredients in this order: vegetables, sausage, shrimp, and then chicken, and clean your work surface in between or use different cutting boards/tools to avoid cross contamination.

2. Heat a large Dutch oven or pot over high heat with your oil. Once your oil is screaming hot, add in your andouille sausage. Sauté for 2 to 3 minutes until your sausage gets nice and browned. Remove from the pan and set aside.

3. Add 2 tablespoons of your Cajun seasoning to your chicken thighs and make sure they are fully coated. Add your chicken thighs to your hot pot and fry until fully cooked and golden brown, about 5 to 10 minutes. Once cooked, remove from the pan and set aside with the sausage.

4. Once you have removed your chicken from the pan, make sure to scrape up all the browned bits from the bottom of the pot. Add in your vegetables with a big pinch of salt. Sauté until soft and translucent, about 3 to 5 minutes.

5. Once your veggies have softened, add in your paprika, coriander, Italian seasoning, red pepper flakes, and black pepper. For a spicier gnomebalaya, add in additional red pepper flakes and some cayenne pepper for a stronger kick. Sauté for another 2 to 3 minutes with the seasoning.

6. Add in your crushed tomatoes, sausage, and chicken. Be sure to really scrape the bottom of the pan to pull up any stuck-on flavor. Bring to a simmer then reduce to medium heat.

7. Rinse your rice thoroughly until the water runs clear.

8. Add in your chicken broth and rice. Mix everything together thoroughly and bring to a simmer. Once simmering, add in your bay leaves, reduce the heat to a medium-low, and cover. Let cook for 25 to 30 minutes, stirring occasionally. Remove bay leaves.

9. After your gnomebalaya has cooked, toss your shrimp in the rest of your cajun seasoning and add it to your stew. Gently mix it in, cover and let cook for an additional 5 minutes or until your shrimp has fully cooked.

10. Enjoy! Top with some chopped chives and a couple dashes of your favorite hot sauce.

CHAPTER NINETEEN
Missing Villagers

Journal,

So, this one's odd. After the "gnomebalaya" fiasco, we decided it would be best to hurry back to the Violet Bastion to restock on supplies and get a few things repaired. Harold's shoelace got snagged by a tree root, so he needs a replacement, and then Karn accidentally stepped on Irabel's tail, so—

Sorry, I'm rambling! Guess what happened on our way back!

The gang and I were passing by the small village of Arvilia, and we were flagged down by a handful of people. They had a mission for us that required some serious detective work.

Twelve people had suddenly disappeared from the village without a single trace. The oddest part was that these people didn't really seem to have anything in common; some were old, some were children, some were human, some weren't. Whatever it was that was taking these people didn't seem like it was targeting anything specific.

We interviewed everybody in town, we studied the villager's personal schedules, we examined footprints, belongings, diaries, and everything else we could to find any hint of a clue. But it wasn't until we decided to check deep within the forest for signs of a villager-eating beast that we finally cracked the case.

I expected to come across a horrible, stinky dire bear with an insatiable taste for everything . . . but that's not what we discovered at all. Lying in the woods amongst the moss and brambles were all the missing villagers, nearly unconscious. They were completely uninjured, but they were all sallow and cold, barely clinging to what little life they had left. The strangest part is that none of them remembered how they got there, or why they were even there in the first place.

With nothing else to go on, we simply returned the villagers home to their families. Harold spent himself healing who he could. Finheld ran ahead to the village for help while Karn and Irabel cleared a decent path for a cart to come through the trees. I stayed back to pass out blankets and comfort to whoever I could. The whole situation was weird and scary. The gang and I left Arvilia confused. We weren't any closer to understanding what happened to the victims—should I even call them victims? What were they even victims of? Sleepwalking? The creepy psychic influence of a phantom? Some sort of forest nymph that likes to pull pranks? I have no idea!

    Anyways... I'll definitely let you know if we crack this case, Journal. You let me know if you see anything weird, okay? Hehe, just kidding, I know you're just a bunch of parchment.

    ... Unless?

Pixie Pie

On the road, we came across a huge patch of lavender bushes! While I was foraging, a pixie girl flew up to me and offered me a pie recipe in exchange for a lock of my hair. You know I can't say no to a recipe! So I made the deal. Plus, Harold reminded me I still owed Finheld a pie. Two birds with one apple core!

Makes 8 servings

Prep time: 1–1½ hours | Cook time: 50–60 minutes

Ingredients

Filling:
4–5 green apples
1½ tablespoons dried lavender
¼ cup honey
¼ cup sugar

Crust:
2½ cups flour
2 tablespoons sugar
½ teaspoon salt
1 cup cold butter
2 tablespoons–½ cup water

Extras:
Vegetable oil
Sugar
Lavender

Instructions

Filling:

1. Peel and thinly slice your apples.
2. Crush your dried lavender in a mortar and pestle until it becomes a fine powder.
3. Coat your apples in your honey, sugar, and powdered lavender. Set aside while you prepare your pie crust.

Crust:

1. Mix your flour, sugar, and salt.
2. Cut your cold butter into small cubes and add to your flour mix. Squish your butter into the flour until it becomes a sand-like texture.

3. Slowly start adding your water, a little bit at a time. You want your dough to hold together without crumbling or cracking. You will need more or less depending on how humid your climate is. Just remember you can always add more, but it's harder to take it away once it's added, so start small.

4. Split your dough into 2 even pieces and form each into a small disk. Wrap your pie dough in plastic wrap and let it sit in the fridge for at least 20 to 30 minutes before rolling out.

ASSEMBLY:

1. Sprinkle a large work surface with flour. Make sure to keep some flour close by to dust your surface as needed.

2. Place one of your disks of dough onto your floured surface and dust the top with a bit more flour.

3. Begin to roll out the dough into a large circle using a rolling pin. You want the dough to fit into a 9-inch round pie pan, so make sure your pie dish is close by to check the size. You want the crust to be about ¼ to ⅛ of an inch thick by the time you are don't rolling it out.

4. Once your crust is fully rolled out, carefully place it in your pie pan. For an extra sweet surprise, sprinkle the bottom of your pie dish with a bit of sugar before adding the first layer of dough to give the pie a candied crust.

5. Tip: Leave the excess dough at this step! Don't trim it until after you add the second crust layer or crust. That way, you know for sure you aren't trimming too much of it away!

6. Add in your filling! You can be fancy and arrange it nicely if you want, but I usually just chuck it all in.

7. Repeat steps 1 to 4, putting your pie crust on top of your filling this time.

8. Trim off any excess pie dough then begin crimping the edges. You can use your thumbs for this, squishing the dough between your fingers, but I find it much easier to just use a fork and press the edges together.

9. Cut small ventilation holes in the middle of your pie with a paring knife.

10. You can either bake immediately or store your pie in the freezer until ready to bake.

BAKING:

1. Preheat your oven to 350°F.

(Continued)

2. Lightly brush the top of your pie with vegetable oil. Evenly sprinkle with your extra sugar and lavender.

3. Bake for 50 to 60 minutes. You want the crust to begin turning golden brown and the filling should be bubbling.

4. Serve with whipped cream or ice cream and enjoy!

FAIRY
- Loves berries
- anger issues

170

CHAPTER TWENTY
Trouble Afoot

Oh my goodness, Journal,

Something strange is <u>definitely</u> afoot. We continued down the mountain road that leads back to the city and were approaching the village of Newellin, when we were flagged down by <u>another</u> desperate group of citizens. That's right, a bunch of people had gone missing, just like in Arvilia! We didn't want to jump to conclusions, so we put in a reasonable amount of detective work to see if something a little less unusual happened this time around, but with each clue we didn't find, it only led us to search the village's outskirts.

So, we left, and we searched and we searched . . . until we found them about forty minutes later. Nine missing people were lying nearly unconscious near the steep, unforgiving cliffside. They were all generally unscathed, except one woman seemed to have gotten her purple-spotted dress caught on a tree. Just like in Arvilia, these people had no idea why they were out there or what led them to such a dangerous area.

One thing that I <u>was</u> certain of, however, was the math of it all. (That's right, Cob CopperSpoon doesn't <u>just</u> cook and tell stories!)

The missing villagers of Newellin went missing about a week after the villagers from Arvilia went missing—and how long does the journey from Arvilia to Newellin take? About a week! The villagers in Newellin had already been missing for a few days before we arrived in town, so that meant if there was something influencing these people to act this way, then we were a few days behind it. We had no time to lose!

"How far away is the next village?" I asked once we had finally made our way back to town with the exhausted missing villagers.

Harold gazed at me, frowning uncertainly at the look of concern in my eyes. "About five days, why?"

Before I could respond people began to flood the streets, realizing their loved ones had been returned. Cheers erupted in the crowd and speaking was nearly impossible.

As if speaking directly into his mind, with a single look, Harold knew what I was thinking.

In an attempt not to be rude, I turned to the crowd and began accepting thanks. Many hands where shaken, small pouches of coins were handed to me, as well as gifts wrapped in burlap. I tried to give the crowd my full attention, but my mind was buzzing with possibilities.

<u>If it takes five days to get to the next village then we may already be to late</u> . . .

<u>Should we scour the woods on the way there?</u>

<u>Maybe we can send Finheld ahead, they move much faster than the rest of us</u> . . .

I glanced back to where Harold once stood, but he was lost to the crowd now. I began frantically searching for him, people still surrounding me, thanking me, putting gifts in my hands, touching me.

It was all too much, Journal. Their words began to blend together. I could feel my chest tightening.

<u>Breathe</u> . . . I thought to myself as the world began to spin. <u>Breathe, just breathe.</u>

Everything was becoming too much all at once.

<u>We need to leave. We need to help the next village.</u>

I could feel the tears welling up in my eyes when suddenly a sturdy hand fell on my shoulder.

"Cob," Harold's familiar, strong voice snapped me out of it in an instant. "Cob, are you okay?"

"Yes!" I responded a little too quickly. "Yes, I'm fine."

He eyed me up and down as if he didn't believe me.

"I talked to the burgomaster. She is proving us with their fastest horses as well as some extra rations. It's going to be okay, Cob. We are going to get there as fast as we can."

I was speechless. Chaos still swirled around me but in that moment, I convinced myself it was going to be okay. After a brief hug, Harold pushed his way through the crowd and began softly speaking to the rest of the party. I took a deep breath and excused myself from the celebrations.

Within the hour, all of us had packed our things and began racing away on the horses provided for us. We rode longer than normal but decided to make camp once the path became too dangerous to pass in the dark. At this rate, we should be to Farvenor in three days time . . . I just hope that's soon enough.

I am too anxious to sleep, so instead I started going through the gifts the villagers sent with us. There was a sack of a few coins, a hand-woven shawl, and even a fancy dagger that was a family heirloom to one of the missing people's families. There was also a handmade meal somebody packed up for us. A sandwich made from something I had never tasted before and a salad with these little, tiny balls of dough-y something.

I can't help but feel bad I never got to meet the chef who made this for us. I never even got to thank them. I am vowing right now to go back after we figure this out and get the recipes. I'm even going to leave the pages blank, just so I make sure I come back!

Moorhsum Cap Sandwich

Hello Journal! I kept my promise and journeyed back. It turns out the weird not-meat in the sandwich was a fungus that grows underneath the moss of the forest! A half-elven person named Beren prides themselves on being an expert forager and their husband Chyrie was the incredible chef. It turns out their cousin was one of the missing villagers. They took me foraging with them and I got to see firsthand how it was prepared.

MAKES 2 BURGERS

Prep time: 1-8 hours | Cook time: 15-20 minutes

INGREDIENTS

MUSHROOM PATTIES:
- 3 tablespoons vegan Worcestershire sauce
- 2 tablespoons olive oil
- 2 tablespoons soy sauce
- 2 teaspoons liquid smoke
- 2 moorhsum caps (can use portobello mushrooms instead)
- 4 cloves garlic, crushed
- Sprig rosemary and thyme

EXTRAS:
- Buns
- Your favorite burger toppings

INSTRUCTIONS

1. Mix together your Worcestershire, olive oil, soy sauce, and liquid smoke in a small bowl.
2. Gently wipe all of the dirt from your portobello with a damp paper towel.
3. Add your portobello, garlic, and fresh herbs to a large plastic bag. Add in your sauce mixture and make sure everything is thoroughly coated.
4. Place this in the fridge and let marinate for at least 1 hour. I let mine sit overnight. This can be baked immediately; the flavors just won't be fully developed.
5. When you are ready to cook your portobello, preheat your oven to 425°F.

6. Place your portobellos in a lightly oiled baking dish after patting dry. Bake for 15 to 20 minutes until the caps are a deep brown on the top.

7. Top with your favorite vegan cheese and bake an additional 5 minutes until melted.

8. Slap your portobello on a bun with all your favorite fixins' and enjoy!

Terra-To Salad

It turns out the salad sent with us was made by an elven woman who went by Chani. When I asked her about the tiny dough balls she used she told me it was an old family recipe they call "Terra To" meaning "Drops of the Earth." She told me the dough recipe was an old family secret, but graciously sent me with a jar of the dried drops. Together we harvested some veggies from her garden, and she taught me how to make the salad.

MAKES 6-8 SERVINGS

Prep time: 15-20 | Cook time: 25-35 minutes

INGREDIENTS

- 2 cups water
- Olive oil
- Salt
- 2 cups uncooked terra-to (can replace with couscous)
- 1 (8-oz) package cherry tomatoes
- 1 red bell pepper
- 2 heads garlic
- 1 tablespoon olive oil
- Salt and pepper
- Fresh basil
- 1 English cucumber
- Fresh parsley
- Fresh chives
- 1 shallot
- ¼ cup kalamata olives
- 1 (16-oz) can of chickpeas
- Red wine vinegar

INSTRUCTIONS

1. Bring your water to a boil with a small splash of olive oil and a pinch of salt.

2. Once your water is boiling, remove it from the heat, add in your terra-to, and cover with a lid. Remove from the heat while you prepare your other ingredients.

3. Preheat your oven to 425°F.

4. Cut your cherry tomatoes in half, dice your red peppers into bite-sized pieces and roughly chop your garlic.

5. Throw your tomatoes, red pepper, and garlic into an oven-safe dish. Drizzle them with a splash of olive oil (about 1 tablespoon), some salt

and pepper, and a few ripped up basil leaves. Place your dish in the oven and let roast for about 20 to 25 minutes.

6. While your other vegetables are roasting, you can now prepare the rest of your ingredients. Chop your cucumber into bite-sized pieces, roughly chop all of your herbs, shallot, and olives, and drain and rinse your chickpeas.

7. Once all of your ingredients are chopped and your tomatoes and peppers have been roasted you are ready to mix everything together. Add all of your ingredients to a large bowl with a splash of olive oil and red wine vinegar (about 1 tablespoon each) and mix everything together.

8. Taste test everything, and add salt, pepper, oil, or vinegar to your liking.

9. Enjoy!

CHAPTER TWENTY-ONE
The Web

Journal,

    By the time we arrived in Farvenor, we were too late. Not just by a few days—by <u>three weeks</u>! There goes my math.

    We were absolutely mortified at first, but then the village guards told us that everybody who had gone missing had eventually managed to find their way back. Everyone except for one person: Rosalind Morwen. No one in the village had any clue where she was or what happened to her. What's even worse, was that she had a husband and two young children at home, waiting desperately for her return.

    We were exhausted from our mad dash to the city, but if we were going to help save Rosalind, there was no time to lose. So, we immediately scurried over to her home under the warmth of the morning light.

    We were greeted at the door by Rosalind's husband, Clark. He had dark bags under his eyes from weeks of tormented nights, and his brown hair was dishevelled and unkempt. Once we shared that we were here to help find out what happened to Rosalind, he quickly ushered us inside. Clark led us into a cozy family room decorated casually with several depictions of the sun, where an elderly, silvery haired woman slept soundlessly in a rocking chair.

    "Have a seat," he said, gesturing to the couches as he crossed the room to where the old woman sat. Clark reached down to a basket on the floor, pulled out a large knit blanket, and draped it over her shoulders.

    "Here you go, Maud."

    The woman didn't stir, but I wasn't surprised. The feeling of grief seemed to hang over the house like a thick, wet blanket. Even the children, who we could hear eating breakfast in the kitchen, whimpered silently to themselves. I'd want to sleep through a time like this, too.

    Once we were situated and Clark found himself a chair to sit in, I took out some parchment and ink and began to do some detective work.

    "So, what happened the day your wife disappeared?"

    "Nothing," He said, "It was a normal day—all we did was garden and spend time with the kids and Grandma Maud."

    He gestured with his head to the sleeping woman in the chair.

    "Then . . . I woke up that night and Rosalind was gone."

"Did it look like someone had taken her?"

Clark shook his head.

"The only thing that was unusual was that the front door had been left open."

Nodding, I scribbled down everything he told me.

"I see, I see. Does she often leave in the middle of the night?"

"No, never."

I couldn't help but notice the twisting of growing torment on Clark's face.

"But night has always been . . . a problem, for her, I guess," he added.

"A problem?"

"Rosalind, she . . ." His breath hitched in his throat, and he swallowed his pain. "She seems normal, but privately she's kind of regrettably attuned to . . . I don't know, the magics of this world, I guess you could say. Supernatural stuff. I kind of keep my distance from that topic, due to my upbringing, but I can say that she's almost psychic sometimes. I don't know how to describe it. Anyway, she has nightmares almost every night. Lately, she's been complaining about seeing a well—way, way out in the woods—and in the dream she'd walk there, barefoot."

"Is there a well nearby?"

Clark shook his head.

"We spend a lot of time amongst these trees, and my wife was certain that this place was nowhere near here. These woods feel like home—but what she kept seeing in her dreams was, well . . . anything but. She said it felt wrong."

"Wrong?"

"She told me that the woods in her dreams had weird, twisted trees and no color at all—and there was the kind of silence you get when there's a predator nearby, you know? Like all the animals knew that something terrible was lurking around the corner . . . and there was."

Chills zipped down my spine.

"There was?"

"Something would whisper to her, beckoning her deeper into the trees. She wanted to turn back, but she never could. She said that she felt like . . . like her body was hers, but it wasn't her own."

Clark shook his head and rested his face in his palms, heaving a great, anxious breath.

"That's when she'd see the well—just a stone well that led down into pitch black— and she'd stand at its edge and peer down. And then she'd hear a voice. 'Come . . . come to me,' it would say, 'Give yourself to me.' And then—then the darkness would start writhing, and she'd see two scarlet eyes appearing at the very bottom of the pit."

Weight crushed against my chest. The creature that stalked the water tribe. It touched me and I saw myself standing before a huge pit in the earth. It wasn't a well . . . but it felt oddly familiar. A huge part of me wanted to dismiss it all entirely, though. What business does a creepy ocean-dwelling creature have in the middle of the woods? None!

"And then what happened?" I asked.

He clenched his teeth at the thought.

"She'd jump. And then she'd wake up screaming. I'd try my best to console her and reassure her that it was just a dream, but now I'm not quite sure that it was. Is—is that even possible?"

Silence fell throughout the house. Was Rosalind having some sort of prophetic dream? Was I? Was something sinister truly reaching out to her—us? Or were her nightmares, and that weird vision I had, simply nothing more than our imaginations?

Clark dragged his hands down his face. "You must think I'm crazy."

The five of us each blurted out in quick protest.

"No one here thinks you're crazy," I reassured. "I promise."

Finheld shrugged.

"I think the issue here is that no one wants to say that your wife's horrible dreams came true," they said.

"You think they came true?" Clark winced, as the color drained from his face.

"No, no!" Irabel interjected. "We just don't want to say they did and have it turn out that there's something less . . . unusual, going on. Like demonic possession or the desire for divorce—"

"Divorce?" Clark asked, a different kind of fear passing over his face.

Harold tutted, shaking his head with a sigh. "She doesn't mean it, Clark."

"Yeah," Irabel shrugged. "I'm just spitballing."

I felt something bubbling up inside of me. I had to say something about the fish thing. I wouldn't be able to forgive myself if I didn't.

"Can I ask you something strange, sir?"

The man's torment turned into a cautious frown.

"Sure,"

"Has your wife ever visited the Adva'loran people way beyond the coast of Marlin's Shore? Nautinara?"

The man shook his head. "Not that I'm aware of, I don't know if she had even heard of that place."

"Hmm," I mused. "Has she ever had a pet fish-thing that was creeping her out so much that she set it loose, so she didn't have to look at it anymore?"

The man looked at my friends like I was crazy, "No, I don't think she's ever had any pets aside from a few cats growing up."

I nodded, scribbling down some more notes. Karn heaved a great sigh.

"Aye, we'll get to the bottom o' this Clark." He reached over and patted the man's back with a heavy hand. "Don't worry."

"Thank you," Clark said. "With the utmost gratitude."

This is when I took the time to push the sea-creature theory aside and do some more mental detective work. I was certain that there were only three villages in this area, and if that were true, that means that Farvenor was the very first one to have any disappearances. Which would also mean that Rosalind was likely the first victim of... whatever it was that was doing this.

The fish-creature?

No! no more fish talk, Cob!

What _was_ it, then? The only facts we knew about the creature Rosalind saw was that it had red eyes and liked wells, and it was potentially luring people into the woods, and giving its victims nightmares—although none of the other victims had said anything to us about nightmares.

"Clark," I said. "Are you positive that there isn't a well like that around here? Not even way, way, way out in the woods?"

But he shook his head. "I'm positive, I—"

"Down, down, _down_ goes the well," A tired voice croaked, as each of our heads snapped in Maud's direction. "Don't fall in or time won't tell... what lives within must not come out... or the world shall seethe and burn."

Clark groaned. "Not in front of guests, Maud, please."

"Down, down, down goes the well," She continued. "The walls prolong our last farewell... unless a girl falls in its maw... then the shadows get their turn."

The woman lifted her head, her milky white gaze falling upon us as tears threatened to fall down her cheeks.

"That's where she went. My daughter fell, and now we are all forsaken."

"You promised me you'd stop with the wives' tales," Clark said, a look of pleading on his face.

The woman turned her gaze from us back to the floor, offering nothing more.

"Sorry. She's just a grieving mother. She means no harm."

Well, creepy or not, I'm glad she spoke up. Once we finished questioning Clark, Harold, Finheld, Karn, and Irabel wanted to get a look at the rest of the house to search for any clues that could have led to Rosalind's disappearance. I took this as a perfect opportunity to gently question Maud. She was thrilled that someone was finally interested in her creepy poem, and she shared all the information she had stored away in her mind for an opportunity just like this.

First, she told me that the rhyme was based on a long forgotten—perhaps purposely so—tale of two wizards who sought the key to eternal life. Somehow, they mucked it all up and created a monster instead. Some say that the monster killed the wizards; others say they managed to escape it and hid themselves away in shame, but her opinion was that they let The Abomination free so the rest of the world could deal with it while they continued their quest to no avail.

I gasped.

"That's horrible!"

She nodded, piercing me with her milky eyes.

"But do you know what I think?"

"No, what?"

"I think they managed to find the answer they'd been looking for all along."

What would the consequences be for finding eternal life, not for the wizards, but for the world? Would we have already seen the effects if they <u>did</u> end up discovering it? Honestly, I'm not so sure.

She went on to tell me that The Abomination was locked away by a great hero, in some strange forest-within-a-forest. Something hidden away from this world so no one would be able to access it. Another dimension, maybe?

"But, whatever has a will . . . has a <u>way</u>."

She clung to the blanket around her shoulders, her eyes looking off into the dreadful distance.

"Do you believe in intuition, girl?"

"Um . . . yeah, I think so! My friend, Irabel, is a sorcerer, and she meditates and does a lot of big-brain psychic stuff sometimes—"

She snatched the neck of my shirt and pulled me in, her hot, stale breath and wide eyes inches from my face.

"Think of the dreams my daughter was having! Think of her premonitions! The monster of legend was reaching out to her to set it free! I just know it!"

I had no idea what to say. I tried to straighten up, but she was much stronger than I ever would have given her credit for.

"We—we can find her—"

The woman scoffed. She let go of my collar, gently shoving me away with a shake of her head.

"Rosalind's gone." She uttered. "I have no ounce of joy left in my life."

As I'm sure you can imagine, the conversation took quite a depressing turn, so I think I'll wrap that up right here. Maud gave us a lot to think of though, that's for sure.

After my conversation with Maud, we made our way to the town tavern. While small in size, Farvenor was built around the main road to The Bastion so the town was no stranger to hosting travelers. The building was set up like a big lodge and the owner kindly gave us access to a humble meeting space/kitchen.

We quickly settled in and started workshopping theories. Even with everybody searching, Finheld was the only one to find a clue. I say "clue" but really it was just a very, very old story book. Inside was the poem Maud had cryptically retold. Nothing new, but good to have the original I suppose.

That's when I informed everybody of what Maud told me. Irabel in particular thought it was all very interesting. Apparently, apocalyptic-type secrets and multidimensional realities aren't a super far-fetched concept!

Here's some nerdy stuff for you: The standing theory is that there are strands of magic running through the planet that are all overlapping in one intricate web. There is a beginning and an end to each strand, so—if this theory is true—all we need to do is figure out how to find the general location of the supposed well, find the strand of magic that it's closest to, and get on the other side! It sounded like a longshot, but what did we have to lose?

As Irabel explain this string theory, I decided to brew us up some food and drink. In our hustle to get here, we hadn't had time to cook a proper meal in days. I didn't know about anybody else, but the cold mountain winds still felt stuck to my bones. A warm soup and hot drink was necessary in this moment. We all sat down for a very tense dinner. All of us were on edge, but I had never felt closer to my team either. There was no arguing or bickering, there was no shooting down of ideas. I think we all know that this case is different. Something weird is going on here.

After we filled our bellies, Irabel offered to spend the night meditating to look for any signs of this magical web while we slept. Apparently when she meditates for long periods of time she can actually sense these magical threads and interact with them. We took her up on the offer, hoping to learn anything we could. I hope she finds what she's looking for. I really don't want any more villagers to go missing because of some well-monster in the woods.

These last few days have been really stressful on my friends, and I'd be lying big time if I said no one was worried about a dream-walking creature that could snatch people up in their sleep.

Red Ruby Spiced Cider

Guess what? I still had a <u>bunch</u> of apples left from Finheld's pie. What more perfect way to use the rest of them than making a big ol' jug of spiced apple cider! I did not have any sugar though. When I went asking around for a sweetener I was given the tavern keep's special stash of red ruby syrup, made from the ruby trees that grew in this area. It was absolutely delicious!

MAKES 12–16 SERVINGS

Prep time: 5–10 minutes | Cook time: 3–5 hours

Ingredients

- 8–10 medium apples
- 1 orange (can replace with ¼ cup orange juice)
- 1–3-inch nub fresh ginger (can replace with ½ teaspoon ground ginger)
- 2 cinnamon sticks
- 1–3 whole cloves
- ½ teaspoon ground nutmeg
- ¼–½ cup red ruby syrup (can replace with maple syrup)
- Water

Instructions

1. Chop all of your apples, slice your orange, and peel your ginger.
2. Place your apples, spices, orange, red ruby syrup, and ginger into a large Dutch oven or pot.
3. Add water until the apples are fully submerged.
4. Bring to a boil then reduce to a simmer. Let simmer for 3 to 5 hours, stirring occasionally. If the water level seems like it is going down, just top it off with a little more until it's full again.
5. After your cider is done simmering and your apples are fully soft, remove from the heat and mash everything together with a potato masher.
6. Strain your cider through a fine mesh sieve and cheese cloth, making sure to get as much pulp separated as possible.
7. Add extra sweetener as needed.
8. Your cider can be stored the fridge for 2 to 3 weeks.

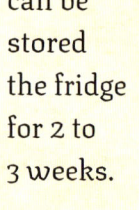

Squashling Soup

Farvenor specializes in growing butternut squash. They even figured out how to grow some of them in cool shapes like dogs and geese—oh, and there's one shaped just like a little lad dancing! I named him squashling! That's the one we used for the soup.

MAKES 4 SERVINGS

Prep time: 10-15 minutes | Cook time: 1½-2 hours

Ingredients

- 1 butternut squash
- 2 onions
- 3 heads garlic
- 2–3 tablespoons olive oil
- Salt and pepper, to taste
- Bundle thyme
- Bundle rosemary
- 1 cup coconut cream or milk
- 3 cups chicken or vegetable broth

Instructions

1. Preheat your oven to 350°F.
2. Start by slicing your squash in half lengthwise and spooning out all of the seeds. Butternut squash are very hard and difficult to cut, so make sure you're using a large, sharp knife, and you're very careful while you are cutting it.
3. Once your squash is cut in half, score it about every inch, both horizontally and vertically. This will help it cook evenly and faster.
4. Peel and quarter your onions and snip or slice the tips off your garlic heads.
5. Add your squash, onion, and garlic heads to a large baking dish and drizzle with your olive oil. Sprinkle your salt and pepper over the squash, then add your thyme and rosemary sprigs to the baking dish.
6. Cover your baking dish with aluminum foil and place in your oven. Bake for 1 hour or until your squash is fully cooked. You will know it's cooked when you can easily stab and remove a fork in the thickest part of the squash.

(Continued)

7. Once your squash is fully cooked, let it sit, covered, for about 30 minutes. Remove the sprigs of rosemary and thyme then scoop out the meat of the squash and place into a large Dutch oven or pot. Add all roasted garlic (minus the husk) and onions to the pot, too.

8. Add your cream to your pot and mash everything together with a potato masher. Slowly mix in your chicken broth while doing this until you get the consistency you desire. You can also use an immersion blender or regular blender to get a smoother, creamier soup.

9. Taste and add salt and pepper as needed.

10. Enjoy! Feel free to eat as-is or add bacon bits or sausage to the top!

CHAPTER TWENTY-TWO
Markings

Eek, Journal!

When Irabel meditates, she hovers mid-air using the sheer power of her mind, sitting cross-legged as though she were on a comfy bench. It's always so peaceful to behold, and tonight was no exception . . . until it was.

Irabel and I shared a room that night. I awoke to the sound of her crashing to the floor. She convulsed, digging into the wood with her sharp claws. Then her eyes rolled back into her skull and her jaw went slack. Where I expected to see a twisted expression of pain, I saw . . . nothing. If she wasn't moving, I would have thought she was dead.

I screamed out for Harold as I ran to her side, but I had no idea how to help.

"Do we pin her down?!" I cried out as I heard the door burst open.

I looked up to see the alarmed faces of Karn, Harold, and Finheld. Karn nodded.

"Grab her arms."

Finheld and I did as instructed, but Harold gently pushed our hands out of the way.

"Wait."

He sat at her side, gripped the sun-shaped pendant on his necklace, and muttered something under his breath. It must have been a prayer because soft light grew in his hands, and with a simple press of his palm to Irabel's forehead, whatever was troubling her had vanished.

I wanted so badly to ask her what happened, but she was sound asleep.

"Will she be okay?"

"I think so, she just needs to rest," Harold assured.

Karn carried her off to his bed, but before I could follow, something on the floor caught my eye.

"Guys, look at this!" I said, pointing at the floor.

Irabel's scratches didn't just look like scratches—they looked like symbols! There were six overlapping lines and strange characters carved into the wood. The writing looked <u>nothing</u> like Irabel's elegant cursive.

Finheld had the bright idea of overlaying a piece of parchment on the scratches and making some impressions with charcoal. They wondered if there was any correlation between Irabel's markings and the areas with the scratch marks. There was only one way to find out, but we weren't going to disturb Irabel after what had just happened to her.

So, we all went back to sleep.

Well . . . we tried to at least.

I was too busy tossing and turning. I couldn't stop thinking about Irabel, and the scratches she made in the floor and all of the missing people that needed our help. It got so bad that I couldn't even stand laying down in bed. I had to do <u>something</u> to take my mind off all that was happening.

I crawled out of bed and krept to the little room we were using as a work space. To my surprise I found Karn there, sipping on a glass of dark liquid.

"Oh! Karn, hi!" I said with a pause. "Couldn't sleep?"

"Nah. And neither could anyone else. Harold and Finny are keeping an eye on our girl while she sleeps."

Concern plastered Karn's face but he smiled through it. "What keeps you up lass?"

There was a long pause as I looked for the right words. I didn't know what to say. I sat frozen, until I heard a soft laugh coming from Karns direction.

"Cob CopperSpoon not knowing what to say. Now that's a first."

A small giggle escaped me. Then a chuckle, then a laugh. Karn and I sat there, laughing into the silence of night for far too long.

"What have we gotten ourselves into?" I asked.

"I don't know." Karn replied, pouring me a small glass of whatever he was drinking. "But I know sittin and moping about it will do us no good. Come on, we have work ta do."

Karn quickly downed his drink before leading me outside. In the soft light of the barely rising sun we wandered the woods looking for ingredients. After gathering a batch or mushrooms, some wild rosemary, and a wild onion we went inside and got to work creating some soup.

We dropped off a couple bowls to Harold and Finheld before trading places with them. Karn and I stayed together keeping watch over our friend until at some point I fell asleep on his shoulder.

Melodious Mushroom Soup

While gathering soup ingredients, I heard a weird singing sound in the woods, so of course Karn and I went to check it out. We quickly came across a happy little trio of mushrooms with arms, legs, and little lutes made out of sticks, grass, and logs. They were singing about how badly they just wanted to be chopped up and turned into soup, and . . . well, you don't have to ask me twice! There is nothing more healing than a magical singing mushroom, right?

Makes 4-6 servings

Prep time: 10-20 minutes | Cook time: 25-35 minutes

Ingredients

- 1-2 (8-oz) packages cremini brown mushrooms
- 2 tablespoons fresh rosemary
- 1 medium onion
- 1 tablespoon olive oil
- 2 tablespoons butter
- 1 teaspoon paprika
- 1 teaspoon white pepper
- ½ cup white wine
- 4 cups beef broth
- ¼ cup flour
- 1¼ cups heavy cream, divided
- 3 heads roasted garlic (see page 15)
- Salt and pepper, to taste

Instructions

1. Clean your mushrooms! Do *not* run your mushrooms under water. Get a paper-towel damp and wipe any dirt off gently. For an extra mushroom-y soup, use 2 packs of mushrooms!

2. Remove the mushroom heads from the stems. Slice the head of the mushrooms and chop up the stems into small chunks. Mince your rosemary and dice your onion into very small pieces

3. Heat a large pot or Dutch oven over medium-high heat with your oil and butter inside. Add in your chopped onions, rosemary, and a pinch of salt. Cook until your onions become translucent, about 2 to 3 minutes.

(Continued)

4. Once your onions are fully translucent, add in your paprika, white pepper, and mushrooms. Mix together, making sure everything is coated in your seasonings.

5. Add in your white wine and cook until the wine has reduced by half.

6. Once your wine has reduced, add in all of your beef broth and bring to a boil.

7. In a small bowl, mix your flour as well as ¼ cup of your heavy cream until smooth. This will be used to thicken your soup.

8. Bring your broth to a boil and add in the rest of your heavy cream, the heavy cream-flour mix, and all of your roasted garlic. Mix thoroughly and cook for about 5 minutes to thicken the soup.

9. Enjoy!

CHAPTER TWENTY-THREE
Irabel's Journey

Hey Journal,

    So, I bet you're wondering what happened to Irabel. By the time I awoke, both Karn and Irabel where nowhere in sight. I made my way to our temporary headquarters and found everybody sitting around the large table.

    Irabel smiled at me but she looked really, really tired. She was very . . . hunchy—kind of not quite able to hold herself as high as normal, you know? Plus, I'm one hundred percent positive that if she didn't have fur we would have been able to see huge dark circles under her eyes. A bowl of mushroom soup sat in front of her that she would occasionally stir but never take a bite.

    Our poor girlie!

    "Mornin' sleepy head." Karn prodded while handing me a warm cup of cider. "You're just in time, Irabel just woke up."

    "So, what happened?" I asked, taking a seat next to Irabel.

    "I found the web. It's real." She muttered into her cup. "I was wandering through the nearby forest in my meditative state, and I found one of the strands."

    "Is that what made you all . . . creepy and wiggly? Its magical influence?" I asked.

    Irabel shook her head.

    "No. It was something else, a—a strange darkness. I wasn't strong enough to fight it at first. It overwhelmed me and I lost control of myself."

    An icy chill coursed through my veins. "And then what?"

    "It pulled me alongside the strand and made me follow its path deeper and deeper into the woods. Eventually I saw a point in the distance where it connected with five others, but an awful feeling grew inside of me. I wanted to turn away, but the darkness became stronger every time I tried. I fought as hard as I could—"

    Karn nodded.

"Aye, is that why you were thrashing?"

Her eyes were wide.

"Well, I suppose it's a good thing that you saw that, because that meant I forced myself out of my meditative trance just enough to do something in . . . the real world—for lack of a better term."

I nodded vigorously.

"If you hadn't then Harold wouldn't have known to help cure you."

Irabel looked at Harold and gave him a thankful smile. "I really appreciate it, Harold."

"Look, I know you said you were fine, but you should get some rest," he said, returning her smile. "You can tell us more when you've recovered."

I really, really, really wanted to hear more and see if Finheld's map theory was worth looking into, but Harold was right. Irabel didn't look great, and her wellbeing means more to me than any information she may or may not have found in her trance.

Harold helped Irabel back to bed while the rest of us stayed behind. After some brief discussion on what to do next, we decided it would be best to stay a little longer and do some more digging. For now, Finheld ended up going to get some rest while Karn began writing a letter to Hutar explaining the situation.

In the meantime, I thought it would be a good idea to interview some more villagers about the disappearances. I wasn't able to learn anything new, but on the plus side, I did gather some new recipes! So, it's not a total loss.

Crimson Berry Soup

Some lady named Lisa said that this was her family's cold remedy. If you serve it cold, maybe it could be your family's <u>hot</u> remedy! Just Kidding! Please don't serve this cold.

Makes 2-4 servings

Prep time: 5-10 minutes | Cook time: 30-45 minutes

Ingredients

Soup:
- 3-4 large crimson berries (can replace with tomatoes)
- 2-3 red bell peppers
- 1 large yellow onion
- 1-3 heads garlic
- Olive oil
- Salt, pepper, and paprika, to taste
- Bundle of fresh basil, divided
- ½-1 cup heavy cream or milk

Cheesy Garlic Bread:

Makes 4-6 slices
- ½ cup softened butter
- 1-3 tablespoons minced garlic
- ½ cup Parmesan cheese (fresh or powdered will work)
- 1 teaspoon Italian seasoning
- Salt and pepper
- Slices of your favorite bread

Instructions

Soup:

1. Preheat your oven to 425°F.

2. Cut your crimson berries into large chunks. De-seed your bell peppers and chop into large chunks. Peel your onion and chop it into large chunks, too.

3. Crush and peel your heads of garlic. You can use as much or as little garlic as you want here.

4. Place your crimson berries, peppers, onion, and garlic into a large baking dish. Drizzle with olive oil and top with a big pinch of salt, pepper, and paprika. Make sure to mix everything up, so it is evenly coated.

5. Rip up a bunch of your basil and sprinkle it on top of your vegetables. Make sure to save some fresh basil for a garnish at the end.

(Continued)

6. Roast all of your vegetables for 20 to 25 minutes or until everything is soft and starting to turn a nice golden-brown color.

7. Once your vegetables are done roasting, let them cool for 15 to 20 minutes.

8. Transfer your vegetables into a blender and blend until smooth. Note: It is very important that you let your vegetables cool if you are using a closed-lid blender. The steam released from the heat will cause pressure to build up while it's blending, and it can lead to hot soup flying all over your kitchen if you aren't careful. You can also transfer your vegetables straight to a large pot and use an immersion blender if you have one.

9. Add your blended vegetables to a large pot. If you like a smoother, creamier soup you can pour it through a fine-mesh strainer to collect any large chunks or seeds left unblended.

10. Add your heavy cream to your soup before bringing it up to a simmer. Give it a final taste test and add any extra salt or pepper as needed.

Cheesy Garlic Bread:

1. Mix together your softened butter, minced garlic, Parmesan cheese, Italian seasoning, and a pinch of salt and pepper.

2. Spread your butter mixture in a thick layer over your slices of bread.

3. Heat a griddle or pan over medium-high heat. Place your bread butter-side down on the griddle.

4. You want to cook your bread until it starts turning golden brown and crispy, which should take about 4 to 7 minutes.

5. Flip your bread over and let cook for 1 to 2 minutes. You just want it to start getting toasty.

6. Remove from heat and serve with your soup! Now all that's left is to enjoy!

Everything-but-the-Dragon's-Hoard Scones

You know, Karn told me this was way too many ingredients for a scone recipe, but I strongly disagree. We got cherries! We got chocolate! We got pistachios! We got flour! We got sugar! We got salt! We—you get the picture.

The villager who kindly shared this recipe told me their uncle had found it written on parchment in the middle of a dragon's lair! Unfortunately, it was the only thing they were able to escape with as they were being chased away. It has been a treasured family heirloom ever since! They even have the original framed on the wall!

MAKES 8 SCONES

Prep time: 15-25 minutes | Cook time: 30-40 minutes

INGREDIENTS

- 1 (15-oz) can dark sweet cherries, drained
- ½ cup chopped chocolate (use your favorite, I combined milk and dark)
- ½ cup chopped pistachios
- 3 cups flour
- ⅓ cup sugar
- ½ teaspoon salt
- 2 teaspoons baking powder
- ¾ cup cold, cubed butter
- 1 large egg
- ¼–½ cup buttermilk

INSTRUCTIONS

1. Preheat your oven to 350°F.
2. Chop your cherries, chocolate, and pistachios. Set aside for now.
3. Mix together your flour, sugar, salt, and baking powder in a large bowl.
4. Add your cold, cubed butter to your dry ingredients and cut into the mix. You can do this by using a pastry cutter or by using your fingers and squishing the butter into your dry ingredients. Your dough should have a crumbly texture by the time it's all mixed in.

(Continued)

5. Add in your cherries, half your pistachios, and half your chocolate. Mix until coated in your dry mix.

6. Add in your egg and half of your buttermilk. Mix by hand until just combined. You don't want to over-mix this and make a firm dough, you want it to be a little crumbly and floury. If it's looking too sticky, add a little extra flour. If it's looking too floury and not clumping together at all, add a bit more of your buttermilk.

7. Once your dough is mixed, place in a well-oiled pie pan or cast iron. Flatten into an even layer then top with your remaining pistachios and chocolate. Score your unbaked scones into 8 wedges with a sharp knife or pastry cutter.

8. Bake for 30 to 40 minutes. When you poke the top of it, it should feel firm (it won't brown too much in the oven so use your best judgment).

9. When you take the scones out of the oven, they will be very moist and cakey. You can enjoy them hot and gooey, but when given time to fully cool for a night, uncovered, they will firm up and become super crumbly and more "scone-like."

Gruble Kebab and Cucumber Salad

Have you ever heard of a gruble before? Well, neither had I! Apparently, a gruble is a small creature around the size of a raccoon. They have large eyes, purple and yellow fur, and big ole' pot bellies. They are mischievous creatures who only dwell in this part of the forest and survive off the stolen rations of passing travelers! Well, that is if you believe the stories of Crazy Joe. I wonder why the other villagers call him that? Either way, he gave me a recipe for gruble kebabs! (It tastes a lot like chicken!)

MAKES 4-6 SERVINGS

Prep time: 1-1½ hours | Cook time: 15-20 minutes

INGREDIENTS

GRUBLE KEBABS:
- 2-4 tablespoons fresh parsley
- 5-8 cloves garlic
- 1 cup plain Greek yogurt
- 1 tablespoon za'atar seasoning (can replace with all-purpose seasoning)
- 1-2 tablespoons seasoning salt or chicken seasoning
- 1 lemon
- 1-2 tablespoons olive oil
- 3-4 large gruble filet (can replace with chicken breast)
- Cherry tomatoes (optional)
- Red onion (optional)
- Bell peppers (optional)

TZATZIKI:
- ½ cucumber
- 1 cup plain Greek yogurt
- ½ lemon
- 1 tablespoon fresh mint
- 1 tablespoon fresh dill
- ½ tablespoon fresh parsley
- 1-2 cloves garlic
- 2-4 tablespoons olive oil
- Salt and pepper

CUCUMBER SALAD:
- 1½ large cucumbers
- Cherry tomatoes
- Salt
- ¼ red onion
- 2-3 tablespoons fresh dill
- 2-3 tablespoons fresh parsley
- 2-3 tablespoons fresh mint
- 3-4 tablespoons olive oil
- Drizzle of honey
- ½ lemon

(Continued)

1 teaspoon za'atar seasoning blend
1 clove garlic
Pepper
½ cup crumbled feta

EXTRAS:
Naan bread
Lettuce
Feta
Pickled red onions (see page 148)

INSTRUCTIONS

BASILISK KEBABS:

1. Finely mince your fresh parsley and garlic.

2. Mix together your parsley, garlic, Greek yogurt, za'atar seasoning, seasoning salt, the juice of one lemon, and your olive oil in a large bowl.

3. Chop your gruble (chicken) into medium-sized chunks. You want them to be thick enough to fit on your kebab sticks but not too big that it's hard to eat.

4. Add your gruble chunks to your yogurt marinade and mix well, making sure to massage your gruble into the marinade.

5. Cover with plastic wrap and place in the fridge for at least 1 hour. This is the perfect time to prepare your cucumber salad and tzatziki!

6. Now it's time to skewer your marinated gruble! If you are using wooden kebab sticks, make sure to soak them in cold water for 10 to 15 minutes before using. This will help prevent them from catching on fire while grilling. Skewer 3–5 pieces of gruble onto each kebab until you use up all of your gruble. You can also skewer on cherry tomatoes, red onion, or bell peppers between your gruble pieces, if you'd like.

7. Heat a grill or grill pan over medium-high heat. If you are using a grill pan, lightly spray with some oil.

8. Grill your gruble for 5 to 8 minutes on each side until it starts to get some nice grill marks. Depending on how big your gruble chunks are, it may take more time to fully cook through. Double check that the internal temperature of your gruble is 165°F.

TZATZIKI:

1. Grate your cucumber into a small bowl lined with a clean cloth. Using the cloth, bundle up the shredded cucumber and squeeze out as much liquid as possible. You can either reserve the cucumber juice to drink or you can discard it now.

2. Add your shredded cucumber to your Greek yogurt as well as the juice of half a lemon.

(Continued)

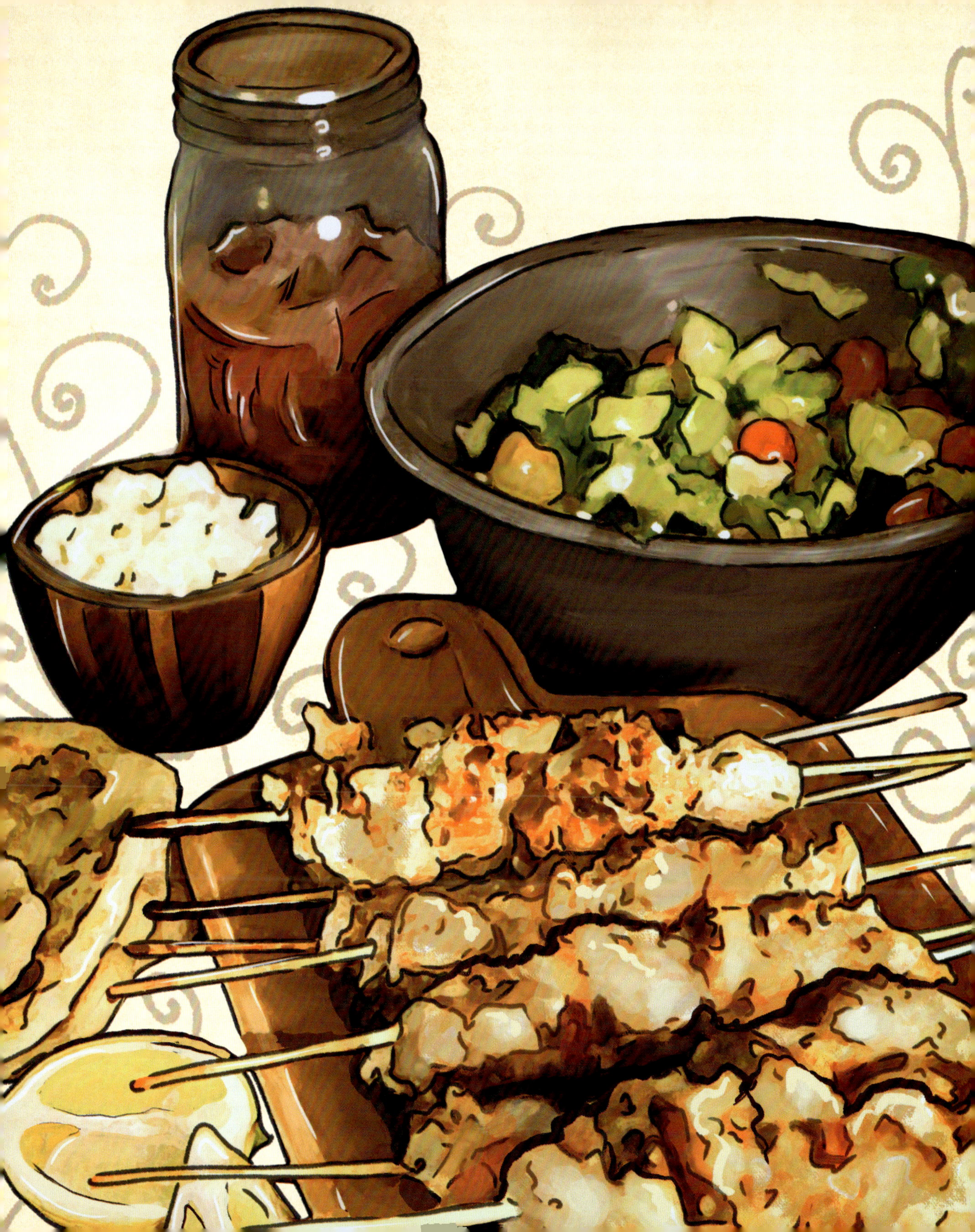

3. Finely mince your dill, mint, and parsley then add to your yogurt mix.

4. Grate in your garlic and then start mixing everything together. Slowly add in your olive oil until you reach your desired consistency.

5. Taste your tzatziki, then add salt and pepper as needed.

6. Cover with plastic wrap and store in the fridge while you make the rest of your meal.

CUCUMBER SALAD:

1. Chop your cucumbers into bite-sized pieces and slice your cherry tomatoes in half. Put them in a large bowl with a couple big pinches of salt. Toss everything around and let sit for 10 to 15 minutes. The salt will help extract any extra liquid from the vegetables and will be rinsed off later.

2. Finely chop your red onion, then throw it in a bowl of ice-cold water. This is going to help dull down the super pungent raw onion flavor. Set aside for now.

3. Finely mince your dill, parsley, and mint.

4. Add your olive oil, honey, the juice of half a lemon, and za'atar to a small bowl. Grate in your clove of garlic and whisk until well combined. Taste your dressing and add any adjustments as you see fit! If you like a little sweeter dressing, add more honey. If you want more spice, add in some salt and pepper or za'atar. Taste as you go and trust your instincts!

5. Drain your cucumbers and tomatoes of any excess liquid. Also give them a little rinse to get off any excess salt. Pat them dry with a clean paper towel and place back in your large bowl.

6. Drain your red onion and add to your other veggies. Also add in your fresh herbs, dressing, and crumbled feta.

7. Toss your salad well and give it a taste. Add in any extra seasonings as you see fit.

8. Cover your bowl with plastic wrap and set in the fridge. The flavors will spend time developing while you grill your chicken.

ASSEMBLY:

The last step of this process is to enjoy whichever way you like! I enjoy heating up some naan and piling it up with the freshly grilled gruble, some lettuce, pickled red onions, feta, and a bunch of tzatziki. I eat that with the cucumber salad on the side, but there is really no wrong way to enjoy this one!

Sweet Dream Soup

I wish I could just cut open a ravioli and sleep inside of it for just one night. I know I'm short, but imagine being <u>that</u> tiny?! Think of all the things you could get away with. I think I'd sneak candies from Harold's backpack.

I got this recipe from a half-goblin named Traver. He says its great for using up leftovers if you have them. Traver recommend sea serpent, but leftover chuck roast or chicken work, too!

MAKES 4-6 SERVINGS

Prep time: 5-10 minutes | Cook time: 35-40 minutes

Ingredients

- 1 pound meat of your choice
- Vegetables of your choice (see instructions for some suggestions)
- 2 tablespoons butter
- 1-2 tablespoons minced garlic
- 4-5 cups broth
- Your favorite ravioli
- 1 teaspoon paprika
- 1 teaspoon Italian seasoning
- 2 bay leaves
- Fresh herbs (optional)
- Salt and pepper, to taste

Instructions

1. Prep your meat! This is a fantastic recipe for using up any leftovers. We made this one with leftover chuck roast, but you can use shredded chicken, sausage, or ground beef. Whatever you have on hand! If you are using anything that needs to be cooked like raw sausage, make sure to cook it up in a large pot first.

2. Prep your vegetables! You can use any of your favorites in this. Here we used onions, carrots, canned tomatoes, and steamed broccoli. I just chopped everything into bite-sized bits and cooked it in butter and garlic until it was nice and soft. This soup would be great with spinach, mushrooms, potatoes, even zucchini, and squash! This is perfect for using up anything you have laying around that needs to get used up.

(Continued)

3. Once your vegetables have softened, add in your meat, broth, ravioli, and seasonings. Bring the broth to a boil and then reduce it to a simmer.

4. Simmer your soup for 20 to 30 minutes then remove your bay leaves.

5. Serve up with some Parmesan cheese and enjoy! This is a great time to experiment if you aren't super comfortable making your own recipes yet—you really can't go wrong with this one!

CHAPTER TWENTY-FOUR

Maps and Mushrooms and Bears, Oh My!

Journal, hey, hey!

Well, Finheld and Irabel's map thing actually worked out perfectly. It led us to this absolutely stunning and lush forest. It was picturesque, awash with vibrant shades of green that could have come straight from a painting. There were chirping birds up high, and the warmth of the sunlight cutting through the treetops reminded me of home. I wouldn't trade my adventurer's life for anything, but I miss home <u>so</u> much. Sometimes, I wish I could go back for even just a moment, but the life of a traveling chef, storyteller, and best friend doesn't wait for anyone!

It took us a day and a half to get within a five-mile radius of our destination, and we all got off our horses to make camp. Once we finished, everyone collectively agreed to start searching for signs of a planar portal. I think that's what Irabel called it. We had no idea what this thing looked like, but I was determined to find it!

So, to start, we walked east for three whole miles.

We found <u>nothing</u>.

We tried again the next day, and guess what?

Nothing again!

Well, that's actually not entirely true. I did some foraging along the way, and I found some pretty neat, lumpy little mushrooms. The moment I saw them—and after Harold confirmed they weren't poisonous, at least—I knew I wanted to treat my friends to a mushroomy meal.

So, a little defeated and with mushrooms in hand, we headed back to camp . . . but then something waggling in the breeze caught my eye. Something you don't normally come across in the woods. Caught up in a bush, torn by branches and stained with dirt, was a shred of fabric—purple-spotted fabric, exactly like the lady in Arvilia's torn dress! The thing is, though, she lives miles away from this forest. How could she have made her way here and back? Was it all just a coincidence?

I collected the piece of fabric, and we headed back to camp. It felt like we found an obscurely shaped piece of the puzzle, but it was far from falling into place.

What did this all mean?

I was so wrapped up in trying to connect the dots I didn't notice the party had stopped moving until I ran smack dab into Finheld's back. In one swift motion they gently placed a hand over my mouth and dragged me low to the ground behind a bush. Holding a finger to their lips they removed their hand from my mouth and pointed towards where we had made camp.

There, in the middle of the clearing was a massive bear with large boney protrusions jutting out of its shoulders. A gasp escaped my lips at the sight.

"What is that?" I asked.

"A bear, a <u>really</u> big bear." Harold whispered from his hiding spot behind a tree.

"Did you tie up the supplies like you were supposed to?" Irabel's voice hissed from a low hanging branch above us.

"Maybe!" Finheld jabbed back. "I . . . may have forgot."

"You <u>forgot?</u>"

While Finheld and Irabel began bickering in whispers my eyes never left the bear.

"Well," Karns voice rang out entirely too loud. "Only one thing to do about this."

I watched in horror as he stood up from his hiding spot. A war cry escaped his lips as he charged towards the camp. We all froze staring at each other in shock for a moment before leaping into action.

Karn certainly does have a way with these things.

Looks like we are going to be having more than just mushrooms for dinner tonight!

Braised Dire Bear Belly and Eggs

Listen up, you better take bear safety seriously, <u>especially</u> if you're camping! Do you think I <u>wanted</u> to make braised dire bear belly and eggs?! While delicious, this did <u>not</u> go with my plan.

Makes 4 servings

Prep time: 10-20 minutes | Cook time: 1½-2 hours

Ingredients

- 5–6 cloves garlic
- 4–5 medium tomatoes
- 1 large yellow onion
- 2½ pounds dire bear belly (can replace with pork belly)
- 1 tablespoon olive oil
- Salt and pepper
- ½–¾ cup red wine
- 2 tablespoons fresh oregano, plus extra for garnish
- 4 eggs
- Parmesan cheese, to taste
- Bread of your choice

Instructions

1. Crush and peel your garlic, quarter your tomatoes, dice your yellow onion, and cube your dire bear into bite-sized chunks.

2. Heat a large cast iron pan or sauté pan over medium-high heat with your oil. Add in your dire bear with a pinch of salt. Sear until you get a nice golden-brown color on most of your dire bear and then remove from the pan. There will be a lot of excess fat in the pan. Drain about half of it then leave the rest to cook your veggies in.

3. Add your garlic and onion into the pan with the leftover pork fat. Sauté until the onions start to turn a golden brown, about 5 to 10 minutes.

4. Once your onions are starting to caramelize, add in your tomatoes with a big pinch of salt and pepper. You want to gently nestle the tomatoes into the onions so that they make good contact with the cast iron. We want the tomatoes to get a nice golden-brown color on them as well. Leave your tomatoes alone for 2 to 3 minutes before giving your whole pan a good stir.

(Continued)

5. Add your wine and fresh oregano to your pan. Let the wine simmer down and reduce by about half.

6. Reduce your heat to medium-low, then grab a potato masher and start crushing your tomatoes. They should be tender enough by now to easily mash.

7. Let your tomato mix come to a simmer before re-adding all of your pork belly. Make sure the dire bear is evenly coated in the sauce before covering with a lid. Leave your dire bear on medium-low heat for 1 hour or until the meat is nice and tender.

8. Once your dire bear is fully cooked, make 4 small wells inside your sauce. Crack an egg into each of these wells, season with some salt and pepper, then cover your pan back up for 5 to 10 minutes. Be sure to keep a close eye on your eggs so you don't overcook them. The whites should look glossy but cooked, with a yellow runny yolk underneath.

9. Garnish with some oregano and Parmesan cheese and enjoy! I like this best with a soft flatbread, but it's also great served on tortillas or even crunchy toast!

Forager's Pillows

Irabel told me that some mushrooms can make you hallucinate. I hope it's not these ones!

Makes 4 servings

Prep time: 40-60 minutes | Cook time: 40-60 minutes

Ingredients

Gnocchi:
- 2 large russet potatoes
- 2 cups flour
- 1 large egg

Sauce:
- ¼ cup dried morel mushrooms
- ¼ cup dried chicken of the woods mushrooms
- 5–7 cloves garlic
- 2 lemons
- ¼ cup fresh chives
- 1 cup mushroom juice
- 5 tablespoons butter
- Bundle rosemary and thyme
- Salt and pepper, to taste
- ¼ –½ cup pasta water
- ½ cup Parmesan cheese

Dried Mushroom Substitution: If you do not have dried mushrooms, you can use fresh as well! Instead of adding mushroom juice to the sauce, deglaze your pan with ¼ cup white wine or a white tea and follow the same steps as before.

Instructions

1. Add your dried mushrooms to a large mason jar or bowl. Cover until fully submerged in water (about 2 cups), then cover and set aside.

2. Bring a large pot of water to a boil with a pinch of salt added.

3. Peel and quarter your potatoes. Add to your boiling water and cook for 20 to 30 minutes until soft.

4. Drain your potatoes and mash them. You want these as smooth and fine as possible, you can use a ricer or fine-mesh sieve to get super fluffy potatoes or just mash them by hand. Let these cool for at least 5 to 10 minutes before moving to the next step.

5. Add your 2 cups of flour and an egg to your potatoes. Mix until roughly combined, then pour the mixture onto a lightly floured surface. Knead your

(Continued)

dough for about 5 minutes until it becomes a smooth ball.

6. Wrap your dough ball in parchment paper and place in the fridge for about 20 minutes while you prep your other ingredients.

7. Smash and peel your garlic, halve your lemons, and finely mince your chives.

8. Retrieve your now-hydrated mushrooms from your mushroom juice and roughly chop. Be sure to save the mushroom juice for the next steps.

9. Start boiling another large pot of water, then add about half of your mushroom juice and a big pinch of salt to the water.

10. Pull your gnocchi dough from the fridge and place on a lightly floured surface. Using a pastry cutter or sharp knife, cut your dough into 8 even pieces.

11. One by one, roll your 8 slices into long thin logs. Make sure you are using enough flour, or the gnocchi noodles will stick to each other. Cut your long logs into bite-sized chunks and set aside.

12. In a large pan or cast iron, melt your butter over medium-high heat. Once your butter is fully melted, add your garlic, rosemary, and thyme bundles. Cook for 5 to 6 minutes, stirring constantly. You want your butter to start turning a golden-brown color. If your garlic looks like it is starting to burn, move on to the next step.

13. Add your chopped mushrooms to your butter mix with a pinch of salt and pepper. Sauté for 3 to 5 minutes in the butter mix.

14. Once your mushrooms have cooked for a few minutes, start boiling your gnocchi. Be sure to stir them occasionally in the water to make sure they aren't sticking together. They will be fully cooked once they start floating to the water surface, which should only take a few minutes.

15. After you start boiling your gnocchi, remove the rosemary and thyme from your pan and add in your remaining mushroom juice and the juice of one lemon. Let this cook down for 2 to 3 minutes and then taste. Add additional lemon juice or seasoning if needed.

16. Once your gnocchi are fully cooked, start adding it to your sauce. You can strain your gnocchi, but if you do, make sure to reserve 1 to 2 cups of your pasta water. Otherwise, you

can scoop out with a slotted spoon or spider strainer.

17. Toss the gnocchi in your sauce. Add in your cheese with about ¼ cup of your reserved pasta water. Mix together until the sauce becomes smooth and creamy. Add more pasta water as needed if your sauce is looking too thick or sticky. Stir in half of your chives at the very end.

18. Serve with a little extra lemon squeezed on top with extra cheese and your fresh chives, and enjoy!

CHAPTER TWENTY-FIVE
Stepping into the Darkness

Dear Journal,

    Karn gently nudged me awake in the middle of the night. Something wasn't right with Irabel. She was tossing and turning in her sleep, clearly having another strange dream.

    "Should we wake her up?" Harold asked, his forehead creased with worry.

    Before any of us could reply, Irabel stood and walked out of the tent.

    I hopped to my feet in an instant. Where was she going?!

    "Irabel!"

    "Hold on, the two of you!" Karn called.

    I heard Finheld utter a tired '*what now?*', but I had no time to fill them in. Irabel was heading somewhere, and I wasn't going to let her go alone! I dashed out the door after her

    The rest of the party caught up to us in the dark woods soon enough.

    We were transfixed by Irabel and driven to silence with both concern and curiosity. She moved as if she were a puppet, being pulled along through the dark by imaginary strings. She moved with an odd intent—a strange familiarity with terrain she's never traveled.

    The further we let her walk, the faster she moved.

    Jogging, running, sprinting—she was nearly gliding over rocks and fallen trees that we, in contrast, found ourselves stumbling over as we scrambled to keep up.

    I was gasping for air. My lungs burned in my chest, but I wasn't going to give up on Irabel. I would have chased her to the ends of the earth if it meant she'd be okay.

    She came to an abrupt stop before an odd, empty clearing where the forest didn't seem to dare grow. At its center stood a massive, leafless tree with branches that curled oddly towards the moonlight. The forest fell silent in this part of the woods, no chirping crickets or hooting owls—even the wind seemed uninterested in rustling the leaves. All I could hear was my heart thumping in my chest and my heaving lungs.

    "Where are we?" I asked.

    Harold grunted and took a slow, careful step back from the clearing.

    "Something's wrong with that tree."

"How do you know?" I questioned.

"I can just feel it."

Finheld nodded.

"We should wake her up."

Oblivious to our presence, Irabel moved towards the strange tree. As if it were welcoming her like a long-awaited guest, its massive trunk split into creaking tendrils and opened like a gaping, tooth-filled maw. A doorway? Only darkness waited inside, but Irabel strode in without hesitation. I couldn't let her go alone, so I rushed after her, and Karn, Finheld, and Harold trailed close behind.

What laid within was beyond my imagination. Beyond sense, even! It was as if we'd stepped into some twisted, mangled version of the forest we'd just left behind. Everything was comprised of miserable shades of black, white, and grey—even us! The trees were dead, the ground was covered in dreary fog, and the sky was an endless, ominous black. No clouds. No stars. No moon. Nothing.

I saw a pair of old bare footprints leading off into the dark, and they sent a cold shiver down my spine. I wondered who they belonged to, but we didn't have much more time to look around.

Irabel headed north, to a shadowed corner of the forest—we followed, but the trees turned against us. Twigs, exposed roots, and branches reached out like gnarled fingers, grabbing at our clothes and yanking us back as we did our best to trudge forward.

"Irabel!" I called, exasperated, as she slowly disappeared into the darkened distance. "We have to keep going!"

Karn swung at the roots around his ankles with his hammer, crushing them with heavy blows.

"Don't give up!"

I pushed, clawed, and cut myself free, but every restraint I broke away from seemed to return only a few steps later. Panicked, my breath came in ragged gasps while Irabel grew smaller and smaller in the distance.

"Help!" I called to her, "Irabel, wake up!" but the forest swallowed my words.

"What do we do?" Harold asked. Sweat beaded over his brow.

Finheld grunted and used their free leg to kick a swiftly approaching branch in two. "We aren't going to make it to her like this!"

Irabel finally stopped, giving us a chance to start closing some of the distance. As we neared we realized she stood at the mouth of a massive, sixty-foot-wide, black hole in the ground surrounded by inky looking cobblestone. The darkness within seemed to seep out of the hole like starved serpents, nearly warping the area around it. My stomach lurched and my blood ran cold. This was it, wasn't it? This was the <u>well</u>.

Irabel stood near its edge.

A horrified wail broke from my lips.

"We have to save her!" I yelled. We were getting closer but not fast enough.

"Irabel!"

In that panicked moment the Harold I knew seemed to transform before me. A roar bellowed from within his chest, and his usually kind eyes blazed with a terrifying intensity. Something within him had been set ablaze. His great sword glowed with a golden light that betrayed the suffocating dark, casting long, harrowing shadows throughout the forest. With a strength I had never seen in him before, he tore and sliced his way through the forest that gripped him, kicking dirt and roots across the ground until he reached Irabel.

Harold grabbed her hand just as she began to teeter over the edge, and he pulled her into a protective embrace, curling away from the pit. The golden light from his sword leached into her skin, and she gasped. The forest was quiet and the branches retreated, Her trance had been broken.

"W-what . . . where are we?!" Irabel panicked, pushing Harold away in surprise.

"You're okay," Harold answered, his concerned eyes on us as we scrambled towards them. "You brought us here, Irabel."

"I . . ." Irabel looked at the looming darkness, and then at the palms of her hands. "How did . . ."

"Irabel!"

I wrapped my arms around her in a tight embrace.

Finheld scowled and wiped fragments of chipped wood from his sleeves.

"How about the next time you wind up in a weird trance you lead us to, oh, I don't know, a happy little carnival or an ice cream shop?"

"Go easy on her, Fin," Karn grunted. "It's not her fault."

"Agreed," Harold said, "I do think we should get out of here as soon as we can, though."

Irabel nodded, but her eyes lingered on the dark hole in the earth.

"This is the well from the poem, isn't it?"

"Aye, I think so."

I could see the dark fur on her shoulders rise as a chill traveled up her spine. Irabel pulled her arms closely to her chest.

"Let's go."

I didn't follow. Not right away. I found my own gaze caught by the darkness of the well. There was something about it that I didn't quite understand. Something I wanted to understand. Maybe even _needed_ to. Something . . . _something_.

Was it calling to me? Was it urging me to step closer?

One . . . two . . . three steps.

I peered over the edge into the pit—the endless expanse of dark. Would my eyes adjust and show me what was inside? Did something move? Did I hear a quiet voice upon the wind? Hmm . . . jump in? I shouldn't . . . right?

What if I _did_?

"Cob!" Harold's call cut through my thoughts, clearing my mind entirely.

"Woah." I took a breath, reeling back from the well. A presence washed over me and I was certain whatever lurked down in the darkness was evil, dark, wrong.

I shuddered and scurried back to my to friends. I didn't want to think about the well anymore. I just wanted to get back to camp.

Hey, there's no better way to calm your nerves than some tea . . . right? Maybe chamomile? Oh, and maybe some almond cookies to go with it.

Wildwinter Tea

The journey back was tense. I filled the time by gathering flowers for my tea. First, I found a wild patch of wildwinter flowers, then not far from that, some linden flower. I was slowly building the tea in my mind as we traveled, and I knew the perfect cookie recipe to go with it too.

MAKES 1 SERVING

Prep time: 5 minutes | Brew time: 5-7 minutes

Ingredients

- 1 tablespoon wildwinter buds (can replace with chamomile)
- ½ tablespoon lemon balm
- ½ tablespoon orange peel
- ½ tablespoon linden flower
- Honey, to taste

Instructions

1. Mix together your wildwinter buds, lemon balm, orange peel, and linden flower.
2. Add to a tea strainer or empty tea bag. Steep in boiling water for 5 to 7 minutes.
3. Add your honey and feel the calming effects. This is perfect for dipping sweet breads or cookies.

Kappa Cookies (Gluten-Free)

Remember how I told you my nana made a bunch of recipes without any wheat in them? Well, this is another one of those recipes she learned on her travels. I miss Nana. And Mom and Dad. And my siblings. I wonder what they are doing right now? I hope all this craziness hasn't reached them in Honeystar . . .

MAKES 40 SMALL COOKIES

INGREDIENTS

COOKIES:
- 1 cup unsalted butter, softened
- ¾ cup sugar
- 1½ teaspoons almond extract
- 2 cups Gluten-Free Flour Blend (see page 19)
- ½ teaspoon gluten-free baking powder
- ¼ teaspoon salt
- Slivered almonds

ALMOND GLAZE:
- ¾ cup powdered sugar
- ½ teaspoon almond extract
- 4–5 teaspoons milk

INSTRUCTIONS

1. Preheat your oven to 400°F.
2. In a large bowl, mix together your softened butter, sugar, and almond extract until it gets light and creamy.
3. In a separate bowl, combine your flour, baking powder, and salt.
4. Add your dry ingredients to your wet in small batches, making sure to mix well until fully combined.
5. Drop tablespoon-sized balls of dough onto a parchment-lined baking sheet about an inch apart. Flatten the dough balls slightly.
6. Bake your cookies for 7 minutes. They will not look done, but that's okay!
7. Immediately after removing from the oven, place a few almond slices onto each cookie.
8. Let your cookies cool for a few minutes before transferring them to a wire rack. If you don't have one, just transfer them to a plate or other flat surface.
9. In a small bowl, mix together all of your glaze ingredients until a smooth glaze forms.

(Continued)

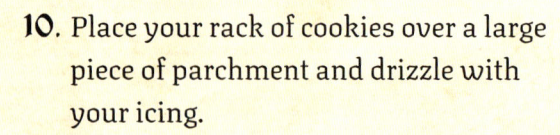

10. Place your rack of cookies over a large piece of parchment and drizzle with your icing.

11. Let the cookies sit until the icing has fully set.

12. Enjoy! Store your cookies in the fridge in an airtight container.

CHAPTER TWENTY-SIX
Something More

Hey Journal,

My last entry was definitely weird, but something about that well in particular really creeped me out . . . can I tell you a secret?

I've been thinking about what's at the bottom of the well almost non-stop ever since I laid eyes on it. Once we got out of the black-and-white realm, we immediately set course back to The Violet Bastion, but instead of daydreaming about food the whole way, I've been daydreaming about what would have happened if I jumped. I'm glad I didn't, though—and I won't be going back to find out, so don't worry.

Unless . . . ?

No, I'm just kidding, I won't!

When we arrived at The Violet Bastion, the first thing we did was find Hutar and tell him about everything we learned. All we really knew, though, was that the strange rhyme that Maud shared with us kind of . . . seemed correct? I mean, we found that weird tree-doorway (the forest-within-a forest?!) and a creepy well. Maybe the creature that was created by those wizards of legend really <u>did</u> exist after all? But then, what does that mean for us? What does that mean for those villages, for the kingdom—or even the whole world?

"If we go by the words in the poem, then it would seem that whatever's down there might want a girl or a woman or something to fall in," I told Hutar.

I couldn't fight the chills that zipped over my skin—<u>I'm a girl</u>. Is that why I can't stop thinking about the well?

"I wonder why," I said.

"Well, perhaps it was abductin' all of those people in order tae find someone with enough power tae actually do it some good." Karn shrugged. "Rosalind had premonitions and stuff, right? It seemed pretty fond of' Irabel in what sounds like a right similar way."

I felt chills throughout my whole body.

The guild leader, perhaps unmoved, leaned back in his chair, the wood creaking under the weight of his frame.

"I see."

"What do we do?" Harold asked. "I don't want anybody else to get hurt."

"Aye, but if we don't look intae it, folks will keep getting hurt." Karn said as a sadness flooded his face. "Innocent folks."

I shook my head.

Hutar, who had been mostly quiet since we arrived, reached into one of his desk drawers and took out a small writing pad. He made sure to keep it somewhat hidden from our view behind a framed picture on his desk.

"First, consider doing more research," he grunted, dipping his quill into a pot of black ink.

Exasperated, I threw my arms into the air before letting them swing by my sides.

"But how do we get more information? I mean, we could always try going down that well—"

The immediate sound of all four of my friends barking curt "no!" in unison was enough to remind me what a bad idea that probably was. I sighed and looked around Hutar's office, hoping one of the trinkets from his adventures or his old dusty books would give me an idea big enough to help solve our mystery. Nothing came to mind.

"There has to be something we can do."

Irabel shrugged.

"We could question that old lady with the rhyme again?" she suggested.

"Please don't make me go back to another one of those villages," Finheld groaned.

"I think she told me everything she knew," I admitted. "I'm not against going back, though."

Hutar cleared his throat and across his desk he slid a fancy piece of paper with militaristic swirls of metallic red foil.

"Here."

"What is it?" I asked, lifting it from his desk.

"The Regal Anthenaeum of the Violet Bastion has a collection of ancient and historical tomes in the north wing. Not many visitors in that section."

I raised an eyebrow.

"What's a regal anth—anthenae—"

"A library, Cob." Hutar grumbled, "One that's reserved for people of certain status, myself being one of them. This will give you access to its—"

A library!

"Thank you, sir!" I blurted out. I could have leapt across the desk and hugged him so tight that he'd burst into confetti!

"But please just . . ." Hutar huffed. "Behave yourselves. You're representing me, but most importantly the guild. Understood?"

I gave him my most noble salute.

"Understood, sir!"

Hutar sighed.

"Now, I'm no member of the high court so you won't have access to everything, but this could be a good start," he said.

Harold carefully took the paper from my hands and tucked it away somewhere safe.

"Thank you so much, Hutar. This will be very helpful," Harold said.

Hutar grunted in the cranky way he did when he didn't want to smile. "Now, get out of here. I have work to do."

And who were we to defy someone as kind and grumbly as Hutar?

The others headed straight to The Regal Anthenaeum of the Violet Bastion—RAVB for short—while I stayed behind to pack us some snacks. When I arrived, an attendant kindly showed me the way to my friends. It was just as silent as I heard big fancy libraries like this were. Seriously, it was so quiet that if a mouse tooted in the basement, we would have heard it from the third floor!

Thanks to Hutar's cool permission slip, we were granted access to an even quieter, nearly deserted section at the top of the library, which sat underneath a very colorful stained-glass dome roof. This is where the rest of the Tag-Along's awaited me. Armored guards stood tall at the entrance, and we were even assigned an attendant to help us along on our literary journey.

Now, I won't bore you with every single thing we read because we'd be here for hours, but I will tell you about something very, very, very interesting that Harold discovered. There was a book that held records of all the wizards hired by the crown and the twelve knights of legend, particularly the disgraced ones. Harold dug through it and found a record of Vorak'neel Hak and Belund Morwennson, two wizards hired long ago for "undocumented research." According to the author, there was speculation that they were working on discovering the impossible: the secret to eternal life.

Just like the old lady said!

According to the author, during their research, the wizards allegedly discovered an ancient device simply called the "Anchor." Apparently, the wizards ended up perishing and weren't ever seen again. That's all the book said, though, which sucked because I was kind of hoping we'd find all our answers right then and there!

But Karn thought it would be smart to seek out a book about arcane devices. Finheld was our resident tinkerer, so with his knowledge we were able to find exactly what we needed. The book we unearthed from the shelves was tattered, and it looked like it had been sitting in a stinky basement for a century.

It had a small chapter dedicated to a device none other than the rare and elusive Anchor. Apparently, it was a mythical apparatus that, by the time people started documenting things on paper, was already sort of lost to time. It was created by an ancient society, and it was originally intended to act as an anchor for souls of those who have passed on to let them stick around. Creepy, but also kind of nice?

Harold told us that there are spells that only extremely powerful magic wielders can conjure that will temporarily bring back deceased loved ones to communicate with the living, but the key word here is "temporary." This is what made the Anchor so special because it could keep a soul tethered to this world for an eternity, whether the individual liked it or not.

We went on to find the book hinted that the Anchor might have been majorly tampered with by two "very powerful but very unnamed wizards" in their search for eternal life and knowledge—bingo.

Perhaps they tampered with it too much, because things backfired. They wanted the Anchor to anchor them and prolong their lives, but not take their souls? Either way, their very beings were caught by the arcane powers within the device . . . and it shredded them and combined them. The chapter describe how after the tampering their bodies and souls were ripped apart and rejoined every moment of every day, ultimately turning the wailing, wounded mass of life-energy into a horrific, invincible Abomination.

The book said the tangled creature mutated often, absorbed knowledge, and caused destruction everywhere it went. Yet, oddly enough, many people across the country were drawn to it in search of power. They essentially fed off its evil essence in one way or another—some of them were even able to snatch little bits and pieces of the creature for their own evil-doing.

"Excellent find, Fin," Harold said. Meanwhile, I tried to pick my jaw up off the floor.

I could have sworn Finheld smiled, but I had much bigger things to focus on.

"What about the creature?" I asked. "Why hasn't it destroyed us all?"

Irabel nodded.

"Yeah, wouldn't this big, evil indestructible thing have torn through The Violet Bastion a time or three hundred since then?"

I scanned the book again, making sure that there was nothing I missed. "Well . . . okay, so the knights of legend were mentioned in the first book alongside Vorak'neel and Belund, right?"

Karn nodded, looking down at the first book. "Aye, it says that right here."

"So, maybe we can do some research on the knights. What happened to them? Did they die, or something?"

Irabel piped up, looking up from a little brown book she held in her hands.

"Well actually, I was just reading in this book here that says they all sort of disappeared on one last mission. It was some sort of final pushback against a great evil—but it says specifically in here it was an evil composed of nothing but pain and greed."

"Well, if that story about the indestructible Abomination is true, then that makes perfect sense!" I spoke frantically. "What else does it say?"

Irabel took her time to scan the page.

"It's kind of strange. It says, 'with the aid of the formidable beacons, the twelve knights sacrificed their lives to seal The Abomination away in another world until the very end of time.' But there's no mention of beacons anywhere else on the page, though—"

"Wait, sealed in another world? Like, a dimension?!"

Were we actually close to solving the puzzle? I leapt from my seat in excitement—realized the book on arcane devices was in front of me—and sat back down. I flipped through the pages like a madwoman, uttering "beacons, beacons, beacons," as though it would manifest the information we needed.

It did not.

In fact, we couldn't find anything about these so-called beacons in <u>any</u> of the books we read. I asked the custodian if we could go back even further into the forbidden section—I even told her that the safety of the world was on the line—but she told us that we'd need express permission from the king himself to access them. Ugh!

Well, at least we found more answers than we started with. Now, if only there's a way to convince the king that we need help. Maybe Hutar could write a letter for us?

I don't think I've ever read this much in my life, though. Libraries are great, even if it's hard to stick to their "be quiet" and "no food" rules. And all this reading certainly worked up an appetite.

Spoiler alert: No one tells Cob CopperSpoon not to eat! When the attendant turned away, we all nibbled on the snacks I prepared before arriving.

PS Journal:

Before we left the northern wing, I made sure to check for any cookbooks. To my dismay there were no super secret hidden recipes. What a shame! That would have made a <u>great</u> addition to our collection.

Piggy and Onion Cheesy Melt

After getting halfway through my sandwich, I realized this is <u>not</u> suitable food for a library. Everything was fine until I went to turn the page. Who knew buttery fingers wouldn't mix well with ancient tomes? Nobody warned me about it!

MAKES 1 SANDWICH

Prep time: 5-10 minutes | Cook time: 30-45 minutes

Ingredients

Bacon Onion Jam:
Makes enough for 2-4 sandwiches

- 1 large onion
- 1 teaspoon fresh rosemary
- 1 teaspoon fresh thyme
- 8–10 slices bacon
- 1 tablespoon butter
- ¼ cup dwarven whiskey, or dark liquor of your preference
- 1–2 heads roasted garlic (see page 15)
- 3 tablespoons brown sugar
- Salt and pepper
- 1 teaspoon paprika

Grilled Cheese:

- 2 tablespoons softened butter
- 2 slices your favorite bread
- ¼–½ cup shredded Italian blend cheese
- Bacon onion jam

Instructions

Bacon Onion Jam:

1. Roast your garlic (see page 15).

2. Slice your onion, mince your fresh herbs, and dice your bacon into small, bite-sized pieces.

3. In a medium saucepan or cast iron, fry your bacon bits until crispy on a medium-high heat. Once fully cooked, remove from the pan and let drain on a paper towel–lined plate. Drain the majority of bacon grease from your pan, leaving about 1 teaspoon leftover.

4. Add your butter and onion to your pan. Add in a pinch of salt and sauté until golden brown, which should take 5 to 10 minutes.

5. Once your onions have caramelized, add in your whiskey and fresh herbs. Cook for 2 to 3 minutes until the whiskey has started to evaporate.

6. Add back in your bacon, your roasted garlic, brown sugar, and the rest of your seasonings. Sauté until brown sugar is dissolved and everything starts to come together, about 2 to 3 minutes.

7. Remove pan from heat and let cool a bit. Make sure to keep stirring the mix every couple minutes to make sure it doesn't burn.

Cheesy Melt:

1. Heat a large pan over medium heat.

2. Spread half of your butter onto each slice of bread. Place one slice of bread butter-side down into your pan.

3. Top your bread with your shredded cheese. Then add on your other slice of bread, butter-side facing up.

4. Fry your sandwich until your cheese is fully melted and your bread starts to turn golden brown on the bottom. This will take 5 to 10 minutes, so be patient. If you cook it at too high a heat your bread will burn, and the cheese won't melt. Just take it low and slow.

5. Flip over your sandwich and cook for another 2 to 3 minutes until the other side turns golden brown.

6. Remove from your pan and carefully peel apart your grilled cheese. Add 2 to 3 tablespoons of your bacon onion jam to your sandwich then put the sandwich back together.

7. Enjoy! I like to serve with some extra jam on the side for dipping.

Scrumptious Scholars Pasta Salad

This is also not a suitable food to eat in a library, but it's not as bad as grilled cheese. Don't touch any books if you have dressing on your fingers; it's a bad idea, believe me!

Makes 6–8 servings

Prep time: 15–20 minutes | Cook time: 10–15 minutes | Cool time: 1 hour

Ingredients

Salad:
1 (16-oz) package tri-color pasta
Salt
1 (8-oz) package salami
¼–½ cup garlic stuffed olives
¼–½ cup roasted red peppers
1 large shallot
Bundle fresh basil
Bundle fresh parsley
½ cup Parmesan cheese
½ cup feta

Dressing:
¼ cup red wine vinegar
½ teaspoon Italian seasoning
½ tablespoon minced garlic
1 tablespoon honey
1 tablespoon stone-ground mustard
½ cup olive oil
Salt and pepper

Instructions

1. Heat a large pot of water over medium-high heat. Bring to a boil with a generous pinch of salt.

2. Boil your pasta for 10 to 12 minutes or until cooked to your liking. Strain and pour into a large bowl to cool.

3. Chop up all of your meat, vegetables, and herbs, and grate your Parmesan cheese. You can add as much or as little of each ingredient as you want. If any of these vegetable options aren't your favorite, feel free to get creative and add what you like! You can add broccoli, pickled asparagus, and spinach. You can add cherry tomatoes and banana peppers. Even try adding extra of your favorite cured meats. The world is your pasta salad, make it whichever way you like!

4. In a medium bowl, whisk together your red wine vinegar, Italian seasoning, garlic, honey, and mustard until fully combined.

5. While continuing to whisk, slowly add in all of your olive oil. Make sure to try it out and season with salt and pepper to your liking.

6. Add all your chopped up vegetables, meats, and cheeses to your pasta. Start by adding half your dressing. Mix everything together and then taste your pasta salad. Add more of your dressing to taste.

7. Enjoy! For ultimate flavor melding, let your pasta salad cool in the fridge for at least an hour but it is fully ready to be enjoyed immediately.

CHAPTER TWENTY-SEVEN
Code Name: Bread Pudding

Okay Journal,

Last we left off we made many a great discovery but there were still a few missing pieces.

- Missing piece number 1: What are the beacons? What do they do, and how do they fit into this story?
- Missing piece number 2: What happened to the Knights of the realm? After all of our research and sleuthing nobody had a solid answer. Even local legend turned up nothing.
- Missing piece number 3: How do we fight this incorporeal Abomination that is seemingly slipping back into our realm from its other-planar prison?

With these questions swirling in our heads, we made our way back to the guild. After some brief discussion with Hutar, he told us of an elusive wizard named Quibby Spruce. Hutar was vaguely aware of the circumstances, but told us even he was not trusted with the full truth. The questions we were asking supposedly had highly classified answers. Quibby was an honored historian who worked closely with the crown. If anybody had the information we needed, it would be her.

But it wasn't going to be as simple as walking up and probing her for answers. She wouldn't be a very good asset to the crown if she walked around telling just anybody these stories. Hutar warned us that our efforts may be futile and would probably lead to nothing.

What other choice did we have, though? We had to do something. Good thing for us it sounds like Hutar <u>still</u> underestimates Cob CopperSpoon's power of persuasion! That's right journal! I didn't know how I was going to do it, but I left determined to convince Quibby Spruce we needed answers!

This mission started with a healthy dose of reconnaissance. I started at the library. Historians <u>loved</u> libraries, so I figured there had to be somebody there who knew Quibby. As I approached the front desk asking if the attendant or anybody knew of the wizard. I was surprised to learn that not only were they familiar, but

Quibby herself had actually just stopped by. I was told if I hurried, I would probably catch her on the way to her favorite café in town.

With a quick "thank you," I darted in the direction of Café Minit, pushing my way through the crowded city. How could I forget how busy the Violet Bastion gets?! I guess I've traveled through so many remote places lately that the big city life feels slightly overwhelming.

In my haste I almost darted right past the quaint shop decorated in black-and-white pin stripes. The only thing that stopped me was a passing glance from a woman sitting on the small patio outside. She wore long, deep blue wizard robes that were decorated with silver stars. Her black and graying hair was tied in a messy bun, strands falling in pieces over her pale lavender skin. She looked at me through slitted, almost cat-like eyes, an air of judgment across her face that she quickly hid behind a dusty-looking tome the second our eyes met.

<u>A History of Botany and Entomology</u> was written in gilded letters across her book. This <u>had</u> to be Quibby.

As gracefully as a halfling possibly could, I skidded to a halt, spun around, and walked back past probably-Quibby, whistling an un-suspecting tune. Once I was sure I was out of her sights, I rushed to the counter. There stood an tall, gray-and-brown-speckled minotaur behind the counter wearing a name tag labeled "Bozzi."

"Hi, welcome to Café Minit, what can I get you today?"

Bozzi's voice was much lighter than I was expecting, and I realized she must be a teenager.

"Actually, first I have a question for you. Do you know who that is?" I asked, gesturing to the woman sitting outside.

"Oh yeah, that's Quibby! She comes in all the time."

"Does she now?! Do you by chance know her favorite pastry?"

Bozzi gave me a confused look, unsure of whether to answer.

"You see," I urged on. "I kind of have a crush on her and I want to make her a nice basket as a gift."

"Oh!"

Any hesitation Bozzi may have felt immediately disappeared. She told me that Quibby's favorite three menu items were the homemade hot chocolate, the pistachio mousse cake, and every year for her birthday she orders a special chocolate cherry brioche.

"Chocolate cherry brioche, you say?" I asked quietly as I glanced over at Quibby. Her nose was deep in her book; she didn't suspect a thing.

"There isn't any way you would be willing to share that recipe now, would you? I want to make it homemade, feels more special that way."

A mischievous look stretched across her face.

"I will do you one better, follow me!"

I followed Bozzi around the counter and she led me to the back of the café. There, she introduced me to an enormous minotaur who I learned was Bozzi's dad,

Colvi. He had all black fur aside from a patch of gray on his chest and massive horns that protruded from his head. It didn't take much convincing for Bozzi to get me a special one-on-one baking tutorial with her dad.

I spent the rest of the afternoon baking bread with Colvi. He told me stories of his old herd, of how he had always dreamed of owning a bakery in the city, and how when Bozzi was just a child, he finally decided to take the leap with years' worth of gold he had saved. Apparently, the first shop he bought failed miserably and he spent years working odd jobs to try and make it by.

Things became a bit sticky when he started asking <u>me</u> questions. I might have blown my cover if I wasn't such a professional! I kept my cool and gave him vague answers, then focused mostly on him. Which was perfect because he <u>loved</u> to talk.

"So, how did you and Quibby meet?" He prodded.

"At the library!" I coolly lied. "She loves books, I love books. What's your favorite book?"

Hook. Line. <u>Sinker!</u> He effortlessly took the bait, and I was in the clear.

I promised myself right then and there that one day I would come back and tell this nice family the truth of my schemes, but, for now, I will do what I must!

By the time the bread had risen and fully baked, it was dark out and the shop had closed. Quibby had obviously left, which distressed me. Luckily, Bozzi reassured me that Quibby stops by the shop every day at three for an afternoon snack. So Bozzi and Colvi wished me luck with Quibby and I headed back to the Bastion for some much-needed sleep.

Now, just the bread probably would have been enough, but I knew I needed to go the extra mile. There was only one way to get the answers we needed and that was going to be by baking the most knock-your-socks-off, best-in-the-world, cookbook-worthy recipe ever! And to do that, I was going to turn Quibby's favorite bread into bread pudding.

The recipe is simple, but in my experience, the best ones always are. A few eggs and one messy kitchen later, I was armed and ready to go.

I set out from the guild in the direction of the café. If Bozzi was right, Quibby should have been hanging out there for some time now. Sure enough, as I approached the shop, Quibby was once again sitting outside. I waited around the street, watching patiently. It only took her a few minutes before she began to pack up her things and leave.

I followed closely behind her. I darted into alleys, kept to the shadows, and glided swiftly between people's feet to stay as hidden as possible. Luckily, Quibby didn't seem to notice anything.

Somehow, though, when we reached a district lined with multicolored townhouses and she rounded a corner, she slipped from my view. Good news is that means she had to be in one of the houses on that block, right?

Only one way to find out! I studied each of the houses with great detail, and decided the one painted a dark blue looked the most like her style. The color matched her robes from the other day, so the chances of this one being hers had to be pretty high.

As I took my first step towards what would inevitably be a full evening of ringing doorbells, a voice rang out from behind me.

"Excuse me."

Startled, I turned quickly on my heels only to look up into the face of my target. "Have you been following me?" Quibby asked.

I could feel my cheeks turning a bright red as I quickly searched for a good lie.

"Uhm . . . No . . . I mean yes . . . I mean—"

"Because I first noticed you in the Library yesterday as I was leaving."

She began to circle me as she spoke. Her voice was calm but her eyes assessed me like a predator stalking its prey.

"Then you ran past me at Café Minit, only for you to double-back to ask questions about me inside."

Oh no! She was on to me!

"And now today you slink behind me as I'm trying to walk home."

"Uhhh . . ."

"The question is . . ." She knelt to the ground putting her face in mine. Menace dripped from her next word. "Why?"

"Well, uhm . . . that's kind of a long story. One I would happily tell you! Perhaps over some bread pudding?"

Her look of intimidation quickly twisted into confusion.

"Bread what?"

Quibby led me to her house as I gave her a thorough explanation of bread pudding.

She brought me through a thin side yard that led to a lovely garden at the back of her home. There, she excused herself for a moment and came back with some plates and a pot of tea.

That's when I told her everything. And I mean <u>everything</u>: about the villages, the missing people who were found randomly dropped in the forest, about the corrupted fish monster, and even the unicorn we came across. Then I told her about our research, how we found out about the wizards and the knights and the "beacons" and anchor. I told her about Irabel's dream and her crazy sleep-walking adventure into what seemed like an alternate dimension.

The entire time Quibby just listened quietly, nibbling at the bread pudding and sipping tea, while I rambled on and on and on, her face never faltering. Not once did she looked shocked, horrified, or surprised.

"So that's what led me here. I'm sorry I was sneaking around and following you, I just figured if I could learn your favorite treat and explain to you the situation it might—"

"Might convince me to reveal classified information to a stranger? A stranger with no real evidence besides an admittedly well-told story?"

"I mean . . . <u>maybe</u>?"

I pursed my lips out and made my eyes as large and pleading as possible as Quibby eyed me up and down. If the bread pudding and story didn't do it, maybe the puppy-dog eyes could. The silence between us must have only lasted a moment or two but it felt like hours as I prayed she would listen to our plea.

"Look, it is my job to keep certain things a secret."

My heart dropped as I felt our last lead slipping away.

"But . . . I might know somebody who <u>can</u> help you."

I could have jumped for joy! Cob CopperSpoon strikes again, folks!

"Don't look too excited," Quibby warned, noticing my obvious excitement. "It is going to be a very difficult journey to get to him."

I tried to somber my excited expression, but I couldn't help it! We were on to something. This was the lead we needed.

Chocolate Cherry Allure

Bread pudding is the process of tearing up pieces of bread (day-old works best), covering it in a mix of sugar, eggs, and cream, then baking until the top is nice and crispy and the middle is soft and gooey. It was a hit with Quibby! She even asked me for the recipe and said this might just be her new day-after-her-birthday tradition!

MAKES 6–8 SERVINGS

Prep time: 1½–8 hours | Cook time: 1½–2 hours

Ingredients

Brioche: Makes 2 Loaves

Dough:
½ cup milk
1 tablespoon yeast
¼ cup + 2 teaspoons granulated sugar
4 medium eggs + 2 additional egg yolks
½ tablespoon vanilla
4¼ cups flour
1 teaspoon salt
1 cup butter

Swirl:
1 cup frozen cherries
1 tablespoon sugar
½ cup chocolate chips

Extra:
1–2 eggs for egg wash

Bread Pudding:
3–4 cups day-old bread
2 cups milk
4 eggs
½ cup sugar
1 teaspoon vanilla

Instructions

Homemade Chocolate Cherry Brioche:

1. In a large bowl or mixer with a dough hook attachment, combine your warm milk, yeast, and 2 teaspoons of sugar. Let sit for 5 to 8 minutes until yeast has bloomed and become foamy.

2. Once the yeast mix has foamed, add your eggs and vanilla to the mixture and whisk together until fully incorporated.

(Continued)

3. Add your flour, remaining sugar, and salt to your wet ingredients and combine until just starting to come together. If using a mixer, start at a slow speed.

4. Once your dough is firm enough to hold together, pour it out onto a clean work surface. Knead your dough until there are no dry spots and it starts pulling away from your work surface without sticking. If using a mixer, turn up to medium speed and mix until your dough starts to pull away from the bowl.

5. Once your dough has started to come together, you can start adding your butter. Knead the butter into your dough ¼ cup at a time until it is fully combined. It won't look like it will mix in easily, but just keep kneading, it will combine with time. Keep incorporating until all of your butter has been used. Once fully mixed in, knead for another 3 to 4 minutes.

6. Next, place your dough into a clean bowl and let rise covered at room temperature for an hour or until it has doubled in size.

7. Once your dough has doubled in size, punch your dough to release some of the gasses. Fold it back into itself in the bowl a few times and then cover it back up. Place it in the fridge for 1 to 8 hours. You can skip this step, but the dough will be a little harder to work with.

8. Right before you are about to use your dough, crush your frozen cherries and sugar in a mortar-and-pestle or blender.

9. Take your dough out of the fridge and roll out into a large square until it is about ½ inch thick.

10. Spread your cherry mix evenly over your dough and sprinkle on your chocolate chips.

11. Fold your dough into thirds over itself until it forms into a large rectangle. Cut your rectangle in half and then roll each half into a log roughly the size of a loaf pan.

12. Butter 2 loaf pans and sprinkle with a bit of flour to prevent your bread from sticking. Place one log into each loaf pan.

13. Cover your dough with a dish towel or plastic wrap and let rise one last time for 30 minutes while you preheat the oven to 350°F.

14. Right before putting your bread into the oven, whisk up an egg and brush onto the surface of the dough.

15. Bake for 30 to 45 minutes, until the top is a deep brown color and the bread has reached an internal temperature of 190°F.
16. Let your bread fully cool on a wire rack.

BREAD PUDDING:
1. Preheat your oven to 350°F.
2. Tear your bread into bite-sized pieces and place in an oiled 8 × 8-inch baking dish.
3. In a large bowl, mix together your milk, eggs, sugar, and vanilla.
4. Pour your milk mix evenly over your torn up bread.
5. Mix the bread into the milk mixture to make sure all the bread gets soaked in some of the mix. (Note: If you are using store-bought bread, you can mix in chopped up cherries and chocolate chips at this point.)
6. Bake your bread pudding for 45 minutes, until the top is golden brown.
7. Top with powdered sugar and enjoy!

You can use so many different flavors for this recipe so have fun and feel free to experiment!

CHAPTER TWENTY-EIGHT
How to Cheat the Heat

Okay Journal,

Here's the update I <u>know</u> you have been waiting for:

It turns out the guy we are looking for lives in a realm covered in flames. The people there adapted to the environment over time but for normal people like us, we would need to brew a fire resistance potion just to travel there.

Luckily, Quibby lent me a book of alchemy from their personal collection, being sure to bookmark the page of fire resistance. She also told me we would need to send word ahead to Ru'uk-Kraak, the stone-bodied chief of a large village in the fire realm called Ignisanti. They don't get visitors very often, so this was a very important step. She told me Ru'uk-Kraak was not the man we were looking for but that he would lead us to him.

After she sketched out a crude picture of him on a piece of parchment, Quibby had one final request:

"Please, nobody must know that I was the one to send you. Our little secret, ok?"

So, everyone's been prepping for our trip. At first, Finheld was hesitant about traveling to a realm of literal fire, but Harold was able to sway him. We're not sure what to expect from that place other than fields of fire. I've never met anyone that's been to another realm before—except for us, I guess. Shout-out to the monochrome realm.

While Harold and Finheld were off making sure we have what we need to keep healthy and hydrated on the road, Karn was making sure everyone had access to fire-friendly weapons, and Irabel and I were . . . well, she was meditating. I was sitting in a chair across from the bed, watching her meditate. Why? Well, Irabel has a special way of contacting people with her mind. Sometimes she can even contact people she doesn't know, as long as she has a baseline description of who they are and what they look like. This, however, requires immense focus. Apparently, it's way harder to contact someone you don't know than someone you do.

Irabel and I had spent the better part of an hour in one of the guild bedrooms trying to get her in the right state of mind to contact him. This was the quietest place we could find, but I could still hear the distant sounds of the bustling city, people sparring on the grounds, and the sounds of guild members coming and going.

Irabel had her eyes closed for a very long time, but she wasn't floating on the bed the way she usually did when she meditated. At first, I wondered if she was practicing a new technique, but the longer I sat there in silence, the more I wondered if she was even meditating at all.

"Irabel?" I whispered.

Irabel opened a single cat-like eye, her pupil slitting into a razor thin line as she looked at me.

"What?"

"Are you okay?"

"Are <u>you</u>?" she challenged.

"No," I laughed. "Not if you're not."

She closed her eye and let out a deep exhale.

"I'm fine."

"Can I tell you something?" I asked.

"I suppose you're gonna tell me either way."

"I'm kind of glad you're not fully meditating right now."

"Why?"

"Because," I shrugged, looking down at my palms. "I'm worried you're gonna . . . I don't know . . ."

"Wander off?"

I nodded, remembering the fear we felt when she ran through the woods, and how helpless we nearly were when she teetered before the edge of the well.

"I hate that place."

Irabel exhaled again. "Can I tell <u>you</u> something?"

"Of course."

She opened her eyes, but her gaze met the floor. "Maybe I'm . . . a little worried too."

I leaned back in my seat so I could fight the urge to give her a hug—she doesn't really like when we get too sappy.

"Really?"

"Yeah, it's, um . . . not very fun to know something can take control of you when you're in your most vulnerable state. Especially something like <u>that</u>."

"I couldn't even imagine what it must have felt like. I'm so sorry, Irabel."

"Maybe I should have asked Harold to stay behind instead," she said, idly hugging her long tail. "Not because I don't want you here, but because he's the only one that can do that spell."

She was right, with the power of his god, Helirion, Harold was the only one of us that could purify Irabel's mind of that wretched thing in the well. I couldn't deny that I felt a little useless now, but I would never leave her alone by herself either way.

"There's gotta be a way I can learn a spell like that," I said, scratching my chin.

"Well, Harold gets his powers from a god, right? Where do your powers come from?"

I thought about it for a moment, but I wasn't too sure. My ability to create illusions didn't really come from family—unless it did, and everyone's been keeping it a secret? Maybe there was a sorcerer born way, way, way down the line and the power trickled down to me, somehow.

"I don't know," I said with a shrug. "It's just something I've always been able to do."

"Here, let me see your hands," Irabel mused, taking my palms. She examined them with her big cat-like eyes, looking over every little line and callous.

"What are you looking for?"

"Sometimes you can see people's magical capabilities in their palms. See, this line right here?" she said, pointing at a thin line I had seen millions of times. "You got the juice, kid."

"I hope it's lemonade."

"You know that's not what I meant," Irabel laughed. "When you make illusions, where do you feel it coming from? Your hands, your veins, your chest, an arch-demon?"

Now *that* was a thinker.

"Uhhh—"

"There's no wrong answer."

"I think . . . I think it just comes from my soul."

Irabel smiled.

"Your soul?"

"Yeah," I nodded. "It just feels like it comes from the very essence of . . . me. Is that a thing?"

"Maybe you're a sorcerer, too." She said with a laugh.

"I don't think so," I sighed. "I think stuff just comes to me when I'm inspired, you know? The things that usually move me the most are food and telling stories."

But the more I thought about it, the more I realized that other things inspired me, too: adventure, knowledge, and my friends.

My friends were pretty much the most inspiring things I could think of! I wanted to protect them, and feed them, and swat away every bit of sadness they felt. I wanted to be like . . . that cozy feeling you get from a blanket when you're tucked in bed at night. I wanted to wrap my arms around them like I was made out of a million quilted squares and comfort them when they were scared. I wanted to—I wanted to—

"I have an idea!" I straightened up and placed my palms on both sides of Irabel's face.

"Oh, Cob, I'm flattered, but you're not really my type."

"I'm not trying to kiss you!" I pouted. "Shh!"

When I was just a young girl, I remember when my older sister came back from her adventure. I had been having nightmares for weeks and weeks, worried she would never make it home. My parents didn't know what to do with me until one day my sister visited town. I thought the nightmares would go away now that she was back but they never did. Until she came to my room one sleepless night. She grabbed the sides of my face and focused on nothing. At first I thought she was just being a weirdo, but then I felt a weight lift from my shoulders.

"What did you do?" I remember asking all those years ago.

"I learned in my travels that nightmares can be real. But, just because those nightmares are real, doesn't mean you can't fight them. A dream walker taught me how."

For months I begged her to teach me her ways but she never did. I practiced for years but was never able to figure out the trick to the magic. I remembered the magic in this moment, and for the first time in my life I thought to myself I can do this.

I closed my eyes and focused on that feeling of love in my heart when I thought about my friends, but this time I fixated specifically on Irabel. I imagined that creature in the well reaching out to her with an evil grin, and I pushed every bit of myself between them as I could. Using the same energy I put into my illusions, I came down between them like a knife on a chopping block. I was a cozy blanket, but where Irabel felt soft fuzz, the creature felt nothing but ice-cold steel. I had her mind on lockdown, and no one was getting in.

"Wait, what did you just do?" Irabel asked.

"Try meditating now!"

She frowned with skepticism.

"I don't know."

"You're safe, Irabel." I smiled, "I promise. Go ahead."

"Okay," she drawled. "But if I take off, you better call Hutar."

I gave her a thumbs up.

Irabel straightened her back, closed her eyes, and let out a soft exhale. The room was filled with silence yet again—or, at least, the guild's closest version of it—and I watched her attentively for any hint of funny business. She sat there for one minute, then two, then three—and then slowly, like a basket of cookies with a bunch of balloons tied to it, she began to float.

"You're doing it!" I whispered, silently clapping my hands, "You're meditating!"

Irabel didn't answer, but that was a good thing! She was finally immersed in her own mind, and I'm beyond happy I was able to help.

While Irabel meditated, I busted open the alchemy book to start doing some research. Turns out that alchemy is a lot like cooking! Sure, there are a few fancy ingredients and weirdly specific rituals, but other than that its basically just like making soup. For the potion of fire resistance, it looked like the hardest part was going to be finding our main ingredient: phoenix tears.

Phoenix tears?!?! That means phoenixes were real! How cool!

I eagerly waited for Irabel to finish up. I was so excited to tell her the good news! She floated on the bed for about an hour before her butt touched the mattress and she opened her eyes.

"Charcoal," she said.

I ripped a blank page from my journal and handed her the piece of charcoal I was using to scribble with. Irabel wrote down a bunch of information so fast that I couldn't even keep up.

"What did you see?"

"I spoke with the chief, Ru'uk-Kraak. I think Ignisanti is at these coordinates," she said, circling the numbers she wrote down. "But that's a little difficult to keep track of in the field. There's a part of the web nearby a—well, some of their words just sound like rocks rubbing together, so I'm not sure what to call it, but there's a thread near the mountain range that's particularly potent. If we get some of the guild mages to teleport us there, all we have to do is head south. The chief's expecting us, I filled him in with all I could. He said he'd do his best to help us."

"And you didn't even get possessed!" I beamed

"Thanks, Cob, you're the best."

"Any time, really! More good news, though, I was doing some research while you were meditating and guess what! The potion we need is basically just fancy soup! We already have most of the ingredients we need here, but the biggest one we are missing is phoenix tears. Do you have any idea where we might find something like that?"

"Not sure," she shrugged. "I think we have a little shopping trip of our own to go on."

I hopped to my feet in an instant. I loved spending time with Irabel, of course, but I was starting to get a little bit stir crazy.

"Let's go!"

"Wait."

Irabel reached into her pocket, and when she didn't find what she was looking for, she crossed the room and dug around in her satchel. She pulled out a small, shiny, silver ring encrusted with garnet and a streaked, burnt orange and black crystal. "I want you to have this."

"What?!" I gawped. It looked <u>expensive</u>. "Really?"

"I have one, too," she said, showing a nearly identical ring on her index finger. "These rings get warm when they're near each other. If I go missing again, it won't really point you in my direction, but at least you'll know if I'm nearby. I'd like you to have it . . . if that's okay? It'll tell me when you're nearby, too."

I looked up at her with big puppy dog eyes.

"Really? Not Harold or Karn or even Finheld?"

"Of course not, Cob. I could have asked one of them, but I want <u>you</u> to have it."

She handed me the ring, which seemed to have been made with someone my size in mind, and I slipped it on my index finger.

"Thank you!" I said, unable to resist giving her a hug. She barely hugged back, but she didn't push me away.

"I enchanted it when we got back to the city. I just wasn't sure anyone would want the other ring. I felt kind of silly."

"The only thing that's silly is you thinking that no one would want it," I said, smiling.
"We love you! You're so cool! And smart, and funny, and you have such soft fur, and you have an amazing sense of fashion, and you're caring, and interesting, and—"
"Okay, okay!" She laughed, wiggling from my grasp. "Stop complimenting me before I get a cavity."
And so, bravely, determined, and with Irabel's mind on lockdown, we dared to set foot from the quiet room and out into the busy streets of the Violet Bastion, matching rings and all!

Firebird Stew and Rice

I bet you're probably thinking to yourself, "How is a potion of fire resistance like a stew?"

Well, Journal, let me tell you how!

For one, a bunch of these ingredients are just normal things you would find at the market. Dried chilies, cloves of garlic, they are just called by their magic name in the alchemy book. For example: Vampire's Bane and Fire of the Earth.

And for two, you basically just stir things in a very specific order. There's no way adding a couple extra ingredients could mess it up that bad!

Makes 4-6 servings

Prep time: 10-15 minutes | Cook time: 1½-2 hours

Ingredients

Stew:
- 3 tomatoes
- 1 large onion
- 5–7 cloves garlic
- 2 pounds boneless skinless chicken thighs
- 2 dried pasilla chile
- 4 dried California chile pods
- 1 tablespoon of olive oil
- 1 tablespoon Mexican oregano
- 2 bay leaves
- 3 cups chicken broth
- Salt and pepper
- Queso fresco
- Tortillas
- 5 phoenix tears (one for each bowl, can replace with hot sauce)

Rice:
- 2 cups white rice
- Cilantro
- 1 lime
- Salt and pepper

Instructions

Stew:

1. Start by prepping all of your ingredients. Cut your tomatoes in half, peel and quarter your onion, and crush your garlic cloves. Season your chicken thighs with some salt and pepper.

2. Heat a large pot or cast iron over high heat until smoking hot. Once heated add in your tomatoes, onions,

and dried peppers. Cook until they get good char marks on them—you want areas of it blackened, but not completely burnt. If you are using a smaller pot, do this in batches as to not overcrowd the pot. Remove all of the charred vegetables from the pan and set aside.

3. Add your oil to the pot and let it heat until rippling hot. Once ready, sear your chicken thighs in batches until they are nice and golden brown.

4. Remove your chicken from the pot and add in your garlic, oregano, and a splash of your chicken broth. Scrape up any stuck bits from the bottom of the pot before adding back in your vegetables, chicken, and the remainder of the chicken broth.

5. Add in your bay leaves. Stir 9 times clockwise while repeating an incantation of protection: "Fire burn, fire toil, protect me from the dancing coils."

6. Cover your pot and let it simmer for about 20 minutes. (Start your rice now while this cooks!) After 20 minutes, remove all of the chicken from the pot and set aside for now.

7. Add all of your veggies into a blender with about 1 cup of your chicken broth. Blend all of your veggies until smooth, adding more broth as needed.

8. Drain the remaining broth from the pot before moving on. You can either save the remaining broth for a different recipe or get rid of it—just be sure that the chicken was fully cooked if you want to save it for later.

9. Use a fine mesh sieve to strain your blended mixture back into the pot. There will be a lot of pulp leftover, that's OK, just try to get as much of the liquid out as possible.

10. Add your chicken thighs back into the mixture and stew, covered, for 1 hour on medium-low heat, stirring occasionally.

RICE:

1. Rinse your rice. Cook according to your package instructions using either water or chicken broth.

2. While your rice cooks, roughly chop your cilantro and cut your lime in half.

3. Once your rice is fully cooked, add in the juice of your lime and as much cilantro as your heart desires. Taste and add salt and pepper as needed.

(Continued)

ASSEMBLY:
1. Shred your chicken and serve with your cilantro lime rice and your favorite tortillas! Top each serving off with a single phoenix tear, then add some queso fresco and lime for the ultimate protecting bite!

CHAPTER TWENTY-NINE
Into the Flames

Hey Journal,

We made it to the fire realm. Teleporting there was a breeze, but the spell conjured a bright flash of light that kind of hurt my eyes a little bit. Once the light subsided, it was replaced by a world awash in a red hue, and a scorching heat that was <u>way</u> higher than what's safe to cook with. The air burnt our lungs as we coughed through the stench of sulphur that stung the back of our nostrils. At first, all I could see was ashy smog through teary eyes, but as my vision adjusted fields of red, orange, and black appeared—every rock and geographical formation in between was either burnt or burning. Most of the ground crumbled at the slightest movement of my feet. The small vents between the cracks sometimes released plumes of hot stream or glowed with what looked like veins of fiery magma.

Without the benefits from my Firebird stew, I was certain we wouldn't last more than an hour here before burning to a crisp. Even now I wonder if I maybe should have just followed the recipe instead of taking delicious liberties. I must admit I myself didn't know exactly how the magic worked, but I'm sure glad it does!

What a strange, oddly beautiful place this was. Terrifying, yes, but also new and beautiful.

"Is everyone okay?" Harold asked.

"I'm okay!" I nodded, certain my eyes sparkled with an undeniable curiosity.

"Aye," Karn masterfully grunted away a cough.

Finheld and Irabel were entirely mystified by the flames that licked at our clothes but left us entirely unharmed.

"This is so weird," Finheld uttered. He squatted low, reaching his hand into the crumbly dirt. "I'd like to find some ore to take back with us. Maybe I can do something with it." I looked at the earth, too. "I wonder what kind of—"

But then, a low grumble thundered in the sky. All of our eyes darted up and we barely caught a glimpse of something impossibly large slithering through the thick vermillion clouds, glowing in streaks of white and orange.

Needless to say, we weren't gonna stick around!

So, we hightailed our way out of there and headed south, avoiding spewing crevices and gurgling, glowing puddles of molten rock. We could feel the rumble of the earth shifting in the distance, and with a deafening boom we witnessed a river of lava break free from the side of a charred mountain and pour slowly into a crevasse deep into the cracks of the flame-ridden earth.

The smoke seemed to get thicker the further we traveled, making it hard for us to even see past our sore noses. But we pushed forward until a shimmer of black cut through the gloom. The smoke started to clear, revealing a forest of obsidian, jagged and branched like petrified trees. According to Irabel, that was where we had to go.

Fortunately, the closer we traveled to the mountain range in the distance, the kinder the terrain soon became. The air even felt lighter once we passed the tree line—maybe the obsidian trees were absorbing the smoke? Eventually we saw the outline of a building, and then more, and then even more! Nestled near a vast range of deep, cherry-red, plateaued mountains was the village of Ignisanti.

We made our way to the entrance by crossing an obsidian bridge over a river of lava, which gradually and quite gently curved around the village's outskirts. The river almost looked intentionally placed, like it was carved to keep those inside safe from whatever creatures lurked around this strange place.

We wandered through the village to meet with the chief, Ru'uk-Kraak. The people that lived in this village—some made of pure fire, some made of rock and crystal—kept their eyes on us in curiosity as we passed through. I waved at what I think was a young child made entirely of vibrant blue flame. They giggled but hid shyly behind their parent's legs. So cute!

We found the chief at the very center of the village, standing within a black gazebo that surrounded a massive, star-shaped gong. His seven-foot-tall body was composed of an incredible blend of dark red stone, veins of gold, and shimmering red crystal. His outfit mirrored the essence and intensity of the fiery world he lived in: the cloak that rested on his shoulders and dangled behind him in the ashen wind looked to be made of shiny, polished scales of rock, woven together like chainmail. Tiny droplets of lava dripped endlessly from stems of glowing red feathers in its collar, streaking down the stone and dripping onto the ground below.

He stretched his long, rocky arms out in greeting, and when he spoke his voice sounded like rocks scraping, cracking, grinding, and crunching against each other. I heard a voice in my head, though—something that sounded much more familiar. I looked to my friends and noticed something strange. A barely perceivable string of bright orange connected us, and when I followed it to the source it emanated from Ru'uk-Kraak's "mouth." I deduced this must have been how he communicated.

"You must be the The Tag-Alongs. I'm glad you made it safely through such foreign terrain."

"Thank you so much for allowing us to visit. We're on a really important mission." Irabel expressed, bowing her head respectfully.

"So, I have heard," he said, turning his head to the tall, red mountain behind the village. "Tell me a bit more about what you are looking for."

We all exchanged glances, silently deciding who would be the one to explain the situation. Ultimately, I started but everyone ended up chiming in. After a very rushed and vague explanation I finally asked outright.

"We were told that you knew of somebody who could help us. Somebody with information on the beacons, is this true?"

"I believe you will find the assistance you need atop—"

It was here that I heard only the sounds of shifting boulders, splintering stone, and the earth quaking below, I guess it didn't translate very well. "—I can lead you up the trail myself, if you do not mind pausing so I may rest every so often."

We nodded, and prepared to begin the treacherous ascent.

With Ru'uk-Kraak as our guide, we exited the village and made our way up Rock-Sounds Mountain. The trail was oddly peaceful. Ru'uk-Kraak stopped every so often not only to rest, but to light lanterns along the trail with odd, sparkling, golden fire. He told us that it was sacred flame, lit specially to appease the mountain, which was especially important since such unusual visitors were traversing it.

I wasn't quite sure what was awaiting us at the top of the mountain, but I was surprised when we came to a large plateau that was almost completely flat. At the center stood a strange stone platform, its stair-like edges carved with thousands and thousands of unique looking symbols and runes that glowed in ebbing shades of orange and red. Standing at the top was what appeared to be a middle-aged elven man! That's right, someone else from our plane had managed to find their way here.

He had dark hair, and was dressed in similar leathers and fabrics that the chief was wearing, and the sword he brandished in his hands glowed pinkish-orange with the heat. Silently, eyes shut, he swung the sword to his right, just as a plume of terribly hot looking steam burst from the platform. He paused for a moment, completely unphased by the heat, and swung again, moving his sword to the left just as another plume of steam burst from the ground. He did it again and again, commencing what looked like a ritualistic dance. The air crackled with glittering embers and fluxed with anticipation each time he raised his glowing sword, and with each downward swing, steam and burning hot flames swirled in the air, almost mimicking his movements. He finished with a heavy exhale, digging the glowing blade into the earth before him, as steam erupted from the metal. The flames around him slowly receded, and the embers drifted softly through the air. When he opened his eyes, I could have sworn I saw a flicker of orange light in his irises as his eyes turned toward us.

"Who are you?" he asked. The sword before him slowly cooled and returned to silver metal.

The chief bowed kindly in greeting.

"Not long ago I received a message from the mortal realm."

His face darkened, "The mortal realm?"

"They wish to discuss something of dire importance with you. Admittedly, I do not know much, but my divination revealed to me it has something to do with the . . . Eternal Malice."

Eternal Malice? Did he mean The Abomination?

I could have sworn that I saw a flicker of fear on the man's face, but he steeled himself, clenching his jaw hard.

"No," the man said, as he turned from us, and began to head to the path.

"Sir Storncrest!" The chief said, doing his best to scurry after him.

"Don't call me that!" The man growled back to the chief.

Ru'uk-Kraak's voice trailed off to the sound of rock against rock. It seems that he no longer wished for us to understand his words because the thin orange string disappeared from us and now only led to Sir Storncrest.

"Sir Storncrest?" Karn gasped.

I raised my eyebrow.

"Do you know him, Karn?" I asked.

Harold placed his hand on my shoulder but kept his astounded gaze on the man and the chief, who now stood mid-bicker.

"Cob, that's one of the twelve knights—"

"Huh?!"

"Not one of the twelve knights, the twelfth knight!" Karn laughed in disbelief. "The namesake of our very own guild, amongst other things."

I blinked in pure shock.

"But aren't they all dead?"

"Apparently not," Harold shrugged. "Come on."

We approached Sir Storncrest and Ru'uk-Kraak, but tensions were high.

"You think I care about the right thing anymore? After what happened . . . after what I saw?"

A pleading look crossed Ru'uk-Kraak's face as a low rumble came out.

"I am not scared, I am realistic. I did not come here just to be dragged back to my death. I'm very grateful for you letting me stay but I'm not a hero anymore Ru'uk. You shouldn't have—"

"Sir Storncrest," I interrupted. "We're The Tag-Alongs, members of a guild named after you, actually."

The man grimaced in such a way that you would have thought my words were deeply offensive.

"That is not my name. I don't know what you want from me, but please leave," he replied.

"We can't, though! That creature you and the other knights sealed away in the well is trying to escape! We need your help."

He rolled his eyes and slung his sword over his back.

"If you think that I'm the right person to help solve this problem, you are sorely mistaken." He spoke in a low grumble. "Obviously, I failed to stop it once before, so I doubt any intervention by my hand will do you any good."

"But sir!"

"Do yourself a favor and go home to your loved ones. Spare yourselves and find another realm—another world, I don't care."

Sir Storncrest turned his back to us and began to walk away.

"I am not who I once was," he said. "And you will do me the respect of keeping your distance."

I couldn't believe what I was hearing! The world was in danger, and the only person who could help keep that thing at bay was being a huge jerk!

"Wait!"

The chief put his heavy, rocky hand on my shoulder. "Do not push him, child. I am sure he will come around in time."

"Time?! We don't have that!"

People were getting snatched from their homes left and right.

A defeated sigh left Harold's lips.

"Why don't we give him room to consider it, at least," he said. "We can get in contact with him again later. I'm sure that he's been through his fair share of troubles. He's probably just scared, Cob."

"Scared? We're *all* scared, but at least we're doing something about it!"

My friends all agreed with Harold in one way or another, though, and the last thing I wanted was another big argument like the one we had when we visited the Adva'loran's.

"Fine," I conceded.

I wasn't done with Sir Storncrest, though, believe me.

With nothing better to do, I decided to wander the village in search of recipes. I wondered what people ate here considering most of the humanoids we came across thus far had seemed more elemental than biological.

It turns out the villagers had quite a few recipes and some were already in the process of cooking! Supposedly, there was once a time where people could easily travel between realms. It wasn't uncommon to have visitors from the mortal realm, so the people started coming up with recipes. They grew special plants that thrived in volcanic ash, bred certain animals that were a fusion of our realm and this one, and they even stored ingredients from the mortal realm for years and years.

I asked one of the families I was learning from what happened, why people stopped coming to visit their lovely village? They told me was that long, long ago magic flowed freely through all of the realms as one. All you had to do to reach Ignisanti was walk through a gate and appear on the other side. That is until one day a great evil came trying to divide us all. Many gateways were destroyed, and now you can only cross over in "chohr-chohr" or "the bad earth" in common. It is a place guarded by the ancient being who keeps this realm ablaze with fire.

"We miss meeting new people," the woman made of purple flame spoke in my mind, just as Ru'uk-Kraak had. "But we are grateful to still be alive. If that evil had never been stopped, we would all be dead."

"So, if nobody comes by anymore then why do you keep all these recipes?" I asked, curiously. "You can't enjoy them, so why go through the effort of making them?"

"For him, of course! For Lord Araak, he was the one who saved us! Although I may never be able to taste my creations, I know he can. That is one way I honor him for his sacrifice."

I knew she must be speaking of Sir Storncrest. I tried to picture him sword in hand, saving these people, but I just couldn't. He was no hero to me.

Boar Butt Sliders

The boars in the realm of fire are covered in... well, flame. But it's kind of neat because every time they get <u>really</u> mad, the fire turns into a cool color and erupts around them in a big, loud explosion, essentially knocking them unconscious for a few seconds. If I burst into flame every time I got mad, I'd want it to be green!

MAKES 10–15 SERVINGS

Prep time: 15–25 minutes | Cook time: 4–8 hours

INGREDIENTS

PORK:
- 5–10-pound pork shoulder roast
- 2–3 tablespoons mustard
- ½ cup Smokey Copper Spice Blend (see page 13)

SLAW:
- 2 cups shredded green cabbage
- ½ cup shredded purple cabbage
- ½ cup shredded carrots
- 3 tablespoons mayonnaise
- 1 tablespoon stone-ground mustard
- 1 tablespoon honey
- 1 clove garlic
- Salt and pepper, to taste

EXTRAS:
- Slider buns

INSTRUCTIONS

1. Brush your pork roast with your mustard until it is fully coated.
2. Coat your pork in your BBQ Seasoning. Let sit overnight if you can for maximum flavor, but not necessary.

- **Smoker:**

1. Heat your smoker to the smoke setting, about 175°F.
2. Smoke your pork for 4 to 5 hours on the smoke setting before turning the heat up to high, about 350°F.
3. Move your pork to a large pan and cover with aluminum foil.
4. Cook for an additional 1 to 2 hours on high until you reach an internal temp of 190°F.

(Continued)

5. Let rest for 30 minutes to 1 hour before shredding. It's gonna be super juicy and delicious, no sauce needed.

- **Oven:**
1. Preheat your oven to 300°F.
2. Place your pork in a large dutch oven or baking dish. Cover with lid or aluminum foil. Bake for 3 hours.
3. Remove covering from pork and increase heat to 375°F. Cook for about 1 more hour or until pork has reached an internal temperature of 190°F.
4. Let rest 30 minutes to 1 hour before shredding.

Slaw:
1. Mix together all of your veggies in a large bowl.
2. In a small bowl, mix together your mayo, mustard, honey, garlic, and a pinch of salt and pepper. Be sure to taste your dressing and adjust as needed. For a sweetened slaw add more honey, for more acid add more mustard, and so on and so forth.
3. Toss your vegetables in your dressing and let sit in the fridge for 30 minutes to an hour.
4. Once your slaw is ready, just build your sliders and enjoy!

Changeling Chili

Did you know that beans are a very common ingredient found on the realm of fire? Well neither did I! The Ignisanti people have created a special harvesting device to help them separate them from the volcanic ash. They taste a little different than normal beans, but for the most part, they are exactly the same as the ones from home! Just a little extra spicy! I named it changeling chili because it will taste a little different each time depending on where you make it!

MAKES 4-6 SERVINGS

Prep time: 5-10 minutes | Cook time: 1-3 hours

Ingredients

- 1 head garlic
- 1 yellow onion
- Bundle rosemary, thyme, and oregano
- 1 teaspoon coriander
- 1 teaspoon white pepper
- 1 tablespoon paprika
- Salt and pepper, to taste
- 1–3 teaspoons cayenne/chili powder
- 1 teaspoon ground mustard
- 2 bay leaves
- 1 teaspoon turmeric
- 1 pound ground beef
- 4 ounces tomato paste
- 1 cup beef broth
- 1 (28-oz) can crushed tomatoes
- 1 teaspoon Worcestershire sauce
- 1 (16-oz) can black beans
- 1 (16-oz) can kidney beans
- Cheddar cheese, to top (optional)
- Sour cream, to top (optional)

Instructions

1. Mince your garlic and dice your onion into small pieces.

2. Heat a large pot or Dutch oven over medium heat. Lightly toast all of your seasoning in the warm pan until just fragrant, should only take 30 seconds to 1 minute. Remove from your pan and set aside for now.

3. Add your ground beef to your pot and cook until fully browned. Once fully browned, add in your onions and cook until they're soft and translucent, about 5 minutes. Then add your garlic and cook for about a minute, stirring consistently to avoid burning.

(Continued)

4. Next, add in your tomato paste and seasonings. Cook for 1 to 2 minutes stirring constantly.

5. Add in your beef broth to deglaze your pan. Make sure to scrape the bottom of the pan to grab up any bits of flavor that are stuck.

6. Add in your crushed tomatoes, Worcestershire, and beans. Bring to a simmer, reduce heat to medium-low heat then cover.

7. Let your chili stew for at least 30 minutes (The longer it stews the more flavorful it will be!)

8. Grab a bowl and enjoy! Top with cheddar cheese or sour cream if you like!

Phoenix Feathers

Don't worry, no phoenixes were harmed in the creation of this recipe. The peppers just look a little bit like feathers! If you've seen a real phoenix, you'd get it.
Oh, P.S., I saw a phoenix! I was gonna wrestle it to try and harvest more tears, but Harold said that was probably a <u>really</u> bad idea considering they are considered sacred here.

Makes 16–20 stuffed peppers

Prep time: 35–40 minutes | Cook time: 20–30 minutes

Ingredients

- 1 (8-oz) package softened cream cheese
- ½ cup shredded cheddar cheese
- ½ cup shredded pepper jack cheese
- 1 tablespoon fresh garlic
- 1 teaspoon paprika
- Salt and pepper
- 8–10 medium jalapeños
- 10–15 strips of bacon
- Cajun seasoning or Smokey Copper Spice Blend (see page 13) (optional)

Instructions

1. Preheat your oven to 350°F, or turn your smoker onto its smoke setting.
2. Mix together your 3 cheeses and 3 seasonings.
3. Cut your jalapeños in half lengthwise and de-seed them.
4. Fill your jalapeños with 1 to 2 spoonfuls of your cheese mix.
5. Wrap with half a strip of bacon and place on a parchment-lined baking sheet, leaving a little room between each popper. If you want, you can also sprinkle the jalapeños with your favorite Cajun seasoning or Smokey Copper Spice Blend (see page 13) before throwing in the oven or smoker.
6. Bake until bacon is fully cooked, about 20 to 30 minutes, or smoke for 1 hour, then increase heat to high and smoke until bacon is fully cooked and crispy.
7. Enjoy!

Golem Grub

Get ready for some golem scraping!

What's that, you ask?

Well, the people of Ignisanti village don't herd cattle, they herd rock golems of all shapes and sizes. And I really mean it, because some don't look like creatures at all! The villagers like to scrape the endlessly growing crystals on their sides and use them as spices! I have never tasted <u>anything</u> like it. I can't wait to make this recipe for my cousins. They will be so jealous I basically discovered a new spice.

MAKES 4-6 SERVINGS

Prep time: 10-15 minutes | Cook time: 1-1½ hours

INGREDIENTS

- 1-2 pounds boneless skinless chicken thighs
- 2 tablespoons olive oil
- 1 large yellow onion
- 3-7 cloves garlic
- 3-5 Yukon gold potatoes
- 3 large carrots
- 4 tablespoons golem powder (can replace with curry powder)
- 1 teaspoon white pepper
- 1 cinnamon stick
- 1 teaspoon ground ginger
- 1 teaspoon coriander
- 1 teaspoon cumin
- ½ tablespoon paprika
- 1-3 teaspoons red pepper flakes (optional)
- 2 bay leaves
- 3 tablespoons tomato paste
- 1 (16-oz) can coconut cream
- 1½ cups water or broth
- 1 tablespoon brown sugar
- 1 (8-oz) can bamboo shoots
- Salt, to taste
- Chili oil (optional)

INSTRUCTIONS

1. Chop up your chicken into bite-sized chunks, dice your onion, mince your garlic, and chop up your potatoes and carrots.

2. Heat a large pot or Dutch oven over medium-high heat with your olive oil.

3. Add your chicken to the pot first and cook until it starts to turn golden

brown. It does not have to be fully cooked at this step. Just look for the right coloring then remove it from your pot.

4. Add your onions, garlic, and carrots to your pot with all of your seasonings. You not only want to soften your vegetables, but you also want to toast all of your seasonings. Cook for 5 to 10 minutes stirring often.

5. Add your tomato paste to your spices and vegetables. Cook for 3 to 5 minutes, stirring constantly.

6. Add your potatoes, coconut cream, water, and sugar to your pan. Bring to a slow boil then reduce your heat to medium-low.

7. Cover your stew and let it simmer for 30 minutes to 1 hour. Once your potatoes are fork tender, you know it's ready.

8. Add in your bamboo shoots and enjoy! Serve this over rice or with a side of naan!

CHAPTER THIRTY
The Twelfth Knight

Journal!

    Listen, I'm not gonna lie, Sir Storncrest's behavior <u>did not</u> sit right with me. I'm mad. <u>Really</u> mad! How dare he not only give up on himself, but on the whole entire world?! Think of all the children, animals, and good people who could get seriously hurt or even <u>die</u> at the hands of that thing the knights sealed away. Sir Storncrest made an oath to the realm with the other knights, didn't he? He swore to protect us, and now here he is hiding like a coward in the fire realm. Nuh uh, <u>not</u> on my watch!
    But I wasn't gonna say all those things to him, because if my mom taught me one thing it's "You catch more flies with honey than you do with . . . well, most things." Kindness is the way here! At least, I hope so.
    The word around town was that Sir Storncrest liked to meditate on Rock-Sounds Mountain three times a day, once in the morning, once sometime in the afternoon, and once at exactly midnight. I recruited the help of some of the Ignisanti chefs and together we developed a brand-new recipe. We dubbed it: Ranchero's Adventeros, and included some of Storncrest's favorite ingredients. I hoped it would be enough. Plate in hand, I began the trek up the mountain.
    The cool thing about the fire realm is that when the sun sets, the fire still keeps things pretty bright. The ambient lighting of the land, and the now waning golden flames in the lanterns that lit the mountain trail, made the trip feel almost a little bit relaxing. . . . at least until I saw <u>him</u> on the platform. I grumbled under my breath as I approached, my eyes fixed on his swishing glowing sword and the swirling motes of fire that surrounded him. How could he be calm at a time like this?!
    One thing that I didn't want, though, was my own frustration to get the better of me. So, I sat down in the dirt and respectfully waited for him to finish his routine. He noticed I was there without even looking at me.
    "What now?" He grumbled, spinning once in a ceremonious, fiery circle.
    "Oh, hello, Sir Storncrest," I smiled, swallowing my rage. "I thought you might like something to eat."
    "That's not my name," was all he muttered before ignoring me and continuing his dance.
    "I hope you like potatoes," I said in a melodic voice.

Still no answer.

Clenching my jaw tight, I muttered, "Sir, I really hate to bother you, but—"

"I said I'm not interested." he replied, flicking a burst of embers into the air. "What more do I need to do to convince you?"

Ooooooh he was making me so _mad_! I could feel the tension in my chest and in my throat, I just wanted to . . . to . . . punch him in the head! I forced myself to plaster the kindest, widest smile on my face, and said, "Maybe we can talk it through?"

"I'm done talking. Go home."

"Please, at least hear me out—"

"Don't you have something better to do?" He barked. "You can't be any older than thirteen. Why don't you head back before your babysitters notice you're missing?"

Rage bubbled up inside me like a boiling teapot. "I am _not_ a kid." I angrily dropped the plate I had so kindly made for him on the ground. "I am _sick_ and _tired_ of grumpy old men with nothing better to do calling me a kid!"

"What do you think you're doing?" he asked, as I pulled out my dagger—the very same dagger I used to slay my first Imp on the top of the guild hall named after _him_.

"I don't care what you have to say!" I charged at him, dagger straight out in front of me. He stepped to the side, dodging my attack with ease. "I don't care that you're jaded and that you feel like the world isn't worth saving! I _love_ the world! How could you turn your back on it?!"

"We were all doomed the moment that thing was created, and there's nothing we can do to stop it—"

"Don't say that!" I roared, turning around and jabbing at him again.

"Can you even comprehend the power that it took to weaken and seal The Abomination in the first place? And we failed! What a _waste_."

"But it wasn't—"

He scoffed, swinging his sword slow enough for me to leap out of the way.

"How will you live with yourself when you befall the same fate?" he asked.

"Well, if that's the case, at least we tried! You think I'm the kid? At least I'm not the scaredy-cat who isn't brave enough to believe in a better future!"

"There _is_ no future! Don't you understand?!"

"There is, you just _have_ to believe in one!"

He practically snarled.

"How can there be when the ones I love were taken from me?"

"Without the other knight's sacrifice, things would have ended a long time ago—"

"I'm not talking about the knights," he snapped. "I'm talking about my family."

Family? The surprise was just enough to knock me off balance. I grunted, as the hilt of his sword whacked me in the back, just enough to knock me to my knees.

"I don't know what happened to your family, but at least do them the honor of paving the way for a future where they'll be remembered." I don't know if it was the frustration, I don't know if it was the hopelessness, but silent tears began falling down my soot-stained cheeks.

"Believing in this world is a waste, child."

"All the bad things in the world make the good things so much more meaningful, and I <u>know</u> I'm brave for believing in that—braver than you. You're a coward. If you're going to act this way, you don't deserve to call yourself a knight."

I got to my feet and threw my dagger to the ground with a clang. I wiped away my tears before turning to face him. We glared at each other in silence for a few long moments, the tension in the air refusing to wane.

"We'll stop The Abomination with or without your help, Sir Storncrest," I wiped away a bead of sweat from my forehead.

He said nothing, that same stoic, almost cold look still plagued his face.

"I can't believe Hutar named his guild after you." I said, then I stormed off, fuming.

But then, as I turned my back and began to head down the mountain, I heard a single, uttered "fine" faint in the distance.

I froze in my tracks.

"What?"

"I'll help," he said under his breath. "I suppose you have my word."

My eyes tingled with tears of joy this time. He was blurry when I turned to face him, but with a wipe of my eyelids, he was clear.

"Really?" I pleaded.

He nodded and stepped off the platform, slinging his glowing sword on his back.

"You're right, I am a coward. I am the worst kind of knight there is." He shook his head, wincing in pain at whatever images must have flashed through his mind. "But . . . if there's more people out there like you then . . . perhaps this world is worth protecting."

"Thank you!"

"Don't thank me yet. I'll help you as much as I'm able to, but I can't make any promises that we'll succeed . . . a little girl I once knew would be disappointed in me if I didn't at least try."

I ran up to him and gave him one of my classic Cob hugs. He reeled back at first, but I could feel him relax a few seconds in.

"You know I'm not a kid right?" I reminded him as I squeezed him tightly. "I'm almost twenty-one."

"Trust me, to me that <u>is</u> a kid," he said. "Come on, I'll walk you back to town."

I looked over to the plate I had smashed on the ground earlier.

"Probably a good idea, we can get some leftovers there."

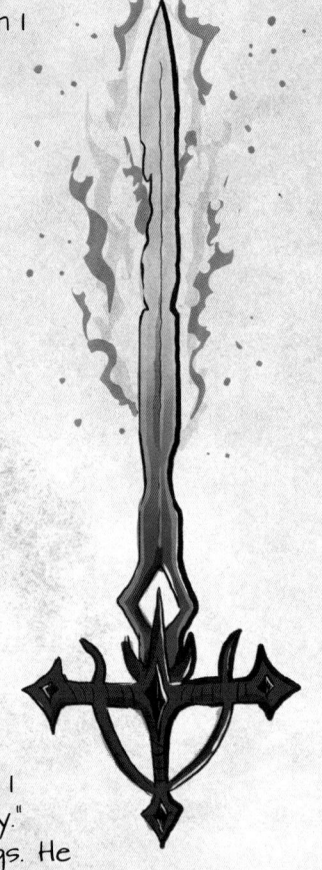

Rancheros Adventeros

Sir Storncrest told me that this recipe reminds him of something his wife used to make way back in the day. I'm not sure I'll ever know what happened to his family, but I hope that he one day finds peace in his heart.

Makes 4-6 servings

Prep time: 25-30 minutes | Cook time: 35-50 minutes

Ingredients

- 3 russet potatoes
- 1 yellow onion
- 3-4 heads garlic
- ½ teaspoon salt
- 2 red peppers
- 1 poblano pepper
- 1 (8-oz) can chickpeas
- ½ teaspoon pepper
- 1 teaspoon paprika
- ¼ teaspoon cayenne
- ¼ teaspoon garlic powder
- 1 tablespoon olive oil
- 1 pound chorizo
- 2-3 cups spinach
- ½ teaspoon red pepper flakes
- 4-6 eggs
- 1-2 cups cheese of your choice
- 1-2 avocado
- Salt and pepper, to taste

Instructions

1. Dice your potatoes and onions and mince your garlic.

2. Fill a medium pot with water and bring to a boil over medium-high heat. Add in a generous pinch of salt and all of your potatoes. Boil until potatoes are fully cooked but not mushy, about 10 to 12 minutes. Once cooked, strain and set aside.

3. Heat a large cast iron over high heat. Place your peppers in the pan and cook for 3 to 4 minutes per side until you start to get a nice char on them. They should start to turn black but not be completely burnt. Cook until all sides are charred, including the tops and bottoms. (Note: If you don't have a cast iron, you can put your peppers under the broiler in your oven, about 5 minutes per side.)

(Continued)

4. As soon as your peppers are done cooking and still warm, place them in a large bowl and cover with a lid. This is going to steam and soften them. Let sit for 5 to 10 minutes.

5. While your peppers are steaming, prep your chickpeas. Strain them and then lay out a large dish cloth. Fold the cloth over them and gently move the chickpeas around through the rag. This will remove most of the peel from your chickpeas. Separate the chickpeas from their peel and place in a small bowl.

6. To your chickpeas add your salt, pepper, paprika, cayenne, and garlic powder. Mix thoroughly so that each chickpea is coated in your seasoning.

7. Remove your peppers from the bowl and chop them up. Make sure to scoop out all of the seeds and get rid of the stems. These don't have to be pretty, just give them a rough chop.

8. Add your olive oil to the cast iron or a large pan. Heat until sizzling hot. Add in your chickpeas and cook until golden brown, about 5 to 10 minutes. To make your chickpeas super crunchy cook for even longer.

9. Remove your chickpeas from the pan and set aside.

10. Add your chorizo to the pan and cook until fully done.

11. Once your chorizo is fully cooked, add in your onion and garlic. Cook until onions are translucent.

12. Once your onions are nice and translucent, add in your peppers, cooked potatoes, and chickpeas. Add a hefty pinch of salt to season everything. Mix together and cook until everything is nice and heated through.

13. Add in your spinach and red pepper flakes, with another small pinch of salt. Do your best to mix everything together. The pan will likely be full at this point but don't worry because the spinach will wilt down.

14. In a separate pan, cook your eggs however you prefer! To do it sunny-side up like me, add a tablespoon of butter to your pan and heat over medium-high. Crack in your eggs and sprinkle with a bit of salt and pepper. Cover your eggs with a lid and cook for 3 to 5 minutes or until the whites of your egg have come together and started to solidify. Immediately remove from the pan and plate. Alternatively, instead of cooking them

separately you can scramble them right into the hash!

15. Top your hash with your favorite cheese and melt in the oven or covered with a lid.

16. Slice your avocado and season with salt and pepper.

17. Top your hash with avocado and your egg then enjoy!

CHAPTER THIRTY-ONE
Beacons of Hope

Journal,

    Well, now that the twelfth knight was on board, all we had left to do was create the beacons. We told Sir Storncrest the details about what we learned, and he said that The Abomination is technically still sealed away for the most part, so we won't need twelve beacons to weaken it enough to seal away again. The power of the first twelve beacons should have weakened it significantly, but it seems to be slowly getting its strength back, perhaps because the seal had been tampered with. Apparently, the black tendrils that were leaking out of the well is a <u>really</u> bad sign. Everything points to the fact that someone did something they shouldn't have. I wonder if it has anything to do with those footsteps I noticed in the nowhere realm.

    That was a lot of information all at once, so I guess I should explain. We learned that the device called a beacon was basically made of the same material that was used to create the old arcane archways. With the right piece of <u>pyromberite</u>—one of this realm's most precious metals—beacons hold the power to bend the magic of different realms and can open and close doorways in the web.

    I know what you must be wondering, <u>How does this help us weaken this thing?</u> Basically, the way it works is the beacons will trap the Abomination in a sort of in-between space. When you teleport, you are jumbling up your physical essence, transmuting it into magical essence, and then relocating your magical essence to a new location in the magic web before hopping back into your physical body. Prolonging the time spent in this weird magical in-between state is enough to tear apart any normal being, but this hunk of evil black goo is already a jumble of magic essence. By prolonging their time in the in-between space, though, it essentially starts to rip apart the mass, scattering it into pieces that can't sustain themselves. Do we think that we can kill this creature on our own? No way! So, our main goal is to weaken it

262

enough to repair the seal, and then we can return some time in the future with an army of people strong enough to take it down for good. Time is of the absolute essence, though—the less beacons they have to forge, the better! Chief Ru'uk-Kraak said that he's going to do his best to make these new ones even stronger than the first, and I really hope that he's able to!

Everyone pitched in to build the beacons in their own way. Finheld has been working closely with Sir Storncrest and the Ignasanti blacksmiths to forge what is an intricate torch handle out of pieces of pyromberite. The process of folding and weaving the metal is extremely complex, so Harold's been helping them take very detailed notes along the way just in case we ever needed this information again. The notes will be left here in Ignasanti for safekeeping.

The key to igniting the Beacon is the rune magic. Ru'uk-Kraak led Irabel to the top of the mountain to teach her an ancient art of rune-writing. The two of them disappeared for hours with the beacons. When they returned, a fiery red energy emitted from the woven metal. Irabel taught us how to activate the Beacons, allowing the magic inside to be used in a spell. We had to utter a word I was told I am not allowed to write down, which caused a light to erupt from the torch. The pyromberite handle acted as a tether to a swirling vortex of chaotic energy that was trapped in a gossamer orb of magic. At the utterance of another word I am not allowed to write down, the handle will absorb the energy once more, rendering it safe to travel with.

Thanks to the extremely light quality of the pyromberite, even I can wield these floating spheres with ease. The thing is, we can't just use these things willy-nilly. Once you expend the energy within using the correct incantation, it cannot be stopped. The beacons will shatter once all their energy is released, so we don't have to worry about their immense power falling into the wrong hands afterwards.

We thanked Chief Ru'uk-Kraak and Sir Storncrest for all of their help. I asked Sir Storncrest if he'd be willing to come along with us to the nowhere realm, but he didn't seem ready. That's fine, he had done enough to help. We have the beacons, and that's all we need. I really believe it!

On our last day in the village, the chief organized a village-wide farewell feast for us! He's so cool. I'd love to come back one of these days and pick his crystally brain—not literally though, of course!

I write this entry now over a delicious plate of "Crispy Lava Lizard Tacos," (see page 264) made with meat from a real lava lizard. I didn't even know something like that existed! I'll be sure to write down the recipe immediately.

Anyway, we're going to eat and then we're off to the nowhere realm. Wish us luck! I don't think we'll need it, though, we got this whole thing under control. It'll be easy!

. . . Right?

Crispy Lava Lizard Tacos

As cute and terrifying as they are, lava lizard meat is very fatty, so it can be hard to cook. The villagers taught me the best way to make them, and I'm so happy they were kind enough to share their knowledge with me!

MAKES 4 SERVINGS

Prep time: 10-20 minutes | Cook time: 2½-3 hours

INGREDIENTS

LAVA LIZARD:
2½ pounds lava lizard (can replace with pork belly)
Salt and pepper

SALSA:
4 medium tomatoes
1-2 jalapeños
½ small yellow onion, divided
3-7 peeled cloves garlic
Chopped cilantro
Salt and pepper, to taste

EXTRAS:
Tortillas
Diced yellow onion
Chopped cilantro
2-3 limes

INSTRUCTIONS

LAVA LIZARD:

1. Preheat your oven to 350°F.

2. Generously coat your lava lizard in salt and pepper, then place on a large baking sheet. Bake for 2 hours. Now is the perfect time to prep the rest of your ingredients.

3. Once your lava lizard has baked for 2 hours, turn your oven on broil. Broil your lava lizard until the top layer gets nice and golden brown and crispy, about 10 to 15 minutes. This part will get a little smoky in a normal kitchen, so be sure to open some windows at this step.

4. Let your lava lizard rest 15 to 20 minutes before slicing into it. It will be very juicy and very hot.

Salsa:

1. Heat a medium-sized pan or cast iron over medium-high heat.

2. Add your tomatoes, jalapeños, a quarter of your onion, and your garlic to your pan. You want to get a nice char on all of your veggies. The garlic will cook the quickest, so pull that out first if needed.

3. Add all of your charred veggies to a blender or molcajete. For a less-spicy salsa, you can de-seed your jalapeños before adding them.

4. Crush or blend your veggies until you get a slightly chunky consistency.

5. Finely mince the other quarter of your onion and rinse it under cold water. Add in a handful of onion and your fresh cilantro.

6. Taste and add in salt and pepper as needed.

Next, just heat up your tortillas, build your tacos, and enjoy!

CHAPTER THIRTY-TWO
Bitter Ends

Well, Journal,

I'm not gonna lie to you, today didn't go like we planned. I don't really feel that awesome right now. This wasn't the story I wanted to tell . . . not anywhere close. You deserve to know, though, I guess.

We traveled back to Farvenor to start setting up the beacons. The tension in the air was thick. <u>Of course</u> we were scared, the fate of the world is in our hands. But we had a plan this time, and it was a <u>good</u> one. The Tag-Alongs have never felt more united than now—in the maniacal, grinning face of doom.

When we arrived at the village, we were expecting to see kind welcoming faces. The plan was to take the night, rest up, set up, and go into it strong the next morning. Instead, we were greeted with empty homes. No one was there, not even Maud, Clark, or his and Rosalind's children. An eerie silence blanketed the village, and though it was the middle of the day, dark clouds hung over our heads, nearly blocking out the sun.

We exchanged a look of not just fear, but of determination, of resolve, of possible goodbyes.

On horseback, we galloped through the forest. When it was time to go on foot, I followed closely behind Karn, knowing I would be able to follow his path through the woods easier than anyone else's. I almost ran right into him when he came to an abrupt stop.

There was a man. It was one of the villagers, walking through the woods. His eyes were fully glazed over; it was like looking at a doll. Soon, we found there were dozens of villagers walking mindlessly through the woods, each of them headed in the same direction as us.

"Don't stop!" Harold's voice shouted from a few feet away. "We help them by ending this. Come on, it's okay."

It was enough to get the rest of us running again.

We ran and ran for what felt like hours, even though it couldn't have been more than twenty minutes. My heartbeat grew louder and louder in my ears the closer we got. More and more people started appearing in the forest. All walking in the same direction, the sky growing steadily darker up above. Finally, we burst out of the tree line to that creepy clearing, ready to sprint through to the nowhere realm.

Once again, though, our plans were foiled.

Looming over the meadow was the tree. Its gnarled, black, dead branches reached out like they were going to grab us at any moment and toss us into the massive black well—the very same one that bore a deep chasm in the middle of the clearing. This was bad, this was really, <u>really</u> bad. For a moment, I wondered if Sir Storncrest was right; maybe there really was nothing we could do.

Hundreds of people from the valley surrounded us, the tree, and gathered at the very edge of the well. Staring into its inky depths—

I found myself caught in a trance, like I had been by the well for a lifetime, staring into the endless black.

The Eternal Malice . . .

   It twists . . .

      It writhes . . .

         <u>It ascends</u>—

I felt a hand on my shoulder. Harold.

"Come on, Cob. We need you right now."

I took a deep breath and readied myself.

"Sorry."

Karn shook his head, nudging me playfully with his elbow.

"Don't be sorry, lass. We'll get through this with nary a scratch, alright?"

I nodded, wishing—praying—that this was possible.

Irabel crouched low, wielding her beacon in hand.

"You all remember the incantation, correct?" she asked.

We nodded solemnly.

"Cob, you're the slowest, so use your beacon from here." Finheld told me.

I wanted to argue, but I felt almost paralyzed in fear. The only thing I managed to do was take the beacon from my satchel and hold it in my shaky hands. The power of the beacon rippled through the metal, and I tried to focus on that sensation for as long as I could. I imagined all my worries fading away—maybe even being absorbed in the beacon—but it didn't work. I was terrified.

Then I felt a hand on my shoulder.

"Count to sixty, then start the incantation," Harold said. His voice was calm, and his beacon was steady. "We'll follow your lead, Cob. Just like we planned."

I had to swallow my fear. I had to steel myself—I had to be brave. I didn't want to be like Sir Storncrest; I wanted to be like <u>me</u>. And what does Cob CopperSpoon do? Cook, spread love, but in moments like this, above all, help others!

"I got this," I said. "Everybody stay safe out there, okay?"

As the words left my mouth, I gave them each a small magical boon. My mind-blanket, something to keep them safe. With that, they ran off.

<u>One</u> . . . <u>two</u> . . .

Karn and Irabel rushed to the left; Harold and Finheld taking the right. I moved myself away from the closest villagers, choosing a spot slightly hidden in a patch of trees. It would be hard for a normal-sized person to reach, but my size was on my side.

<u>Twenty-five</u> . . . <u>twenty-six</u> . . .

I could see the silhouettes of Harold and Finheld. Harold stopped in his position about eighty feet away, Finheld gave him a tight embrace before sprinting onward.

<u>Thirty-nine</u> . . . <u>forty</u> . . .

It wasn't hard to spot Karn—his broad shoulders and powerful stance. Even from far away, he was a beacon of strength.

<u>Fifty-one</u> . . . <u>fifty-two</u> . . .

Irabel was fast. She was one of the hardest to keep track of, especially in the dark. But I spotted her. She was so close. Only five feet away now.

<u>Fifty nine</u> . . .

   <u>Sixty.</u>

I slammed the pyromberite into the ground, with all my strength, commanding the beacon to prepare itself to weaken The Eternal Malice. At the utter of the release word, a powerful surge of bright red energy erupted around me, brightening the dark forest in scarlet light, but deepening the black shadows in the distance.

Hundreds of heads snapped in my direction, jaws slack, eyes dark. The people filling the meadow became feral. Before the first breath of incantation left my lips, they began to drag themselves in my direction.

<u>I hope the others are okay.</u>

I quickly pushed the thought out of my head. They were way stronger than me, way smarter, and way more experienced in times like these. They <u>had</u> to be fine. My focus shifted back to the incantation.

I closed my eyes and began speaking. As the ancient words left my lips, I could feel the energy from the beacon begin to surge. I got through the first sentence when I felt something wrap around my ankle. Before I could even react, I felt myself getting slammed to the ground.

It was a young boy, no older than seven or eight. He was small enough to squeeze into my tree sanctuary, yet he pulled me to the ground with the strength of a full-grown man. I never stopped speaking, though. I <u>could not</u>—<u>would not</u> stop speaking! I wasn't going to fail my friends.

I wiggled out of his grasp and gently kicked him back, the words still flowing over my teeth. But more and more people began to circle around me. Villagers of all shapes and sizes reached their hands towards me, their dark eyes turning milky white. I felt like a rabbit in a wolf's den. Where were my friends?!

<u>They're okay. I know they're okay.</u>

I flicked my wrist towards the small boy and cast a stun spell on him—something Irabel taught me. His grip loosened on my ankle, but it didn't stop the rest of the villagers. They pulled at the bark, they tore at the trees with their teeth and bloodying fingers. And when the protective wall of trees could no longer stand, I dodged swinging attacks and arms grabbing at me while I continued to chant.

<u>You're almost there, you're almost there, you can do this.</u>

My bones started to ache, and it took everything in me to keep speaking the magical words. Finally, I was so close, the incantation was almost complete—

A hand wrapped around my waist and the force started to crush my insides. I writhed in pain, chanting as I battled my attacker. Even in the shadows and red light, I was able to make out their face.

It was Maud, in a delicate white nightgown, now stained with dirt.

I wanted to reach out to her—to beg her to stop, but even when my head slammed back against a tree, I kept uttering the incantation. Then, she squeezed me hard and my ribs crunched under her grasp, leaving me breathless. My vision blurred, the words of the incantation faded from my mind, and I let out a piercing scream of agony.

<u>Is this really how it ends?</u>
<u>After all we've done, do we really lose?</u>

The earth trembled. A wave of oppressive darkness and piercing, dissonant whispers oozed from the well in the distance. The sounds of groaning villagers and clanging metal was drowned out by a deep, guttural roar. I gritted my teeth in pain, the sound almost too loud for my ears to bear.

It's here.

The Eternal Malice had escaped the seal.

The gigantic, constantly shifting mass resisted all interpretation—legs, faces, arms, wings—it had everything and nothing all at once. It was so dark that it seemed to absorb the red lights of the beacons, but occasionally a flash of pale flesh, a terrified face, glowing red eyes, or a tuft of hair would come into view for just a moment.

The creature lurched from the hole, still clearly weakened from the twelve knights, but strong enough, now, to walk on our soil.

Time seemed to stretch like an endless abyss. The only thing tethering me to reality was the pain of my ribs and the stench of Maud's breath. I had to keep going. I had to finish the incantation. This was our last chance.

I felt myself screaming out the last words, but they only came as a soft whisper.

<u>Shelive, shelai, velar</u> . . .

My beacon pulsed, sending a massive wave of fiery energy into the woods that knocked all the villagers around me unconscious. I watched as a beam shot from the beacon like a laser, burning into the core of The Eternal Malice.

Then there was another beam. And another, and another, and another.

The creature screeched in a discordant cacophony of hundreds of different voices. Its piercing, high-pitched wail clawed at my ears and drained what little strength I had left.

To some relief, I saw some of my friends in the distance. Irabel raised her hands to the sky, and a flash of brilliant white lightning struck the creature where it stood. It shuddered, but seemed unaffected. Finheld unleashed several arrows from his crossbow, Karn sprinted into battle, attacking it with his hammer, and Harold blasted it with balls of bright light to little effect. The beast conjured a twitching limb of pure darkness, and with one fell swoop, struck with immense power and sent them barreling into the trees.

I had to do something.

As the beacons steadily unleashed their power, I grit my teeth through the pain and hobbled closer. I reached out my hand and conjured false images of the twelve knights—each of them wielding magic and weaponry, ready to take on the creature. They couldn't really defeat it, but they could keep it distracted enough for me to reach whoever was closest.

Harold.

He hit a young tree when he fell, its trunk cracked and jabbed several splinters under his armor when he landed.

"Cob?" He took a breath, slowly pulling himself to his feet.

"Are you okay?!"

"Don't worry about me," he said. "Are you okay?"

I tried my best to stand straight, but the pain that tore through my torso wouldn't allow it.

"We have to stop that thing!" I wailed, tears streaking down my face. "We <u>have</u> to!"

He smiled and comforted me, placing his hand on my shoulder. That familiar warm light rushed through me, and my pain dissipated.

"Thank you," I cried. "But what about you?"

"That was my last healing spell," Harold told me. "Better spent on you than me."

"But—"

"I'll be okay, Cob. We can do this together."

His confidence reassured me enough to wipe away my tears.

"Okay," I said, taking his hand. "Let's go."

We emerged from the treeline to the sounds of screeching, roaring, and my friends' battle cries. My illusory knights faded, the creature's strength greater than some silly mirages. Karn threw his hammer, which tore a hole clear through the beast's amorphous body and circled through the air right back to his hand. The beast wailed in pain, but the hole quickly filled with more darkness, seemingly healing as it did so.

Irabel struck it with more lightning, and Finheld snuck behind it, slicing at one of its many ankles with his daggers, but nothing worked.

"What do we do?!"

"Cob, look," Harold said, he pointed to the beast's . . . shoulder? I could have sworn that I saw a set of eyes with a wild gaze that looked directly at Harold and I, but as it fluxed with darkness, they retreated.

"What was that?"

"It's back!"

The eyes returned. . . . and then a full face, then a torso. A woman with brunette hair and a tattered green dress emerged faintly from its form, weakly maintaining her presence with the aid of a faintly glowing, warm light—one that looked exactly like Harold's.

"Rosalind?"

Harold stood transfixed for a moment, his eyes locked steadily with hers.

"Harold, come on. We have to do something!" I urged, pulling at his arm.

The beast raged, but Harold turned to me with a strange look on his face. Something close to resolve, closer to pain. He got down on one knee, grunting through the pain in his torso as he did so, and wrapped me in a tight hug.

"I love you, Cob. I love all of you, so, so much."

The timing had me a little surprised, but I returned the gesture.

"I love you too, but why are we hugging?" I asked. "We have to fight."

"I know," his voice broke, tears streamed down his face. "It'll be over soon."

It all felt like a <u>farewell.</u>

Harold stood to his feet, and gave me a strange, heartbreaking smile before sprinting towards the beast. It was then that I found myself wondering, what was he planning?

Overwhelming dread made my stomach lurch.

"Wait!" I called, but he didn't turn back. "<u>Harold!</u>"

The beacons finally shattered, spending all of their strength. Rosalind's form disappeared, her presence exchanged for streaks of blinding, golden light that burst from the very depths of the creature and into the sky, weakly breaking through the dark clouds. The terrible sound of twisted and tangled screams of pain shook the earth. I clamped my hands over my ears, screaming Harold's name as the creature lashed back, launching thousands of black needles out in all directions. Narrowly, I dodged them, and the remaining black ooze sizzled into the earth and trees. "Harold, please!"

Harold reached the beast and extended his hand. An opulent, golden, otherworldly staff appeared in his grasp. He looked to the sky in reverence. Somehow, the sun parted the clouds above him, filling the clearing with warm light. A gift. An <u>agreement.</u>

"Wait, what is he doing?!" Finheld screamed. "Harold, no!"

Harold looked to the ground, perhaps saying something private to himself in his strange moment of calm.

We were then each knocked back by a blinding, white flash of light, then the earth shuttered. And all was quiet.

Suddenly, I awoke back in the treeline. The darkness had subsided. The Eternal Malice was gone. In the middle of the meadow there was no tree, no well, just blackened scars on the earth where they once stood. There was nothing there . . . but then Karn appeared. I could see him running to where the well stood.

Then Irabel, then Finheld.

Then . . .

Harold was nowhere to be seen.

A broken "no!" escaped from my mouth as I rushed to my friends. My eyes darted from tree to tree, from the face of every unconscious villager I could see. Where was he? <u>Where was he</u>?!

I wasn't sure how much time passed after that. Ten minutes? An hour? Days? I felt like I was floating.

"Cob, er' ye okay?" Karns words rang through my ears, but his voice sounded so far away. "Come on, let's get you patched up."

It was dark now, the villagers were long gone. I vaguely remember him starting a fire. I heard Finheld yelling, cursing Helirion—I saw Irabel frantically digging in the earth where Harold once stood, emptying her bag of runes and trinkets on the darkened soil.

I watched them move around me, but I could do nothing.

Where had he gone?

<u>Why didn't I stop him?</u>

Karn boiled some hot water and handed me a mug at some point.

"Here Cob, this will help you feel better."

I barely touched it.

<u>Where was Harold?</u>

Karn's Comfort

Dear Cob,
I know if you were feeling better, you would want this recipe, so I wrote it down for you. Wishing us all healing. If you ever want to talk, you can bend my ear whenever you need to, lass.
    Here for you always.

Love,
Karn

MAKES 96 SERVINGS

Prep time: 10-15 minutes | Cook time: 5-10 minutes

Ingredients

- 4½ cups sugar
- 2 cups cocoa powder
- 1¼ cups plain powdered creamer
- 1 cup French vanilla powdered creamer
- 1¼ cup powdered milk

Instructions

1. In a large bowl, mix together all of your ingredients until everything is sufficiently combined.

2. Store your powdered mixture in airtight containers. This will all fit into a gallon-sized container if you have one.

3. Use 1 to 2 tablespoons of this mixed with boiling water to make your hot cocoa! Top with whipped cream or marshmallows and enjoy!

4. My mom used to use this recipe for homemade gifts. Add in chocolate chips, peppermint crumbles, or even dried mini marshmallows for an extra bit of pizzazz.

CHAPTER THIRTY-THREE
Unwinding

Journal,

We waited all night, just in case Harold showed up from somewhere in the darkness.

He didn't.

Finheld disappeared into the woods some time during the early hours of the morning after a particularly tense conversation with Karn and Irabel. I couldn't seem to utter a word—I wasn't sure I even wanted to. How could I speak while someone I cared for so much was gone forever?

We held a memorial at the guild, but it felt wrong. What else were we supposed to do? I remember Telfina handed me a bouquet of white flowers, their yellow stamens were shaped like the sun. I cried. I cried all day. I felt like I couldn't function—how was I supposed to wrap my head around what was happening? Harold saved the world, but ours ended the moment he left. What were we supposed to do without him?

Hutar called us to his office at one point. He wasn't as gruff as he typically liked to be, but it didn't make a difference. Karn told him everything that happened, so that he could file a report and send it off to the king.

Hutar nodded in silence, writing down every word.

He slipped the papers in an envelope, and sealed it with a blue wax seal.

"And I'm sorry for your loss, of course. Harold was—"

Finheld scoffed, his hands crossed against his chest.

"You're not sorry," he said.

Hutar raised a thick eyebrow.

"Excuse me?"

"<u>None</u> of you are sorry!" Finheld burst into rage like cannon-fire. "No one cared about Harold enough to even <u>try</u> and stop him! Cob, he was with you the whole time, you didn't think to yourself, 'hey, maybe I should grab him,' or something?!"

I felt tears trickling out of my already puffy eyes.

"I didn't know what he was planning, I already told you!" I wept into my palms. "I didn't understand!"

"What a convenient excuse!"

Finheld blamed me for everything, and as much as it hurt, and as much as Karn and Irabel fought for me, I almost agree with him. I blame me, too.

It all ended when Finheld brought his fist down on Hutar's desk. I found myself flinching at the sound.

"I can never forgive any of you," he uttered. "I can't live like this. Hutar, I'm leaving the party and proposing it be formally disbanded. I want nothing to do with any of this."

I didn't think my heart could break more than it already had, but it turns out I was wrong.

"Finheld, no!" Karn yelled. "What about all the good things we've done together? I miss Harold, too, but we need each other now more than ever!"

"Hutar," Finheld said firmly, expectantly.

Hutar looked to us, and even though I wildly and tearfully shook my head in disagreement, Irabel and Karn hung theirs low.

"Fine." He said, standing from his seat. "Let me just get the paperwork."

"Wait, what?! No!" My heart raced in my chest. "All of you think we should disband?!"

Irabel nodded, her eyes filled with a mixture of grief and rage.

"I'm still your friend, Cob, but I can't work with someone who <u>refuses</u> to accept <u>reality</u>." She glared at Finheld as she spit her words. "And someone who is just going to blame what happened on <u>everyone else</u>!"

I couldn't believe what I was hearing.

"Karn?"

"I think we just need some time to recuperate, Cob," He frowned. "It won't be forever, but we—"

I'm not sure what else he said. I stopped listening. It doesn't even matter. Harold is gone, The Tag-Alongs are over, and I have never felt this horrible in my entire life.

There's nothing more to look forward to.

Nothing more to write about.

I'm done.

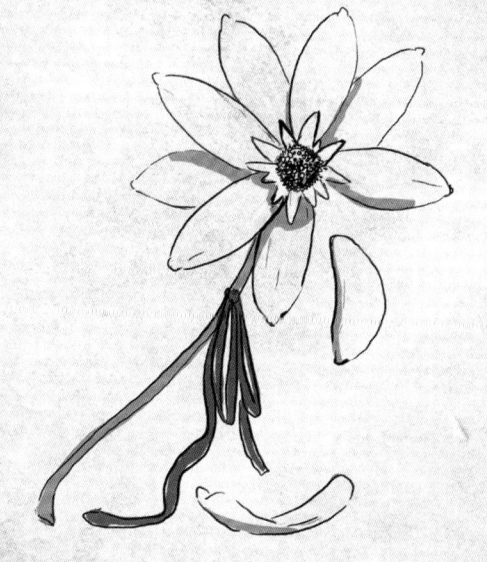

The Tag-Along's Clouds and Cream

As I was flipping through my journal, I saw a random piece of parchment stuffed in its pages. It was a mostly finished recipe that Harold must have been working on for me in secret, I think he slipped it into my Journal right before we split off to plant the beacons.

He titled it The Tag-Alongs Clouds and Cream. What a wonderful name he came up with.

MAKES 4-6 SERVINGS

Prep time: 15-20 minutes | Cook time: 30-45 minutes

INGREDIENTS

BISCUITS:
- 3 cups flour
- 1 teaspoon salt
- ½ teaspoon sugar
- 1 tablespoon baking powder
- ½ cup cold butter
- 1 cups milk

GRAVY:
- 1 pound raw breakfast sausage
- 2 tablespoons butter
- ¼ cup flour
- 2 cups milk
- ½ cup beef broth
- Salt and pepper, to taste
- 1 teaspoon paprika
- 1 teaspoon garlic powder
- 1 teaspoon onion powder

INSTRUCTIONS

BISCUITS:

1. Preheat your oven to 350°F.

2. In a large bowl, mix together your flour, salt, sugar, and baking powder.

3. Take your cold butter and cut it into small cubes, then add that into your flour. Using a pastry cutter or your fingers, mix the butter into the flour until a sand-like texture is formed.

4. Pour in half of your milk and start combining. Keep adding the milk a splash at a time until there are no more dry spots in the flour, but so the dough also isn't too sticky. If you add a little too much milk, just mix in a bit more flour until you get the desired consistency.

5. You can roll these out into traditional biscuits, if you prefer, but I like to grease a pie pan or my cast iron skillet, put all of my dough in it, and score individual pieces with a sharp knife before placing it in the oven to bake.

6. Bake for 20 to 25 minutes until fully cooked through the center.

Gravy:

1. In a large saucepan, brown your sausage in your butter over medium-high heat, breaking it into bite-sized pieces. It should take 10 to 15 minutes to fully cook through.

2. Once fully cooked, add flour and cook for 2 to 3 minutes to get rid of any floury taste. You want a smooth, creamy consistency when you add the flour. Depending on the sausages you use, more butter may need to be added to thin it out some.

3. Add milk and beef broth slowly, about ½ cup at a time, waiting for the previous pour to thicken.

4. Add all of your seasoning. Once thickened turn heat to low and stir occasionally to make sure it doesn't burn.

Harold's Late Night Comforts

This was something that Harold used to make late at night. I figured it would go well with his biscuits and gravy recipe (see page 276).

MAKES 1–2 SERVINGS

Prep time: 5 minutes | Brew time: 3-5 minutes

Ingredients

- 1 tablespoon black tea
- 2 teaspoons dried sage leaves
- 2 dried rose buds
- 1 teaspoon lemongrass
- Honey and cream, to taste

Instructions

1. Mix all of your dried tea leaves, rose buds, and lemongrass and put them into a tea steeper or empty tea bag. Alternatively, you can also add this to boiling water and strain out the leaves later.
2. Boil 2 to 3 cups of water then add to a mug. Steep your tea for 3 to 5 minutes.
3. Add honey and cream to taste.

CHAPTER THIRTY-FOUR
A Big Blur

Hi Journal,

My last entry was a month ago.

I have no idea where Finheld disappeared to, but they probably wouldn't have told me if I asked. Irabel left the city, saying she was going back home for a little while. Karn stayed at my side for a little bit, but eventually we saw less and less of each other. I don't want to lose him—I don't want to lose any of them—but I just need to be alone for a while, I think. Honestly, I'm not sure what I want.

I've been staying at the guild, but I'm not taking on new quests or anything like that. I'm not even cooking, to be honest. I feel like my soul and limbs are full of rocks, and I really don't think I could possibly stomach food right now. Hutar suggested that it might be best for me to head home. I think he's right.

Sluggishly, I packed all my belongings, and I was told I could help myself to some rations from the kitchen and any other supplies I might need for the journey. As I made my way down the stairs and out of the guild, I wondered what my family would think when they saw this version of me. What would I tell them about my adventures? Should I lie to them and pretend everything was fine? Would they be ashamed if I told them the truth? Would they blame me for all of this like Finheld did? I really hope not—and I really don't think so—but something about this headspace that I'm in has me worried about everything.

I waved goodbye to some of the guild members, and just as I put my hand on the door, I heard Telfina calling my name. She wheeled across the guild, a letter in a white, gilded envelope in her hand.

"For you!"

"What is it?" I asked, taking it from her.

The golden seal on the back said all I needed to know—this letter was from the crown. I felt a pit forming in my stomach. Did Finheld reach out to the king to accuse me of murdering someone? Was I being summoned to attend court?

I opened the letter to reveal the fanciest paper I've ever seen. Handwritten by the king himself was a big thank you to me and everyone else for saving the world. He even sent me a small sum of gold to use as I pleased. I wasn't even sure how to process this. Was I even excited? Why does grief always overshadow everything?

"The large chest of gold out front was getting a little too much attention, so Hutar took the liberty of putting it in a vault for you at the bank." Telfina said. "He has receipts and all the information you'll need in his office."

"Thank you," I nodded, but I was still unsure of what to do with myself. How could I spend money that was tied to the death of my friend?

"Hey, Cob?" Telfina said, gently squeezing my free hand. "I know you want to take off, and I don't blame you, but you're always welcome here. Despite it all, this will always be a home for you, sweetheart. . Don't forget us, okay?"

I'm not sure if it was her words, or the way she looked at me with her earnest, motherly eyes, but I broke down. She wrapped me up in a hug, and let me cry. I didn't have to leave, did I? I loved traveling, adventure, and experiencing new things, Was I was really about to give that all up and go back to my old life? Things weren't great—they weren't even good—but they'd get better over time, right?

I pulled away from Telfina, steeling away my emotions for the first time in a while.

"Thank you, Telfina. Thank you."

I set off after that. Not to home, but away from here. From the memories, from the pain. The whole reason I set out on this adventure was to continue the Copperspoon family legacy, to explore the world one dish at a time and bring my stories back home. I haven't filled this book up yet and I will not let my family down by giving up.

Am I ok? No. Will I be? Today, right now, I think I might be.

Burnt Sugar Harvest Brew

I came across a group of farmers who were harvesting some weird beans and making a drink out of it. . . . It was dark and bitter. Karn would have hated it; he was always a sweets kind of dwarf. I made this recipe out of it for him. When I see him again someday, I think I'll make it for him.

MAKES 16–20 SERVINGS

Cook time: 30–35 minutes

INGREDIENTS

SPICED CARAMEL DRIZZLE:
- 1 cup brown sugar
- ½ cup butter
- 1 teaspoon pumpkin pie spice
- ½ cup heavy cream or half-and-half

COFFEE:
- 2½ cups half-and-half
- 1 cup pumpkin or butternut squash
- 1–3 teaspoons pumpkin pie spice
- ⅓–¾ cup brown sugar
- 12–18 ounces coffee
- Caramel sauce

INSTRUCTIONS

SPICED CARAMEL DRIZZLE:
1. Add your brown sugar, butter, and pumpkin spice to a medium-large pot. You will need a larger pan than you think.
2. Heat your brown sugar mix over medium-high heat until starts to bubble, stirring occasionally, then slowly add in your cream, mixing constantly.
3. Once cream is fully mixed in, let your caramel simmer for 5 to 7 minutes, stirring constantly until all of the sugar is melted.
4. Remove from heat and place in a heat-safe container to cool.

COFFEE:
1. Add your half-and-half, squash, pumpkin pie spice, and brown sugar to a medium saucepan. For a sweeter creamer, add in more brown sugar, and for a lighter one, add less.

(Continued)

2. Heat your cream mixture over medium-high heat, stirring constantly until your cream starts to scald. It will be hot but not boiling quite yet.

3. Reduce your heat to medium-low and continue to stir until your brown sugar is fully melted, about 5 to 10 minutes.

4. Strain your cream mixture through a fine-mesh sieve and cheese cloth if you have them available.

5. Store your cream in the fridge until you are ready to use.

6. Brew your coffee in your preferred method. Mix with as much cream as you like and top with your caramel drizzle.

Manticore Noodles

I found myself traveling through the Wildflower Plains when I left the Bastion, mostly just because I never found myself traveling this way. I think I know why that is now. For as nice as this place sounds it is <u>crawling</u> with manticores. Luckily, some locals found and saved me before I became dinner for one. They taught me how to prepare this recipe.

MAKES 4-6 SERVINGS

Prep time: 15-25 minutes | Cook time: 20-30 minutes

INGREDIENTS

- 4 tablespoons soy sauce
- 1 tablespoon sesame oil
- 2 tablespoons fish sauce
- 2 tablespoons hoisin sauce
- 4 tablespoons Worcestershire sauce
- 2 tablespoons ketchup
- 2 tablespoons sugar
- 1 tablespoon minced garlic
- 1 pound thinly sliced manticore (can replace with beef)
- 2-3 cups napa cabbage
- Pinch of salt
- 3-4 green onions
- 2 tablespoons vegetable or peanut oil for pan
- 1 pound yakisoba noodles
- Sesame seeds, for garnish

INSTRUCTIONS

1. In a small bowl, combine soy sauce, sesame oil, fish sauce, hoisin sauce, Worcestershire, ketchup, sugar, and minced garlic.

2. Add your manticore to a bowl. Add about half of your sauce mixture to your meat and make sure to fully coat it, really working it into the manticore. Cover your bowl with plastic wrap and set it to the side for now.

3. Thinly slice your cabbage, piling it in a large bowl once you're done. Add a large pinch of salt and mix it into the cabbage, then let it sit. After 5 to 10 minutes, most of the water in the cabbage will be pulled out. Drain the water and pat the cabbage dry with a paper towel.

(Continued)

4. Thinly slice your green onions while the cabbage and salt are sitting.

5. Using either a wok or large frying pan, heat your oil over high heat. You want the oil to be spitting hot at this step, so be patient and let it get really hot.

6. Once your pan is thoroughly heated, add in all of your green onions and fry just until they are fragrant and soft. This should only take about 2 minutes. Once done, remove from the pan.

7. Let your pan reheat for about a minute and then add in all of your cabbage. Once again, we're only frying this until it's warm and just starting to soften. This should only take 4 to 6 minutes. Like before, remove from the pan.

8. At this point, you may need to add a bit more oil to your pan, just to make sure nothing sticks. Again, let it reheat to a higher temperature and then we are going to add your manticore (beef) in batches.

9. Start with a small handful of pieces so you don't overcrowd the pan. You are going to cook this until the manticore is just browned and then remove it from the pan. Repeat this process until all of your beef is cooked.

10. Once all of the beef is cooked and removed from the pan, let your pan reheat. Once heated add in the remaining sauce. It should bubble very quickly. Add in your noodles immediately after and toss them in the sauce, making sure they are thoroughly coated in the mixture.

11. Add in the rest of your cooked ingredients and toss with the noodles. Cook for 2 to 3 minutes until everything is nice and warm.

12. You can top this with sesame seeds, chili oil, green onions, anything you want.

Island Burger

Guess who I found on my travels?! It's Karn! We somehow ended up on the road to Marlin's Shore at the same time. I am so glad I ran into him; it would have been hard going back without him. This burger is a new recipe from the stand that sold us the crab dip from our last visit.

MAKES 4 BURGERS

Prep time: 30-45 minutes | Cook time: 30-45 minutes

INGREDIENTS

CUCUMBER SALAD:
1-2 cucumbers
Salt
1 green onion
¼ cup rice wine vinegar
Red pepper flakes, to taste
2 teaspoons soy sauce
1 tablespoon sugar
½ teaspoon fish sauce
1 teaspoon sesame oil
1-2 cloves garlic

PICKLED RED ONIONS:
1½ tablespoons sugar
Red pepper flakes, to taste
⅓ cup red wine vinegar
1 medium red onion

BUNS:
2 cups sushi rice
3 cups water
2 tablespoons butter or vegetable oil

GRILLED GREEN ONIONS AND GLAZE:
¼ cup soy sauce
¼ cup hot water
½ tablespoon sesame oil
2 tablespoons honey
1 teaspoon fish sauce
Red pepper flakes
Sesame seeds
1-2 cloves garlic, grated/minced
Bundle of green onions
2 tablespoons cornstarch

BURGER PATTY:
1 pound ground beef or lamb
Salt and pepper, to taste

EXTRA TOPPINGS:
Kewpie mayo
Sriracha

(Continued)

Instructions

Cucumber salad:

1. Slice your cucumber evenly then sprinkle them with a pinch of salt. Let it sit for 10 to 15 minutes. After that time, drain any excess liquid from your cucumbers.
2. Finely chop your green onion.
3. In a medium-large bowl, whisk together your rice wine vinegar, red pepper flakes, soy sauce, sugar, fish sauce, sesame oil, and green onions until the sugar is dissolved.
4. Toss your cucumbers into the marinade until they are fully coated. Give it a taste to see if it needs anything then store in the fridge until you are ready to serve.
5. Note: The longer this salad sits, the better it is, so do this before anything else.

Pickled Red Onions:

1. Mix together your vinegar, sugar, and red pepper flakes until the sugar has fully dissolved.
2. Thinly slice your red onion.
3. Put your onion into a medium mason jar or lidded container.
4. Pour your vinegar mix over your onions.
5. Fill your container with water until the onions are fully submerged in liquid.
6. Give your onions a good shake and then leave them in the fridge for at least 30 minutes. For the best results, though, let sit overnight.

Buns:

1. Rinse your rice under cold water for 3 to 5 minutes or until your water runs clear.
2. Pour your rice into a medium saucepan with your water. Bring to a boil over high heat and then reduce to a medium-low.
3. Cover and let cook for 20 to 25 minutes until your rice has fully cooked.
4. Once your sushi rice is done cooking, set aside for 30 to 40 minutes to cool while you prepare the rest of your dish.
5. Once your rice is cooled enough, lightly coat your hands in water to prevent the rice from sticking, and using about ¼-cup scoops of rice, roll it into a ball then smash it into a disk shape.
6. Heat a skillet over medium-high heat with your butter. Once your skillet is fully heated, place your rice disk into the pan and fry until golden and crispy on each side, about 3 to 5 minutes per side.

GRILLED GREEN ONIONS AND GLAZE:

1. In a medium-large bowl, mix together your soy sauce, water, sesame oil, honey, fish sauce, pinch of red pepper flakes, pinch of sesame seeds, and grated garlic.

2. Chop your bundle of green onions in half and let marinate for 15 to 20 minutes while you form your burger patties.

3. Once you are ready to grill your burgers, remove the green onions from the marinade and cook with the burgers for about 5 minutes, just until they start getting charred.

4. Once you have removed your green onions, whisk your cornstarch into the remaining marinade mixture until there are no more lumps.

5. Dump your sauce mix into a small saucepan and heat over medium-high heat until your sauce starts to thicken.

6. Let cook 2 to 3 minutes to get rid of any cornstarch flavor, then remove immediately from heat.

BURGER PATTY:

1. Divide your meat into 4 even pieces.

2. Trying not to overwork the meat, form each section into a thin disk where the middle is slightly thinner than the edges.

3. Heat a grill pan or skillet over medium-high heat until fully heated.

4. Generously salt and pepper one side of your disk, then place seasoned-side down on your grill pan.

5. Salt and pepper the other side of your patties. Let cook about 4 to 6 minutes on each side until they have nice grill marks and are fully cooked all the way through. If your meat is sticking to the pan, just keep letting it cook on that side and don't touch it. It will unstick once it is ready and fully cooked.

6. Once they are done, set aside to rest for 5 minutes.

ASSEMBLY:

After all parts are finished you are ready to assemble and enjoy.

CHAPTER THIRTY-FIVE
An Old Frenemy

Hi Journal,

I just have to write something down for a sec because Hutar said it's important to document these types of things. (Also Karn and I decided to travel back to The Bastion. It was easier with a friend.)

I was walking back to the guild after some shopping at the market, and I heard a voice calling out to me. Remember, Balador, the chef of the dubious "meal" I had when I visited the Rusty Dog so long ago? Donning his greasy apron, he flagged me down in the middle of the street, practically reeling in excitement to see me. I was pretty confused, and even more confused when he told me that he made some changes to the menu.

"Why?" I asked. He didn't seem interested before.

"Just come try it, please."

I sighed but ultimately agreed. I told myself that if he brought me there just to yell at me again, though, I was going to really give him a piece of my mind. I made sure to keep my back to the table I once shared with my friends and where we first met. How could I have forgotten? I felt sick to my stomach at the thought of it.

"Here you go," Balador grinned, placing a plate in front of me. "The meal."

Those two words alone made my stomach churn even more.

Although, this meal wasn't "<u>the</u> meal," it was still a weird pile of mush, but this time there were green sprigs and garnishes. It smelled somewhat aromatic and appetizing, so I dug my fork in and took a sniff. To my surprise, I could actually make out almost each separate ingredient.

"I hope you like it," Balador said, sitting across from me with a pleased huff. "I was upset about your suggestion when we first met, but then, uh, word started getting around about all those meals you made at the guild. I figured you probably knew what you were talking about or something. I even took a few cooking lessons."

"Oh," I said, half smiling.

Feeling a little better than I've felt in a long time, I dug in and took a brave bite of the meal. And guess what? Not bad! It wasn't the best, but it was <u>leagues</u> better than it used to be.

"Wow, Balador," I said, going in for another bite. "I'm actually really impressed."

His scruffy face lit up in glee.

"Wait, really?"

"Yeah!"

"Do you have any pointers?" he eagerly asked. "Any advice?"

I cleared my throat, pausing to think for a minute. Did I? The old me would have a million things to say, but what about this me? It felt like my mind was a wrinkly, forgotten book, and Balador just blew away a thick layer of dust.

"Hmm," I mused, a little nervous. "Chili flakes?"

He was delighted.

"I knew something was missing! Some spice!"

We sat and enjoyed the meal together, while we talked shop and I offered him a few more suggestions for the menu. By the end of the conversation, Balador reignited within me a deep love for food. I felt refreshed—not entirely back to normal—but it kind of felt like my brain just took a really good shower or had a day at the brain-spa.

All this to say, I finally figured out what to do with all that money from the king. I want to start making everybody happy with my food again, so I'm opening my very own tavern! I'm hoping this will help me rediscover my zest for life along the way.

I think I'll call it The CopperSpoon Inn and Tavern. Cozy and simple! I will need the perfect menu, too, so I guess its time to get back in the kitchen!

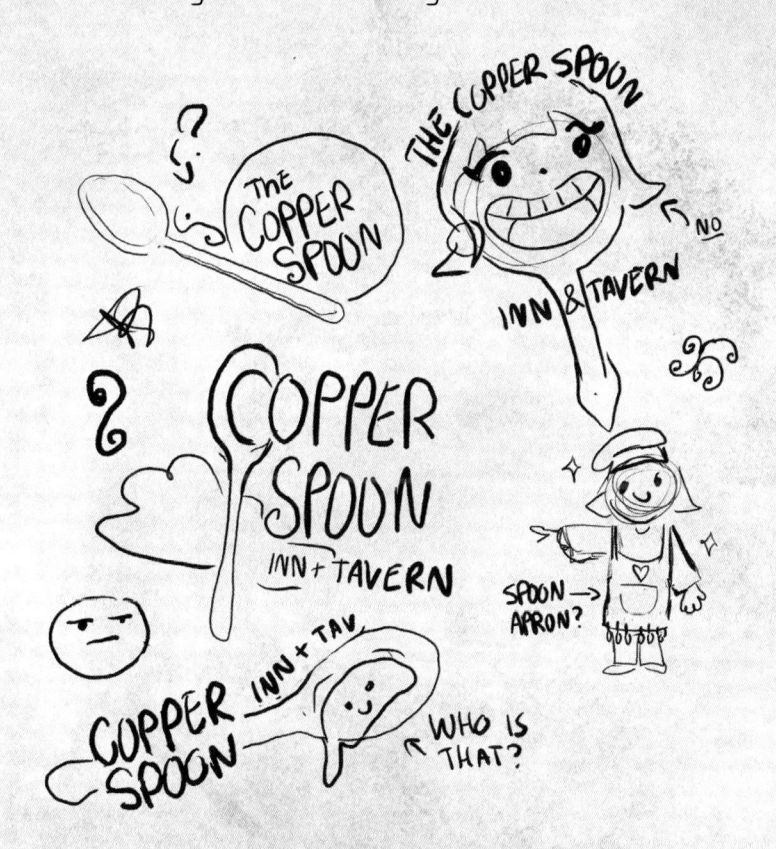

The Meal

I didn't think it right to <u>not</u> copy this recipe down. I followed Balador back to his kitchen and together we made "The Meal." It was a very simple concept, honestly: one pot, one spoon, one hearty dinner. He originally just threw everything in and let it cook, but I taught him to season each part, really crisp the bacon for some crunchy texture, and work in steps. By the end of our fun, Balador and I left friends.

Makes 4-6 servings

Prep time: 5-10 minutes | Cook time: 35-50 minutes

Ingredients

- 1½ heads fresh garlic
- 8-10 slices bacon
- 2-3 large chicken breasts
- Salt and pepper, to taste
- 2 teaspoons paprika
- 3 tablespoons butter
- 3½ cups heavy cream
- 2-4 cups chicken broth, divided
- 1 (16-oz) package pasta of your choice
- 1 cup shredded Parmesan cheese
- ¼ cup grated Parmesan cheese
- Fresh basil or parsley (optional)

Instructions

1. Finely mince your garlic, chop chicken into bite-sized pieces, and slice bacon.

2. In a 5-quart pot, cook your bacon over medium-high heat. Once crispy, remove from the pot and drain most of the oil.

3. Add your chicken to the pot with a big pinch of salt, pepper, and your paprika. Cook until the chicken is fully done and has started to form a golden-brown crust. Remove the chicken from the pot and set aside.

4. Lower the stovetop to medium heat. Add your butter to the pot and let it melt. Once melted, add in your garlic and cook until fragrant. Note: Garlic burns very easily, so make sure to move it around constantly and keep an eye on it.

5. Add your heavy cream and 2 cups of chicken broth to the garlic, then bring to a simmer. There should be small bubbles rising to the very edge of the pot but not a roiling boil.

6. Once your cream and broth are simmering, add in all of your pasta. Leave on a simmer until your pasta is fully cooked, stirring occasionally. The pasta will absorb the liquid as it cooks. If your pasta isn't fully cooked by the time most of your liquid is absorbed, add in more broth, ½ cup at a time, until the pasta is fully cooked through.

7. Once your pasta is cooked, remove from heat and slowly sprinkle in your cheese. Mix until fully melted.

8. Add your chicken and bacon back into the pot and mix until everything is thoroughly coated in the sauce.

9. Top with some fresh basil or parsley and enjoy.

Toadstool and Leaf Pockets

Now that I'm hanging out with the people at the guild a little bit more, I've been spending quite some time with Telfina. She taught me how to make homemade pasta, and we came up with this scrumptious filling to put inside! I had never known before but it turns out she <u>loves</u> cooking. While we rolled out the dough and mixed the filling she told me all about her days in the kitchen as a little girl cooking with her mom.

MAKES 2–4 SERVINGS

Prep time: 1–1½ hours | Cook time: 15–20 minutes

INGREDIENTS

PASTA:
2 cups flour
Pinch of salt
1 tablespoon olive oil
3 large eggs + 2 yolks

FILLING:
1 teaspoon rosemary
1 teaspoon thyme
1 small onion
1 (8-oz) package mushrooms
2 cups spinach
1 tablespoon butter
Salt and pepper, to taste
3 heads roasted garlic (see page 15)
1 (8-oz) package ricotta

ASSEMBLY:
1–2 eggs

SAUCE:
4–6 tablespoons butter
Fresh dill
1–2 lemons
½ cup fresh Parmesan cheese

INSTRUCTIONS

PASTA:

1. Pile your flour into a mound on a clean surface and mix in your salt.
2. Make a shallow well in your flour mix and add in your oil and eggs.
3. Start whisking the eggs and oil with a fork, slowly incorporating the flour into the wet mix.
4. Once your dough just starts to come together, knead it with your hands. Your dough will seem dry at first but

just keep kneading it. It should take approximately 5 to 7 minutes for it to form into a smooth ball.

5. Wrap your dough in plastic wrap and place it in a fridge while you prep the rest of your ingredients.

FILLING:

1. Mince rosemary, thyme, onion, and mushrooms, and roughly chop your spinach.
2. Heat a large pan over medium-high heat with your butter. Add in your onions and sauté until they just start to turn golden brown, about 5 to 6 minutes.
3. Once your onions are starting to caramelize, add in your herbs and mushrooms. Sauté for another 3 to 5 minutes until the mushrooms are soft.
4. Once your mushrooms are soft, add in your spinach and a pinch of salt and pepper. Cook 2 to 3 minutes until the spinach has just wilted.
5. Add your mushroom-spinach mix and your roasted garlic to your ricotta. Mix until fully combined, making sure to taste and see if it needs any extra salt or pepper.
6. Place your mixture in the fridge while you roll out your pasta.

ASSEMBLY:

1. Fill a medium-large pot of water with a generous pinch of salt. Bring to a boil over medium-high heat.
2. Remove your pasta dough from the fridge and cut into 4 even pieces. If you have a pasta roller you can roll it through your machine, but if not, hand roll your dough out into a long rectangle on a lightly floured surface until it is as thin as possible. You want it to be about 2 inches wide and almost transparent.
3. Once all of your dough has been rolled out, dollop about 1 tablespoon of your cheese mix onto one half of your dough in one-inch intervals.
4. Whisk your eggs in a small bowl and brush a small amount around the cheese mixture onto the dough.
5. Fold the dough over the filling and press together, making separate pockets with cheese inside.
6. Cut out your ravioli pieces with a sharp knife and gently press each side down with the back of a fork.

(Continued)

7. Gently place your ravioli into your boiling water. Boil for 5 to 6 minutes or until the ravioli starts to float in your water.

Sauce:
1. While your ravioli is boiling, heat your butter over high heat in a large pan. You want to heat your butter until it starts to turn golden brown.
2. Once your butter starts turning golden brown, add in your dill and lemon juice. Once it's browned (but not burnt), remove from the heat and set aside if your raviolis haven't finished cooking yet.
3. As soon as your ravioli is done cooking, move it to your brown butter mix with about ¼ cup of your pasta water.
4. Add in about half of your Parmesan and toss your ravioli in the sauce, making sure it gets fully coated.
5. Top with the remaining cheese and enjoy!

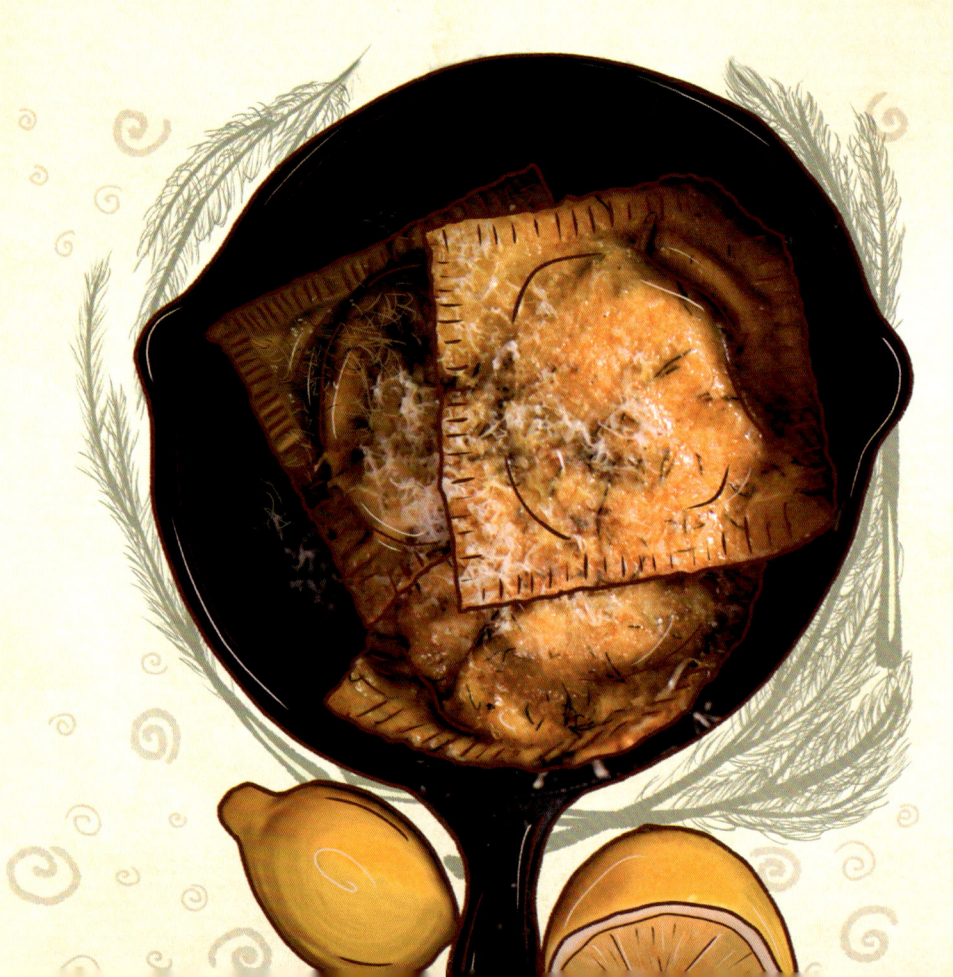

Broccoli and Dire Bull

Telfina told me in confidence that Hutar's favorite vegetable is broccoli, so I went to the market and picked up the broccoli as well as some dire bull they where selling at the butcher. I wanted to make him something to thank him for all he's done for me and the guild. I'm still on my lifelong mission to get him to like me. I will say that he did actually help me chop up a piece of broccoli or two after Telfina pretended she was too tired to help. We are really making some progress here.

Makes 6–8 servings

Prep time: 15–20 minutes | Cook time: 20–30 minutes

Ingredients

- 2 pounds flank steak
- 2 pounds broccoli florets
- 1–4 tablespoons water
- 1/3 cup soy sauce
- 2 tablespoons sesame oil
- 1/4 cup brown sugar
- 1 tablespoon minced garlic
- 1/2 teaspoon black pepper
- 2 tablespoons peanut oil (olive oil also works)
- 1 1/2 tablespoons cornstarch

Instructions

1. Note: The flavor of the beef intensifies if you marinate overnight, so if you wish to do so, complete steps 2 through 4 the day before.
2. Thinly slice your beef and cut your broccoli into florets if they are not already prepared. To easily get really thin slices of beef, cut with a sharp knife while beef is partially frozen.
3. Mix together your water, soy sauce, sesame oil, brown sugar, minced garlic, and black pepper in a small bowl. Start with a small amount of water and add more as needed.
4. In a medium bowl or plastic bag, coat your sliced beef with about 1/3 of your sauce mixture. Let marinate for at least 20 minutes or overnight.
5. Fill a medium pot with about 2 inches of water. You may use a steamer here or just add your broccoli

(Continued)

directly into the water. Bring the water to a simmer, add your broccoli, and cover the lid of your pot. Steam your broccoli until bright green and tender.

6. While your broccoli is steaming, heat a large pan or wok with your peanut oil over high heat. You want your pan to get very hot before adding in your beef.

7. Add your beef to your hot pan in about ⅓ batches to make sure you don't overcrowd the pan. You want to just cook this through. If your pan is hot enough, this should only take about 5 minutes per batch; it's ok if you need longer to cook the beef, though. Remove each batch from the pan before adding the next.

8. Add your cornstarch to the remaining sauce mix and whisk until smooth. There should be no chunks of cornstarch visible.

9. Once all batches of beef are fully cooked and removed from the pan, add your sauce mix to the pan and whisk constantly. Cook 2 to 3 minutes until thickened, then immediately add in your cooked beef and steamed broccoli.

10. Make sure all of the beef and broccoli is coated in sauce.

11. You can eat this with your favorite type of rice or just have it plain with some sesame seeds.

Farvenor's Autumn Harvest

I went back to visit my friends in Farvenor with the really cool butternut squash in all shapes and sizes. It was hard coming back, but I promised myself I would. This village was such a huge part of my story, so I didn't want to hide from it or its amazing people. I was given the warmest welcome upon my arrival. Maud, her grandchildren, and I came up with this recipe using a squash shaped like a star.

Makes 4–6 servings

Prep time: 25–30 minutes | Cook time: 1–1½ hours | Cool time: 30–60 minutes

Ingredients

Bread:
- 2 cups flour
- ½ teaspoon salt
- ½ teaspoon baking soda
- 1 teaspoon baking powder
- 1 tablespoon pumpkin pie spice
- ½ cup brown sugar
- ½ cup white sugar
- 1 cup puréed butternut squash or pumpkin
- ½ cup melted butter
- 2 eggs
- ¼ cup water

Cream Cheese Butter:
- ½ cup butter
- 1 (6-oz) package cream cheese

Spiced Caramel Drizzle:
- 1 cup brown sugar
- ½ cup butter
- 1 teaspoon pumpkin pie spice
- ½ cup heavy cream or half-and-half

French Toast:
- 3 eggs
- ½ cup heavy cream or half-and-half
- 1 tablespoon cinnamon
- 2–4 tablespoons brown sugar
- Sliced butternut squash bread

Instructions

Bread:

1. Preheat your oven to 350°F.

2. In a medium bowl, mix together your flour, salt, baking soda, baking powder, and pumpkin pie spice. Set aside for now.

3. In a large bowl, mix together all of your sugars, butternut squash, and melted butter.

(Continued)

4. Add in your eggs and water and mix until fully combined.
5. Once all of your wet ingredients are mixed, sift about half of your flour mixture into the wet ingredients.
6. Gently fold together your wet and dry ingredients until mostly combined.
7. Sift in the remaining dry mix and once again fold together until fully combined. You don't want to overmix, but make sure there are no dry spots left in your batter.
8. Lightly oil and flour a loaf baking dish before adding in your batter.
9. Bake for 40 to 50 minutes or until you can insert a toothpick to the center of the loaf and have it come out clean.
10. Let this cool completely and slice before using it for your French toast!

Cream Cheese Butter:
1. Soften your butter and cream cheese.
2. Whisk together until light and fluffy.

Spiced Caramel Drizzle:
1. Add your brown sugar, butter, and pumpkin spice to a medium-large pot. You will need a larger pan than you think.
2. Heat your brown sugar mix over medium-high heat until starts to bubble, stirring occasionally, then slowly add in your cream, mixing constantly.
3. Once cream is fully mixed in, let your caramel simmer for 5 to 7 minutes, stirring constantly until all of the sugar is melted.
4. Remove from heat and place in a heat-safe container to cool.

French Toast:
1. Heat a pan or griddle over medium heat with a small amount of butter.
2. In a shallow bowl or pie dish, whisk together your eggs, creamer, and cinnamon.
3. Place your slices of squash bread into the custard mix, soaking it on both sides for a couple seconds.
4. Immediately after soaking, place the slices on your warm griddle. You will know your French toast is ready to flip once it stops sticking to the griddle. This should take 5 to 10 minutes depending on your griddle heat. You can turn your heat up to a medium-high heat once you add the French toast to speed up the process a bit.

5. Flip your French toast and cook for another 2 to 3 minutes. The second time always takes a little less time than the first.

6. Once done, remove from your pan, top with all your fixings, and enjoy!

Baked Apple Cheese

Karn and I took a long vacation to his hometown in the mountains! His family is absolutely amazing. They remind me of my own, honestly. They surrounded themselves with love, family, raucous partying, and a bunch of good food. I fit right in! Plus, they have a <u>massive</u> supply of this ooey gooey delicious cheese hidden deep in a mountain cave. I don't think I ever want to leave!

MAKES 4-8 SERVINGS (DEPENDING ON HOW BIG YOUR WHEEL OF BRIE IS)

Prep time: 15-20 minutes | Cook time: 20-30 minutes

Ingredients

BAKED CHEESE:
Wheel of Brie cheese
1-2 apples
Bundle fresh sage
Bundle fresh basil
Drizzle olive oil
Drizzle honey
Salt and pepper, to taste

CROSTINI:
Baguette
Olive oil
Salt and pepper
1-2 cloves garlic (optional)

Instructions

BAKED CHEESE:

1. Preheat your oven to 350°F.
2. Score your wheel of cheese with a sharp knife. You want the cuts to be about an inch deep without cutting through the bottom of the cheese wheel. This cheese is very sticky, so it helps to have a glass of warm water nearby to rinse off your knife.
3. Thinly slice your apple. Do this by cutting off big sections around the core and then slicing those sections as thinly as possible.
4. Shove your apple slices into the scores you made in the cheese. This is a little difficult because the cheese is so gooey, but don't worry, this doesn't have to look pretty! Once your cheese is stuffed, place your brie into a cast iron or pie pan. You can now either surround your brie with the remaining apple slices or set them aside to use to dip later.

5. Thinly slice your sage and basil. Once sliced, sprinkle on top of your cheese wheel.
6. Drizzle your cheese with some olive oil, honey, salt, and pepper.
7. Finally, bake your cheese until it becomes bubbly, and the cheese begins to ooze. This should take about 15 to 20 minutes.

CROSTINI:
1. Preheat your oven to 425°F. (You can also bake these at the same time as your cheese on the bottom rack of your oven, but you may need to adjust your time for leaving the bread in the oven due to the higher temperature.)
2. Slice up your baguette into about ¼-inch slices. Thinner slices will be crispier, and thicker slices will end up chewier.
3. Lay out your bread slices on a large baking sheet. Brush or drizzle each piece of bread with a small amount of olive oil.
4. Sprinkle your bread with salt and pepper, then place in your preheated oven.
5. Bake your bread slices until they just begin turning golden brown around the edges. This should take 5 to 10 minutes, but make sure you keep an eye on them because they can burn fairly easily. This may take longer if you bake at the same time as your cheese.
6. You can also rub each piece of toast with a clove of garlic right as they come out of the oven for added flavor.
7. Serve your cheese with your crostini and your favorite dried meats or fresh fruits. I personally like it best with prosciutto and jam! I shared this one with Karn, but I really wish the rest of the gang was here to help eat this, too.

CHAPTER THIRTY-SIX

The CopperSpoon Inn & Tavern

Dear Journal,

    Well, it's finally happening! I found the perfect plot of land right around the corner from the guild. Turns out an old apothecary burned down, and they just decided to rebuild elsewhere (no one was hurt though, thank goodness!).

    I forked over the big bucks to get the builders to work as quickly as they could, and soon enough the tavern came to life right before my eyes!

    A delightful combination of the comforts of Honeystar and the big-city vibes of The Violet Bastion (just like me!), the building is a cozy, two-story structure with big windows, white bricks, and the cutest giant copper spoon above the front entrance. The white walls are adorned with wide, warm, brown wooden beams, which are accented by orange shingles that randomly alternate in the color of autumn leaves. There's also a big wrap-around deck with a decent-sized seating area for when the weather's nice.

    I really wanted to combine functionality and comfort on the inside, so the main features are two curved, double staircases, which lead to a landing where people can lounge around on cozy furniture in front of a roaring fireplace. The main floor has several dark wooden tables, the legs and chairs are carved with designs inspired by the many recipes and many adventures I had. The cutlery is, you guessed it, copper, which matches little details and decals on the plates and cups. I also made sure to commission several beautiful paintings by local artists that I've hung on the walls. Some are landscapes of the fire realm, some are portraits of cute little creatures we saw in the woods, and one's even of me in a big chef's hat!

Oh, and the kitchen, don't even get me started! It's state of the art, and there's so much room for me to cook and store every ingredient I could ever imagine. If I can find a wizard that's interested, I'd love to magically link one of the cupboards up to my family's spice cupboard one day so that they can have access to <u>my</u> spices, too!

All in all, this place is my sanctuary. It's all about warmth, happy vibes, and good food. It's all about home!

On opening night, there was a huge crowd out front. I was so happy to see everybody, but I couldn't help but scan each of their faces in hopes I might see a few people in particular. I had sent a letter to Irabel and Finheld letting them know about the tavern's grand opening. Irabel responded immediately and said she would try, but didn't know if she could make it. Then she went on about all her travels in distant lands. Finheld never responded. A little piece of my heart broke when I didn't spot Irabel or Finheld. I fidgeted with the ring that Irabel gave me. I always kept it on, no matter what. And it was always cold.

At least Karn was there, though! He showed up early, actually, to help me get the tavern ready for the biggest day in our lives.

Hutar and Telfina were the very first in line. They were dressed up in their fanciest clothes. Hutar even had a little bowtie around his neck! I shook their hands as professionally as I could, since I'm an important business owner now.

"Thank you for coming."

Telfina grinned.

"We wouldn't miss it for the world."

Hutar cleared his throat, awkwardly looking at the tavern.

"Uh, looks good, Cob."

"Thank you, I'm really happy with how it turned out. I couldn't have done it without you guys, though!"

"We have a surprise for you," Telfina said, waving a small group of five guild members over.

"Oh?"

Hutar nodded, and I could have sworn his green cheeks were flushing red.

"We're, uh, really proud of you—amazed at how far you've come, really. As a gift for your perseverance, we've hired a few mages to give you something special."

"<u>Oh</u>?" I asked, I couldn't wait to see what they had in store.

The mages conjured shimmering magic in shades of purple, white, gold, and green, and with a few choice words, my tavern was enveloped in sparkles and light. The wood groaned, the earth crumbled, and The CopperSpoon Inn and Tavern stood up about a whole foot! Thousands of tiny legs sprouted from the foundations, which swirled with magic and color!

"<u>Huh?!</u>" I gasped.

"We know how much you miss traveling, Cob, so we thought why not give you the ability to take your tavern with you?" Telfina smiled.

One of the mages, Antonio, leaned forward, scratching his mustache.

"When you're ready to settle, the legs should completely hide away at your command."

I grinned. "Tavern, sit!"

And with a surprising amount of grace, my tavern crossed its thousands of legs and sunk back into the earth like it had never moved in the first place. Well, Hutar, Telfina, and the mages were overdue for the biggest hug in the world, and I wasn't going to keep them waiting. My heart has never felt fuller. This was the best gift I've ever received! I couldn't wait to one day take this show on the road!

"Hey Cob," I heard Karn's voice ring out from behind me as I squeezed Telfina one last time. "I got one more thing for ya."

"Another surprise?" I exclaimed as I turned to look at him. "I don't know if my heart can handle many more—"

My words were cut off when at least eight sets of arms tackled me at once.

"Cob!" I heard my mother's voice ring out.

"Mom?"

Tears began welling up in my eyes as I realized what was happening.

"I'm so proud of you, Sweetie!"

For the first time in years, I felt the warm embrace of my family. I couldn't think of a better way to spend my first night as a tavern owner.

Roasted Thunderbird Thighs with Zucchini and Squash

Karn went out and hunted me thunderbird as a specialty ingredient just for the opening night menu! He is so amazing. I am so grateful to have him around.

P.S.: Its so weird seeing my recipes displayed on a menu!

Makes 4 servings

Prep time: 10-15 minutes | Cook time: 20-30 minutes

Ingredients

Roasted Chicken Thighs:
- 4 bone-in, skin-on thunderbird thighs (can replace with chicken)
- 1-2 tablespoons olive oil
- Salt and pepper
- Garlic powder
- Onion powder
- Italian seasoning
- Paprika

Zucchini and Squash:
- 2 zucchini
- 2 yellow squashes
- ½ large yellow onion
- 4-5 cloves garlic
- 1 teaspoon fresh rosemary
- 1 teaspoon fresh thyme
- 1 teaspoon lemon zest
- 1 tablespoon olive oil
- 2 teaspoons salt
- 1 tablespoon pepper
- 2 teaspoons paprika

If making these two recipes together, just bake them on the same baking sheet!

Instructions

Roasted Chicken Thighs:

1. Preheat the oven to 425°F.
2. Place each thunderbird thigh, skin-side up in a cast iron or oven-safe pan. Drizzle them with your olive oil.
3. Evenly coat thunderbird thighs in salt, pepper, garlic powder, onion powder, Italian herbs, and paprika.
4. Bake for 20 to 25 minutes or until your thunderbird has reached an internal temperature of 165°F.
5. Let your thunderbird rest for 10 to 15 minutes then enjoy!

(Continued)

ZUCCHINI AND SQUASH:

1. Preheat the oven to 425°F.
2. Dice your zucchini, squash, and yellow onions into even, bite-sized pieces. Mince your garlic and fresh herbs and zest your lemon.
3. In a large bowl, toss your vegetables in your olive oil, lemon zest, salt, pepper, paprika, fresh herbs, and minced garlic.
4. Spread out evenly on a large baking dish covered in parchment paper. Bake until golden brown and roasted, about 15 to 20 minutes, tossing your vegetables once about 10 minutes into the cooking process.
5. Enjoy!

Wanderer's Savory Porridge

I did a lot of research when creating this menu and I deduced that this was the perfect hearty recipe for people who have a hard time chewing! No matter who you are, you will find a meal here at The CopperSpoon!

Makes 4-6 servings

Prep time: 10-15 minutes | Cook time: 1-1½ hours

Ingredients

- 4–5 cups chicken broth
- Bundle thyme sprigs
- 1 large yellow onion
- 4–5 cloves garlic
- 3 tablespoons butter
- 3 tablespoons olive oil
- Salt and pepper
- 1½ cups Arborio rice
- 1 cup shredded Parmesan cheese

Instructions

1. Heat a small saucepan over medium heat with your chicken broth and thyme.
2. Slice your onions and mince your garlic.
3. In a large Dutch oven or saucepan with a lid, heat your butter and olive oil over medium heat. Add in your onions and minced garlic with a small pinch of salt and pepper. Sauté, stirring frequently until your onions are a deep golden color, about 30 to 45 minutes.
4. Remove half of your onions from your pan and add in your rice. Cook until rice is lightly toasted and starts smelling fragrant, about 3 to 5 minutes.
5. Reduce your heat to medium. Using a ladle, scoop about 1 cup of your warm chicken broth over your rice. Cook, stirring constantly, until the rice has mostly absorbed the broth, about 5 to 10 minutes.

(Continued)

6. Repeat the above step until all the broth has been absorbed and the rice is fully cooked. Make sure you are stirring constantly. If all the liquid has been absorbed and the rice is still not cooked, add in warm water ½ cup at a time until the rice is fully cooked. This process should take 30 to 45 minutes.

7. Once the rice is fully cooked, mix in all of your cheese. Top with extra cheese and leftover onion mix.

8. Enjoy!

Twinebrush Onion Soup

When creating the menu for opening night, I knew I wanted to include ingredients from some of my travels. This one was inspired by Twinebrush and their onions! If only there was another unicorn for me to get some more of that magic fruit from. Now, <u>that</u> would really put this place on the map!

MAKES 4-6 SERVINGS

Prep time: 10-15 minutes | Cook time: 1-1½ hours

INGREDIENTS

- 3½ pounds sweet onions
- 4 teaspoons butter
- 2-3 teaspoons salt
- 1 cup white wine
- 2 tablespoons bourbon
- 6 cups beef broth
- Bundle thyme sprigs
- ½ cup shredded Gruyère cheese
- ½ cup shredded mozzarella cheese
- Baguette
- Olive oil
- 2-3 teaspoons salt
- 1 clove garlic

INSTRUCTIONS

1. Slice all of your onions (it's going to seem like a lot, but trust the process).

2. In a large 5- to 6-quart pot or Dutch oven, melt your butter over medium-high heat. Once the butter is melted, add in all of your onions at once. This should fill up most of the pot.

3. Add all of your salt to the onions and mix around in the pot. The salt will draw moisture out of the onions, helping them cook down. Sauté the onions until they are a nice, golden brown and there is no more liquid in the bottom of the pan. The onions will only fill about ⅕ of the pan by the time the cooking process is done. This will take 45 to 60 minutes minimum.

4. Once the onions are fully browned, add in your wine and bourbon. Cook until the liquid is reduced by half. Add in beef broth and thyme and bring to a boil. Once boiling, reduce the soup down to a simmer and leave for at least 15 minutes, removing your bundle of thyme when you are ready to serve up.

(Continued)

5. While the soup is boiling, shred both of your cheeses and prepare your bread croutons.

6. There are two ways you can eat this soup, so first you need to figure out if you want to dip your bread or if you want to soak your bread in the soup (or if you want to do both).

Soaked Bread:

1. Cut your baguette into thin slices. Drizzle with olive oil, a little bit of salt and pepper, and broil just until the edges of the bread are golden brown. This does not take long so keep an eye on them.

2. Once out of the oven, take your clove of garlic and rub it on the warm bread.

3. To assemble, fill an oven-safe bowl with your desired amount of soup. Place 2 of your croutons on the top and cover with a mixture of your cheeses.

4. Broil, just until the cheese is ooey and gooey, and starts to get a little golden brown on the top.

Dipping Bread: (Great when you don't have oven-safe bowls)

1. Cut your baguette in half lengthwise. Drizzle with olive oil, a little bit of salt and pepper, and broil just until the edges of the bread are golden brown. This does not take long, so keep an eye on them.

2. Once out of the oven, take your clove of garlic and rub it on the warm bread.

3. Take your cheese and sprinkle it over all of your bread. Broil again until the cheese is nice and melted.

4. Dish yourself up a bowl of soup and enjoy!

Baklava in Bloom

While developing my menu I did some international traveling for the very first time! It's springtime in the country of Lilimere, and I spent a day at their yearly flower festival. There were so many colors, and petals floated from the sky on every street in the city. It was so beautiful! I'm really happy I made the trip and managed to collect enough lavender and rose buds to make something super special for dessert.

MAKES 24-30 SERVINGS

Prep time: 1-1½ hours | Cook time: 35-45 minutes | Cool time: 1-2 hours

Ingredients

- 2 cups shelled pistachios
- ¼ cup brown sugar
- 1-2 tablespoons dried lavender
- 1½-2 cups melted butter
- 1 (16-oz) package phyllo dough, thawed
- 1 teaspoon coriander

Syrup:
- 1 cup honey
- 1 cup water
- ¾ cup sugar
- ¼ cup dried rose buds
- Orange Peel (2 long strips or 1 tablespoon zest)
- 1 lemon

Instructions

1. **Important Note:** Before you begin, make sure your phyllo dough is fully thawed in the fridge the day before you plan to use it.

2. Add all ingredients for your syrup to a medium saucepan. Cook over medium-high heat until the mixture has come to a boil.

3. Once boiling, reduce the heat to medium-low and let simmer for 25 to 30 minutes, stirring occasionally.

4. After the syrup is done simmering, it should be a deep golden color. Strain out all of the rose buds and orange peel, then set aside. Let cool at room temperature while you assemble and bake your baklava.

(Continued)

5. Chop up all of your pistachios and mix with your brown sugar, lavender, and coriander. If you have whole dried lavender, make sure to crush it up into a fine powder before adding it to the mixture.

6. Preheat your oven to 350°F.

7. For the next step you will need to set up your assembly station. For a thicker baklava, use an 8 × 8-inch pan, for a thinner one use a 9 × 13-inch pan. Make sure your butter is melted and nearby with a pastry brush. Gently roll your phyllo dough nearby and have your nut mixture on hand. To prevent your phyllo dough from drying out while you are working, place a damp paper towel over the dough.

8. Brush a thin layer of your melted butter on the bottom of your pan. Add one sheet of your phyllo dough to the bottom of the pan. Brush that layer with butter before adding the next. If you are using a smaller pan, you can cut the phyllo dough in half first, or just fold the sheet over itself making sure to add a butter layer between the fold. Repeat this step until you have used about 1/3 of your phyllo dough.

9. Once you have layered 1/3 of the phyllo dough, brush the top with butter then add half of your nut mixture to this layer.

10. Repeat steps 8 and 9 until all of your dough and nuts are used up. If you run out of butter at any step, just melt some more and keep layering. Make sure to add butter to the very top layer as well.

11. Using a pastry cutter or sharp knife, cut your baklava into bite-sized pieces.

12. Bake for 35 to 45 minutes or until the baklava is a deep golden brown.

13. Pour your syrup mix over the Baklava immediately once it comes out of the oven. Let sit for at least 1 hour but ideally overnight at room temperature. The longer it soaks, the better.

14. Garnish with chopped up pistachios, and enjoy!

Sea Dragon and Noodle Stew

Did I mention I wanted to use ingredients from my travels already? Well, these sea dragons where the perfect option for opening night! I had them delivered fresh from Marlin's Shore and I think it will make for a perfect opening night entrée!

MAKES 6-8 SERVINGS

Prep time: 10-15 minutes | Cook time: 25-40 minutes

INGREDIENTS

- 2 pounds sea dragon (shrimp)
- 1 tablespoon creole seasoning
- 3-4 large cloves garlic
- 1 large shallot
- Bundle parsley
- 5-6 green onions (greens only)
- 1 (16-oz) package pasta of your choice
- ½ cup butter
- ½ cup white wine
- 1 (16-oz) carton heavy cream
- 1 cup Parmesan cheese
- 1 lemon

Instructions

1. Deshell and devein your sea dragon, if needed. Once your sea dragon has been prepped, coat them with about half of your creole seasoning.

2. Crush your garlic cloves, chop your shallot, and roughly chop your parsley and green onions.

3. Bring a medium pot of water to a boil with a pinch of salt. Once your water is boiling, add in your pasta. Cook until *al dente*, about 10 to 12 minutes. Reserve about 1 cup of your pasta water then strain and set aside until your sauce is done.

4. In a large pan or cast iron, melt your butter.

5. Add your crushed garlic to your melted butter and sauté over high heat until the garlic and butter start to turn a golden-brown color, should take 1 to 2 minutes. Once they start to turn golden, immediately reduce the heat to medium and remove your garlic from the pan.

(Continued)

6. After removing your garlic, add in your sea dragon, shallots, and white wine. Cook on medium-high until your sea dragon is cooked completely. Once your sea dragon is fully cooked, remove from the pan.

7. There will be a thin sauce left behind from your sea dragon. Cook this down for 2 to 3 minutes until it has reduced by about half.

8. Once the pan drippings have reduced, add in your heavy cream and pasta. Make sure everything is nice and coated in the cream before moving on.

9. Add in your fresh parsley, green onions, remaining creole seasoning, Parmesan cheese, the juice of your lemon, and about ¼ cup of your pasta water.

10. Mix everything together thoroughly. The sauce will look very thin at this point, but the longer it sits and cools, the thicker it will get.

11. Top with Parmesan cheese and parsley and enjoy! Don't forget to whip up some garlic bread too to soak up that sauce.

The Copper Shepherd

Tonight's special menu item! The Copper Shepherd! I hung out at the guild hall enough to know what my people like, and that's meat and potatoes! I hope they love this humble little dish inspired by them.

MAKES 4–6 SERVINGS

Prep time: 10–15 minutes | Cook time: 1½–2 hours

INGREDIENTS

STEW:
- 1–1½ pounds cubed stew beef (pre-cut at local butcher or use tri-tip)
- 1 large onion
- 1 teaspoon basil
- 1 teaspoon oregano
- Bundles fresh sage, rosemary, and thyme
- 1 tablespoon minced garlic
- 2 bay leaves
- 1 tablespoon olive oil
- ¼ cup dwarven whiskey (or dark liquor of your choice) or red wine
- 1 teaspoon salt
- 1 teaspoon white pepper (optional)
- 1 tablespoon paprika
- 1 teaspoon ground mustard
- 1 teaspoon coriander
- 1 cup beef broth
- 2 teaspoons Worcestershire
- 4 tablespoons milk
- 2 tablespoons flour

MASHED POTATOES:
- 3–4 large russet potatoes
- ½ cup Roasted Garlic Butter (see page 16)
- Salt and pepper, to taste
- ½–1 cup milk
- 3 tablespoons sour cream
- ½ cup Gruyère cheese, grated
- ½ cup mozzarella, grated

TOPPING:
- ¼ cup grated Gruyère
- ¼ cup grated mozzarella

INSTRUCTIONS

1. Prep your roasted garlic for garlic butter first. See page 16.
2. Cube your steak, dice your onions, mince your fresh herbs, and peel and dice your potatoes.

(Continued)

3. Heat a 5-quart or larger pot over medium-high heat with 1 tablespoon of olive oil in it. Once spitting hot add in half of your cubed meat. Sear until it gets golden brown and is fully cooked through. The steak will start to release juices, just keep cooking until all of the liquid is gone. Repeat this process until all of your meat is cooked. Set aside for now.

4. Add your onions and garlic into the pot you cooked your meat in. Sauté until translucent and fragrant, about 5 to 10 minutes. Add your whiskey or red wine to the onions to deglaze the pan and cook the onions evenly. Make sure to scrape the browned beef leftovers from the bottom of the pan and incorporate it into the onions. If your pan looks super dry when you add your onions, add a touch of extra olive oil beforehand.

5. Once the onion and garlic are fully cooked, add all of your steak back in and then add your salt, pepper, paprika, ground mustard, basil, oregano, and coriander. Make sure everything is evenly coated in the seasonings.

6. Add your beef broth, Worcestershire, sage, thyme, and rosemary. Bring to a boil, reduce your heat to medium/medium-low so it's simmering, then cover and leave for at least an hour. The longer you let this cook, the more tender the meat will become.

7. Fill a medium-large pot ¾ of the way with water and a big pinch of salt, then bring to a boil.

8. Add all of your potatoes and boil until soft and tender, which should take about 30 to 40 minutes.

9. While your potatoes are boiling, make your garlic butter.

10. Strain your potatoes once fully cooked, then place back in the pan. Start with a small amount of each, add in your garlic butter, half your cheese, sour cream, and milk. You can always add more but you can't take anything away. Taste as you go and make them the way you like them.

11. Once your mashed potatoes are done, it's time to finish the stew. Remove the bay leaves and fresh herbs. In a small bowl, mix your milk and flour until it is a smooth consistency, then pour into your beef mixture, stirring until it's thoroughly combined. Bring to a

boil and cook for 2 to 3 minutes until the consistency is nice and thick.

12. In an oven-safe bowl, add a large spoonful of your potatoes to the bottom of the bowl and then layer some of your stew over the top. Top with cheese and put under a broiler until your cheese is nice and melted (3 to 5 minutes).

13. Enjoy!

CHAPTER THIRTY-SEVEN
And Then There Were Five

Journal,

    My life has changed significantly since we last spoke—I'm not just a bard who owns a cool tavern with legs; I'm an actual business owner! A pretty dang successful one, too. I've served meals and collected stories from the Wildflower Plains all the way to the Frostcreep Tundra. I've served nobles, creatures of all kinds, and I even had a demigod stay at the inn a time or two. If you told me that any of this was possible when I first left Honeystar—or even after the party disbanded—I might have never believed you.

    But something was still missing. Then one day, I found it! And it was the most wonderful day in a very, <u>very</u> long time.

    I recently took the tavern back to The Violet Bastion. Not only did I have a big shipment of fancy cheeses being delivered, but I thought it would be nice to visit the guild for the first time in a few months. I settled the tavern down for the day on my typical plot, and about ten minutes later I had a visitor: a little blue courier pigeon tapping on my window with its beak.

    This wasn't unusual, but the letter wrapped around its leg was.

    It was from <u>Finheld</u>.

    When I scanned the letter and saw his name scrawled at the bottom, I felt a pit in my stomach. You know that feeling you get when you're walking through the dark and you miss a step? Or when your foot finds an unexpected divot in the earth, and it's like your whole world has just been turned upside-down? That's what I felt. Nausea, fear, anxiety, betrayal.

    I replayed our last conversation over and over in my mind—was he writing just to blame me again for everything that happened when we vanquished The Eternal Malice? I almost didn't even want to know. At first, I was tempted to throw the letter into the fireplace, but I couldn't bring myself to do it. I'd forever wonder about its contents. So, gritting my teeth, I began to read.

The letter was only a few sentences and didn't say much; Finheld was in town for a day or two and he had something urgent to discuss with me. He'd heard all about The CopperSpoon, and he thinks that it would be best to meet here—preferably that same night, just as long as we could do it privately.

I really didn't know what to think. Did I even <u>want</u> to deal with the public's disappointment if I kept the tavern closed for the night? My better judgement said "no," but something in my heart, something that I thought had long since dwindled felt otherwise. I sent my reply with the same pigeon and hoped it would reach him safe and sound.

After turning away hordes of customers into the night—to the point where I had to get an obviously illusory version of myself to sit out front and tell them we were closed, I finally got a knock on my door. My stomach lurched in anxiety, but as I reached for the door, I noticed one of my favorite rings was unexpectedly warm. <u>Irabel</u>?

Sure enough, there she was, standing there with a lush purple leather satchel swung over her shoulder.

"Hey, Cob!"

"Irabel!" I gave her a hug, which she happily returned. "You came all the way from the Dreadfern jungle?! It's been forever, how are you?"

"Same old, same old. Nothing's really changed since my last letter."

Irabel and I had been writing every few months for quite some time. Most recently she'd been having some troubles on some supernatural research she was doing with the aid of a small group of traveling monks.

"Well, why don't you refresh my memory over something to eat?" I was actually pretty relieved that she randomly showed up; this way I wouldn't have to deal with Finheld on my own. "I actually have something kind of weird to tell you, have a seat—"

Then there was another knock at the door.

"Oooh, a customer." Irabel smiled. "Should I tell them to go away? By the way, why is the Inn closed?"

I sighed, ignoring the steadily growing sick feeling in my guts. It was time.

"That's what I wanted to tell you, actually. Finheld's coming."

The happy look on Irabel's face turned to pure rage. "<u>Seriously</u>?"

"It's okay, though . . . I <u>think</u>," I found myself putting on a hopeful, probably obviously fake smile. "Yeah, it'll be okay. I'll get the door."

Well, I swung that thing open as casually as I could, only to come face to face with Karn. I hadn't seen him in months! His family's cheese cave had been robbed of some of its stores, so he went home to help them relocate.

"There ya are, ya little rascal!"

Karn's voice was boisterous and loud. He wrapped me up in one of his tight bear hugs and I allowed myself to remember just how much I missed them.

"How are ya doin'?" he asked.

"I'm good!" I laughed, "Irabel's here, too. What odd timing."

"Irabel, you scamp!" he greeted her in the very same way, although she was much tenser when receiving her hug.

"Hey, Karn," she laughed, gently wiggling from his grasp. "This is so weird."

Weird, but probably in the best way possible.

"Karn, come have a seat I was just about to make something for Irabel and I."

"Ooooh, let's have some o' that famous CopperSpoon cookin'." Karn laughed as we made our way to a table. "And you can tell me all about those weird bears."

I stopped in my tracks. "Weird bears?"

"Yeah, you sent me that letter askin' me tae help you with a micro-bear infestation."

<u>Micro-bears</u>? I had never even heard of micro-bears, let alone seen one in my tavern. The even stranger part is, Irabel said that she got a letter where I asked her to come look at a haunted amulet that someone gave me in exchange for one of my recipes. I didn't ask them to do either of these things!

"You don't think . . . you don't think Finheld sent—"

That was when there was a final knock at the door. We froze, exchanging silent glances of confusion. I steadied myself, expecting the worst when I opened the front door.

There was Finheld, a shabby little hat in hand, looking just about the same as they did when I last saw them. Healthier, though, much healthier.

"Cob?" Their eyes lit up in relief.

"Hey, Finheld," I said, awkwardly twisting the ties on my apron. What was I supposed to say? What was I supposed to do with my hands?

"Can I come in?"

Could they? I suppose I agreed to let them visit, but now that it was real, I wasn't quite sure how I felt. I wouldn't be able to forgive myself if I didn't hear them out, though. So, I opened the door a little wider and allowed them inside.

Before they could even pass the threshold, Irabel chewed into Finheld.

"How dare you just show up, you—"

A long string of insults ensued. She even changed languages a few times, giving them a piece of her mind in every way she could. Finheld hung his head low. Karn and I exchanged glances, trying to hide the smiles creeping to our faces in this very serious moment. I had missed Irabel's feistiness.

"So, tell us, why <u>are</u> you here? What could you possibly have to say to us?" Irabel finally finished.

"I deserved that."

Irabel scoffed then turned her back to Finheld, taking a seat at the table.

"I came to say . . . I came to say that I'm sorry."

I was shocked. I always knew Finheld had a good heart, but it was so hard to find it sometimes. In the year I had known them, I don't remember them once apologizing. To anyone.

"What I did, how I acted, what I said. It was wrong. It was so, so wrong." Finheld crouched down and finally met my eyes. For the first time, I could see tears welling up in their eyes.

"Cob, I am so sorry. What happened was not your fault. I <u>loved</u> Harold—"

"So did we!" Irabel interrupted from across the room.

"I know you did. When he was gone, it felt like part of my soul was ripped from my body and I was so caught up in the pain I just. . . forgot that the rest of you loved him too. I'm so sorry."

I looked to Karn and Irabel for some sort of direction. I didn't know how to feel, didn't know what to think. Irabel was glaring daggers, arms crossed in front of her chest. To her, Finheld's words seemed to hold little weight. Karn, on the other hand, wore a different expression. It was one of sadness, but also one of understanding.

"I'm not trying to make excuses. I know that's probably what it sounds like, but I promise it's not. I very quickly realized I had nobody. I had no friends, no family, no home. For a long time, I felt sorry for myself until one day I finally realized. I <u>had</u> a home. I <u>had</u> a family. And I threw it all away."

Tears welled in their eyes and began to fall, and I could feel the dampness on my cheeks that matched his.

"You think <u>we</u> were your family?"

"I know you were. I am so sorry I didn't treat you like it. I could never ask your forgiveness. But I would love the chance to try to make things right."

I heaved a sigh, and with it drifted away the weight of the world.

"You owe me a <u>lot</u> of batches of dishes."

The twisted look of fear and shame broke in that moment as Finheld let out a weak laugh.

"I will do your dishes for the rest of my life!"

I stepped forward and wrapped them in a big hug. After a moment of tension, Finheld melted into the grasp. It wasn't long before I felt the muscular arms of Karn wrap up the both of us, giving us a good shake as he did. Irabel circled around Finny's back and placed her hand on mine.

"<u>Thank you</u>," I mouthed at her silently.

She gestured to Finheld then dragged a claw in front of her throat insinuating she was willing to do what needed to be done if I wanted. I giggled at the offer and we shared a smile.

"Alright, who's hungry?" I asked.

Everybody followed me back to the kitchen. Karn helped me chop and watched over the sauce. We decided on pasta for dinner, so I began to prep the tomatoes and cheese and noodles. I made a nice salad to go on the side and a berry crumble for dessert.

Finheld was on dish-duty of course and Irabel made sure to hover closely. Watching her torment them, glass of wine in hand, reminded me of the old days when they would constantly bicker. I couldn't help but notice the genuine smile on Finheld's face as they took jab after jab from her.

The food was done before long. We set the table with plates and forks, but decided to just bring out all the food to serve family style.

"Alright, everybody! Dig in!"

"Actually," Finheld interupted as hands began reaching for serving spoons. "I have something I want to show you guys first."

Finheld shoved their hands into their pockets and began digging around for something.

"This better be good," Irabel jabbed.

After some excavating, Finheld pulled out a couple items. One was a small, rounded gemstone that glowed the shade of amber honey, another a spell scroll, and the last was a holy symbol to Helirion. Memories of Harold rushed back to me at the sight of it.

"So do you guys remember when we were doing research on the beacons and Harold mentioned a spell that could temporarily bring back your loved ones?"

Karn, Irabel, and I exchanged a confused glance.

"Well, I thought maybe we could share one last night together."

The room was silent for a moment as we all processed what Finheld was suggesting. Do they mean bring Harold back? Like right now?

"If that's alright with you guys of course, we don't have—"

"Yes," It was Irabel who softly placed her hand on Finheld's. There was no malice or sarcasm in her voice as she spoke. "That would be very nice."

Finheld smiled at Irabel before taking a deep breath. They got up from the table and placed the scroll on the ground. Nerves coursed through me as I watched.

What if it didn't work? What if it did? What if—

A bright light erupted in the room before I even realized Finheld was casting the spell. I had to squeeze my eyes closed to keep from being blinded.

As I slowly opened my eyes, there, standing in the middle of my tavern, was Harold. There was a moment of silence as we all stared. Nobody knew what to say. Was this really him? Was this just a parlor trick? Was he really here?

"Hello friends," Harold's voice rang through our ears like a song long forgotten.

Noise erupted as chairs scraped against floorboards and sobs rang out. All of us tackled our friend to the groud in the biggest, longest group hug imaginable.

It was really him.

For one night only, at The CopperSpoon Inn and Tavern, The Tag-alongs were whole again. "Well," I spoke up when we finally stepped away from our overdue embrace. "Who's hungry?"

Cheesy Vine Fruit Manicotti

It's so unbelievably awesome to have The Tag-Alongs back together again, even if it's only for the night. I really hope we all keep in touch from now on! This is the perfect meal to share with friends.

MAKES 4-6 SERVINGS

Prep time: 35-50 minutes | Meal time: 1-1½ hours

Ingredients

- 2-3 heads roasted garlic (see page 15)
- 1 large onion
- 2 tablespoons basil
- 2 tablespoons fresh thyme, divided
- 2 tablespoons fresh rosemary, divided
- 1 teaspoon red pepper flakes
- 1 teaspoon coriander
- 1 tablespoon paprika
- 1 pound ground beef
- ¼ cup tomato paste
- 1 cup beef broth
- ¼ cup red wine
- 1 (28-oz) can diced or whole tomatoes
- 1 tablespoon sugar
- 1 tablespoon Worcestershire
- Salt and pepper, to taste (start with 1 teaspoon)
- 1 (16-oz) box manicotti noodles ¾ cup Parmesan cheese, divided
- 1 cup mozzarella shredded cheese, divided
- 1 (8-oz) package ricotta

Instructions

1. Start by roasting your 2 heads of garlic for the cheese filling (see page 15).

2. While the garlic is roasting, start prepping everything for the sauce. Dice your onion into small pieces and mince all of your herbs. Reserve half of your herbs for the cheese filling at this point, making sure to keep them separated.

3. Once everything is prepped, heat your Dutch oven or 6-quart pot over medium-high heat with a tablespoon of olive oil in the bottom. Add all of your ground beef and cook fully with a pinch of salt and pepper.

(Continued)

4. Once your beef is fully cooked, remove from the pan and add all of your onions and garlic. Cook until the onions are translucent and the garlic is fragrant. Be sure to stir frequently because garlic tends to burn easily.

5. Once cooked thoroughly, add in half your rosemary and thyme, then your red pepper flakes, coriander, basil, and paprika, and tomato paste. Cook for 2 to 3 minutes, stirring constantly so it doesn't burn.

6. After 2 to 3 minutes, add in beef broth and red wine. Bring to a boil and cook for about 5 minutes.

7. Add in diced tomatoes, sugar, Worcestershire, salt, and pepper.

8. Bring to a boil, reduce the heat to medium-low heat, and cook until the tomatoes are soft (around 15 to 30 minutes). Gently mash the tomatoes with a wooden spoon if you like your sauce chunkier or use an immersion blender if you like your sauce smoother. (You can use a regular blender for the latter, too, just make sure you allow your sauce to cool a bit before you do.)

9. Add your beef back into the sauce and cook for another 5 to 10 minutes. You can leave this on low for longer to let it stew. At this point, you can start to preheat your oven 350°F.

10. While your sauce is cooking, mix together your Parmesan, mozzarella, ricotta, roasted garlic, and remaining thyme and rosemary in a medium-sized bowl. (You can substitute cream cheese, if you don't like ricotta.)

12. Fill all of your manicotti shells while the sauce finishes cooking. You can fill them with a spoon or add the filling to a plastic bag, snip the bottom corner off, and pipe the filling into the shells. Set your filled shells aside until your sauce is completely cooked.

13. Once the sauce and your manicotti shells are ready to go, grab an 8 × 8 baking dish. Add a small spoonful of sauce to the bottom of the pan. Layer 8 filled manicotti noodles in the base of the dish. Drench the manicotti completely in the sauce. Add another layer of the remaining 8 manicotti noodles and again cover fully with the sauce. The dish may start to get pretty full at this point, so make sure to place it on a sheet pan to catch any drippings in the oven.

14. Sprinkle it with a little extra Parmesan and mozzarella cheese and cover with a sheet of aluminum foil. Place on the middle rack of your oven and bake for 45 minutes. After 45 minutes, remove aluminum foil and bake for another 15 minutes.

15. Once you remove from the oven, let the pasta cool for 10 minutes. Then dig in and enjoy!

Dryad's Crunchy Morsels

I have found finger food is the superior food, which makes these salad boats the perfect recipe! I was very glad to find all my friends happily agreed with me on this matter.

Makes 5–6 Boats

Prep time: 15–25 minutes

Ingredients

Dressing:
- 1 clove fresh garlic
- ½ cup mayo
- ½ tablespoon lemon juice
- ¼ cup grated Parmesan
- 1–2 teaspoons Worcestershire sauce or anchovy paste
- Salt and pepper, to taste
- 2–3 tablespoons olive oil (optional)

Salad:
- 2 heads romaine lettuce
- ½ cup cooked chicken or meat of your choosing
- 1 cup croutons, divided
- 3–5 tablespoons dressing
- ¼ cup grated Parmesan
- Salt and pepper, to taste

Instructions

Dressing:
1. Finely mince or grate your fresh garlic.
2. Mix your mayo, garlic, lemon juice, Parmesan, and Worcestershire sauce in a small bowl. For a smoother consistency, mix in a blender or food processor.
3. Slowly add in your olive oil until your dressing reaches a desired consistency. For a thicker sauce add less and for a thinner one add more.
4. Taste and add salt and pepper as needed.

Salad Boats:
1. Rinse off and dry your heads of lettuce. Then chop off the root-y end. Set aside 5–6 whole leaves to use as your boats.
2. Chop up the rest of your lettuce. The smaller your pieces of lettuce are the easier it will be to eat your boats so keep chopping away!
3. Chop up your cooked chicken or meat of your choosing. Make the pieces about the same size as your lettuce chunks.
4. Take half of your croutons and smash them into smaller pieces. You can either

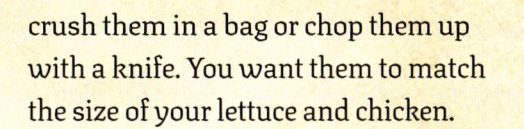

crush them in a bag or chop them up with a knife. You want them to match the size of your lettuce and chicken.

5. Mix together your lettuce, meat, crushed croutons, half of your salad dressing, a squeeze of lemon juice, half your cheese, and a pinch of salt and pepper.

6. Taste your salad mix, and add any ingredients as needed. You can always add more, but you can't take anything away, so move slow here and go with your gut!

7. Scoop your salad mix into the lettuce leaves you set aside. Top with the remaining cheese and croutons and serve with a wedge of lemon.

8. Enjoy! This is the perfect recipe for a light lunch, or a side to a big dinner!

Blackberry Honey Crumble and Ice Cream

Finheld brought me some berries they gathered on their travels. They said it reminded them of me when they came across the big patch of bushes. Don't worry, Finheld made sure to double check with the locals and they are safe to eat. We will not be having poison pie tonight!

Makes 4-6 servings

Prep time: 30-45 minutes | Cook time: 50-55 minutes

Ingredients

Ice Cream:
- 1 pint heavy whipping cream
- ½ cup sweetened condensed milk
- ½ tablespoon vanilla
- ½ cup rock salt
- Ice

Berries:
- 1 (24-oz) package blackberries
- 2 tablespoons brown sugar
- 1 teaspoon lemon juice
- 3 tablespoons honey

Crumble:
- ½ cup melted butter
- ½ cup brown sugar
- 1 cup flour
- ½ teaspoon salt
- 2 tablespoons rolled oats

Instructions

Ice Cream:

1. In a medium-sized metal bowl, mix together all of your ingredients until fully combined.

2. In a bowl large enough to fit the medium bowl inside it with about 1 inch of space, fill about halfway with ice. Sprinkle your rock salt over the ice.

3. Nestle your medium-sized bowl into the ice and start whisking. The rock salt will make the ice extra cold and start to cool your cream.

4. After about 15 to 20 minutes, your cream will start to chill. You can either a) keep whisking it until your ice

cream fully sets or b) you can put your ice cream in the freezer now. (If you chose the freezer, check on it and whisk every 45 minutes until it fully sets).

5. This recipe will take a couple hours to finish. Alternatively, you can also use an ice cream machine instead of doing it by hand.

CRUMBLE:

1. Preheat your oven to 350°F.
2. In a large bowl, lightly toss all of your berry mix ingredients until all of your berries are evenly coated. Once mixed, spread evenly in a pie pan or cast iron skillet.
3. In a large bowl, mix together your melted butter and brown sugar for your crumble. Once mixed add in your flour, salt, and oats until a thick, crumbly dough is formed.
4. Evenly spread your crumble over your berries.
5. Bake for 50 to 55 minutes or until your berries start bubbling around the crumble.
6. Top with ice cream and enjoy!

CHAPTER THIRTY-EIGHT
Onward, Onward

To my dearest Journal,

Hello Journal, it's been many a year, hasn't it? I'm sorry it's taken so long to finish you off, I've been very busy. But don't worry, I won't keep you in suspense much longer. This is how it all ended . . .

After that amazing evening with the whole gang reunited, I'm sure you're expecting to hear that we all walked right into that guild hall, straight into Hutar's office, and got the party back together again. You want me to say we embarked on more wild adventures and slayed massive evil wherever we went! The Tag-Alongs protecting the world once again.

Well, I am afraid that's just not how this story goes. Don't worry, we still have a happy ending, though.

Irabel moved back to the Violet Bastion and opened up a school for young sorcerers. She and a few of her sisters run the academy, teaching magically gifted youths to hone their skills and protect themselves while wandering the veil.

Finheld lives at the guild. They spend most of their days tinkering with new gadgets and repairing adventurers' gear. Occasionally, they'll go out on neglected commissions like the one we did for Granny Fran and Aunt Jo.

Karn was absolutely <u>not</u> going to let me run the tavern alone, and I was happy for it. He now works full time at the CopperSpoon. I insisted he own part of the tavern, but he refused. Half the time he wont even let me pay him! I've never been great at drink recipes, so he's in charge of the bar, and also helps me develop recipes in the kitchen.

Oh, and do you remember that group of kids we found living in that hole at the Old Manor Bazaar? Well, Mindy, Tophius, Ember, Jack, Kieran, Tommy, and Nielson all work full time for me now! It was Karn's idea actually, and they've filled our lives with so much joy.

And then there is me, I guess. I'm still telling stories and finding new recipes. Karn and I have a normal route now and we have made many new friends along the way. Occasionally, we will pick the tavern up and go somewhere crazy, but for the most part we stick to the same path: First, we hit my home, Honeystar. You should have seen the look on me neighbors' faces the first time I pulled up with a full-blown walking tavern! Everybody immediately fell in love with Karn, of course, and he was quickly ingratiated into the family. Sometimes, I think they like him more than me! (It's fine, I'm not sad about it.)

After we're done in Honeystar, we head off to spend a night or two in Twinebrush, the small village where we saved the unicorn. Normally, I serve the people for free while we're there. They don't have much in the way of taverns, so the people are definitely happy and excited when we show up. After that we hit the road to Farvenor, Newellin, and Arvilia. I always make sure to pick up some butternut squash while we are there and visit Maud. I can't believe she's still kicking!

Then we travel south to Marlin's Shore, hitting a few of the major cities along the way. This part of the route always changes a little so that Karn and I can explore a bit. We like to visit the Scovterra Desert frequently. Their food and culture reminds me a lot of the people of Ignisanti village.

To end our route, we always make sure we're back in the Violet Bastion for at least twelve days or more (one in honor of each knight). Every time I'm there, I make it a point to see all of my friends and help them with whatever they're working on. I bring Irabel and her sisters lunch at the academy and even teach cooking classes to the kids every once in a while. Finheld and I have made it a tradition whenever we're in town to spend a day visiting Little Jo's Gator Getaway for lunch. They even help feed the alligators! I always visit the guild hall. Together Telfina and I make a big meal for all the mercenaries who are in town, and I even started playing chess with Hutar. I still have yet to beat him, but I've already won knowing he finally likes me.

Finally, for just one night, we always make time to close the tavern down for a family dinner. Whenever we can we buy a spell scroll and drag Harold back for a night. Finny, Hutar, and Telfina all head over from the guild. Irabel brings all of her sisters. Karn and I cook a massive feast, and for one night, we all eat, drink, laugh, tell stories, and play games.

So, things didn't snap neatly back to the way they were, but I don't think that's such a bad thing. Don't consider this a "happily-ever-after" moment, because that means our story has to end. Life keeps taggin' along, and the world still turns. There's still evil out there, but there's also still a whole lot of good. I still want to make it better.

For now, I think this is just goodbye.

Goodbye to this journey, and hello to the next.

Above all else, I hope you enjoyed.

Metric Conversions

If you're accustomed to using metric measurements, use these handy charts to convert the imperial measurements used in this book.

Weight (Dry Ingredients)

1 oz		30 g
4 oz	¼ lb	120 g
8 oz	½ lb	240 g
12 oz	¾ lb	360 g
16 oz	1 lb	480 g
32 oz	2 lb	960 g

Oven Temperatures

Fahrenheit	Celsius	Gas Mark
225°	110°	¼
250°	120°	½
275°	140°	1
300°	150°	2
325°	160°	3
350°	180°	4
375°	190°	5
400°	200°	6
425°	220°	7
450°	230°	8

Volume (Liquid Ingredients)

½ tsp.		2 ml
1 tsp.		5 ml
1 Tbsp.	½ fl oz	15 ml
2 Tbsp.	1 fl oz	30 ml
¼ cup	2 fl oz	60 ml
⅓ cup	3 fl oz	80 ml
½ cup	4 fl oz	120 ml
⅔ cup	5 fl oz	160 ml
¾ cup	6 fl oz	180 ml
1 cup	8 fl oz	240 ml
1 pt	16 fl oz	480 ml
1 qt	32 fl oz	960 ml

Length

¼ in	6 mm
½ in	13 mm
¾ in	19 mm
1 in	25 mm
6 in	15 cm
12 in	30 cm

Index

#
100 Gold Chocolate Cake, 54–55

A
Adventurer's Comfort, 45–46
allium, 9
almonds
    Kappa Cookies (Gluten-Free), 215–216
apples
    Baked Apple Cheese, 300–301
    Pixie Pie, 168–170
    Red Ruby Spiced Cider, 184
    Sea Moon Charcuterie, 128–129
asparagus, 10
Aunt Jo's Alligator Ranch Biscuits, 143
avocado
    High Elven Garden Tacos, 155–156
    Rancheros Adventeros, 259–261

B
bacon
    The Meal, 290–291
    Ocean's Embrace, 91–92
    Phoenix Feathers, 253
    Piggy and Onion Cheesy Melt, 222–223
    Roasted Coral Bulbs, 134
    Sampler Spuds, 42–44
Baked Apple Cheese, 300–301
Baklava in Bloom, 311–312

bamboo shoots
    Golem Grub, 254–255
basil
    Adventurer's Comfort, 45–46
    Baked Apple Cheese, 300–301
    Cheesy Vine Fruit Manicotti, 323–325
    Chimera Roast and Root Veggies, 144–146
    Copper Cockatrice Caprese, 22–23
    Copper Shepherd, 315–317
    The Meal, 290–291
    Scrumptious Scholars Pasta Salad, 224–225
    Smoke Copper Spice Blend, 13
    Terra-To Salad, 176–177
bayberry juice
    Bayberry Taffy, 98–99
Bayberry Taffy, 98–99
bay leaves
    Adventurer's Comfort, 45–46
    Changeling Chili, 251–252
    Copper Shepherd, 315–317
    Firebird Stew and Rice, 240–242
    Forest Fromage Soup, 40–41
    Gnomebalaya, 164–165
    Golem Grub, 254–255
    Ole Bessy's Legacy, 37–39
    Sweet Dream Soup, 201–202
    Tea Witch Soup, 151–152
beans
    black
        Changeling Chili, 251–252

        Stuffed Dragon Scale, 148–150
    garbanzo, 6–7
    kidney
        Changeling Chili, 251–252
        Grammy Linda's Spoon Tacos, 30–31
    lima, 8
beef
    flank
        Broccoli and Dire Bull, 295–296
        Island Burger, 285–286
    ground
        Changeling Chili, 251–252
        Cheesy Vine Fruit Manicotti, 323–325
        Grammy Linda's Spoon Tacos, 30–31
        Surprise Fries, 86–88
        Manticore Noodles, 283–284
    prime rib
        Chimera Roast and Root Veggies, 144–146
    stew
        Copper Shepherd, 315–317
        Ole Bessy's Legacy, 37–39
    tri-tip steak
        Smoked Centicore Sandwich, 59–61
beer
    Guinness
        Ole Bessy's Legacy, 37–39
        Tavern Classic, 49–50

bell pepper
  alternatives, 9
  Crimson Berry Soup, 193–194
  Gnomebalaya, 164–165
  Gruble Kebab and Cucumber Salad, 197–200
  roasted
    Scrumptious Scholars Pasta Salad, 224–225
  Terra-To Salad, 176–177
biscuits
  Aunt Jo's Alligator Ranch Biscuits, 143
  Tag Along's Clouds and Cream, 276–277
blackberries
  Sea Moon Charcuterie, 128–129
Blackberry Honey Crumble and Ice Cream, 328–329
Boar Butt Sliders, 249–250
bourbon
  Twinebrush Onion Soup, 309–310
Braised Dire Bear Belly and Eggs, 205–206
brassica, 10
bread
  Adventurer's Comfort, 47–48
  Aunt Jo's Alligator Ranch Biscuits, 143
  Baked Apple Cheese, 300–301
  Boar Butt Sliders, 249–250
  Braised Dire Bear Belly and Eggs, 205–206
  Chewy Gnome Bread and Cheese Sauce, 100–101
  Chocolate Cherry Allure, 231–233
  ciabatta
    Copper Cockatrice Caprese, 22–23
  Crimson Berry Soup, 193–194
  Farvenor's Autumn Harvest, 297–299
  Huntsman's Hoagie, 102–104
  Lemony Toadstools with Salty Cheese, 27–28
  Moorhen Cap Sandwich, 174–175
  Nana's No-Wheat Bread (Gluten-Free), 26
  Not Your Papa's Bread Rolls, 24–25
  Piggy and Onion Cheesy Melt, 222–223
  Sea Moon Charcuterie, 128–129
  Smoked Centicore Sandwich, 59–61
  Twinebrush Onion Soup, 309–310
bread crumbs
  Siren Fry, 106–107
bread pudding
  Chocolate Cherry Allure, 231–233
broccoli, 10
  Forest Fromage Soup, 40–41
  Island Burger, 285–286
Broccoli and Dire Bull, 295–296
brownies
  Fudgy Brownies (Gluten-Free), 74–75
brussels sprouts, 10
  Roasted Coral Bulbs, 134
buffalo sauce
  Sampler Spuds, 42–44
Burnt Sugar Harvest Brew, 281–282
butter
  ghee, 4
  goat, 4
  Roasted Garlic Butter, 16
buttercream
  100 Gold Chocolate Cake, 54–55

C

cabbage, 10
  Boar Butt Sliders, 249–250
  High Elven Garden Tacos, 155–156
napa
  Manticore Noodles, 283–284
purple
  Boar Butt Sliders, 249–250
Cajun seasoning
  Gnomebalaya, 164–165
cake
  Uni-Fruit Cheesecake, 157–158
caramel sauce
  Burnt Sugar Harvest Brew, 281–282
cauliflower, 10
  High Elven Garden Tacos, 155–156
cayenne
  Changeling Chili, 251–252
  Rancheros Adventeros, 259–261
  Smoke Copper Spice Blend, 13
chamomile
  Harold's Ginger Peppermint Tea, 114
Changeling Chili, 251–252
charcuterie
  Sea Moon Charcuterie, 128–129
cheese
  Brie
    Baked Apple Cheese, 300–301
    Sea Moon Charcuterie, 128–129
  cheddar
    Changeling Chili, 251–252
    Chewy Gnome Bread and Cheese Sauce, 100–101
    Forest Fromage Soup, 40–41
    Grammy Linda's Spoon Tacos, 30–31
    Sampler Spuds, 42–44
  Cheesy Garlic Swirls, 72–73

cream
- Colossal Crab Cheese Dip, 95–96
- Farvenor's Autumn Harvest, 297–299
- Forager's Impy Rolls, 68–69
- Phoenix Feathers, 253
- Sampler Spuds, 42–44
- Uni-Fruit Cheesecake, 157–158

goat, 4

Gruyère
- Copper Shepherd, 315–317
- Forager's Impy Rolls, 68–69
- Smoked Centicore Sandwich, 59–61
- Twinebrush Onion Soup, 309–310

Italian blend
- Piggy and Onion Cheesy Melt, 222–223

The Meal, 290–291

mozzarella
- Cheesy Vine Fruit Manicotti, 323–325
- Colossal Crab Cheese Dip, 95–96
- Copper Cockatrice Caprese, 22–23
- Copper Shepherd, 315–317
- Surprise Fries, 86–88
- Twinebrush Onion Soup, 309–310

Parmesan
- Braised Dire Bear Belly and Eggs, 205–206
- Colossal Crab Cheese Dip, 95–96
- Crimson Berry Soup, 193–194
- Crispy Roasted Spuds, 70–71
- Dryad's Crunchy Morsels, 326–327
- Forager's Impy Rolls, 68–69
- Forager's Pillows, 207–209
- Lemony Toadstools with Salty Cheese, 27–28
- Roasted Coral Bulbs, 134
- Scrumptious Scholars Pasta Salad, 224–225
- Sea Dragon and Noodle Stew, 313–314
- Tea Witch Soup, 151–152
- Toadstool and Leaf Pockets, 292–294
- Wanderer's Savory Porridge, 307–308

pepper jack
- Phoenix Feathers, 253

queso fresco
- Cheesy Harvest Wands, 97
- Firebird Stew and Rice, 240–242
- Rancheros Adventeros, 259–261

ricotta
- Cheesy Vine Fruit Manicotti, 323–325
- Toadstool and Leaf Pockets, 292–294
- Sea Moon Charcuterie, 128–129

sheep, 4

Smoked Centicore Sandwich, 59–61

cheesecake
- Uni-Fruit Cheesecake, 157–158

Cheesy Garlic Swirls, 72–73

Cheesy Harvest Wands, 97

Cheesy Vine Fruit Manicotti, 323–325

cherries
- Chocolate Cherry Allure, 231–233
- Everything-but-the-Dragon's-Hoard Scones, 195–196

Chewy Gnome Bread and Cheese Sauce, 100–101

chicken
- breast
  - butterflying, 18
- Copper Cockatrice Caprese, 22–23
- Gruble Kebab and Cucumber Salad, 197–200
- The Meal, 290–291
- Stuffed Dragon Scale, 148–150
- Dryad's Crunchy Morsels, 326–327

sausage
- Tea Witch Soup, 151–152

shredded
- Hen and Hearth Stew, 33–34
- Sampler Spuds, 42–44

thighs
- Firebird Stew and Rice, 240–242
- Gnomebalaya, 164–165
- Golem Grub, 254–255
- Roasted Thunderbird Thighs with Zucchini and Squash, 305–306

chickpeas, 6–7
- High Elven Garden Tacos, 155–156
- Rancheros Adventeros, 259–261
- Terra-To Salad, 176–177

chili
- Changeling Chili, 251–252

chili paste
- Huntsman's Hoagie, 102–104

chili powder
- Stuffed Dragon Scale, 148–150

chili sauce
- Colossal Crab Cheese Dip, 95–96
- Surprise Fries, 86–88

Chimera Roast and Root Veggies, 144–146

chipotle peppers
- Siren Fry, 106–107

chips
- tortilla
  - Grammy Linda's Spoon Tacos, 30–31

chocolate
- Everything-but-the-Dragon's-Hoard Scones, 195–196

Chocolate Cherry Allure, 231–233

chocolate chips
- Chocolate Cherry Allure, 231–233
- Fudgy Brownies (Gluten-Free), 74–75

ciabatta
- Copper Cockatrice Caprese, 22–23

cider
- Red Ruby Spiced Cider, 184

cilantro
- Cheesy Harvest Wands, 97
- Crispy Lava Lizard Tacos, 264–265
- Firebird Stew and Rice, 240–242
- High Elven Garden Tacos, 155–156
- Huntsman's Hoagie, 102–104
- Siren Fry, 106–107
- Stuffed Dragon Scale, 148–150

cinnamon
- Farvenor's Autumn Harvest, 297–299

cinnamon stick
- Red Ruby Spiced Cider, 184

clams
- canned
  - Ocean's Embrace, 91–92

cocoa powder
- 100 Gold Chocolate Cake, 54–55
- Fudgy Brownies (Gluten-Free), 74–75
- Karn's Comfort, 273

coconut aminos, 8

coconut cream
- Golem Grub, 254–255
- Squashling Soup, 185–186
- Tea Witch Soup, 151–152
- Tropical Cream, 105

cod
- Siren Fry, 106–107

coffee
- 100 Gold Chocolate Cake, 54–55
- Burnt Sugar Harvest Brew, 281–282

coffee beans
- Smoke Copper Spice Blend, 13

Colossal Crab Cheese Dip, 95–96

cookies
- Gold Coins, 153–154
- Kappa Cookies (Gluten-Free), 215–216
- Kelpie Cookies (Gluten-Free), 135

Copper Cockatrice Caprese, 22–23

Copper Shepherd, 315–317

coriander
- Adventurer's Comfort, 45–46
- Changeling Chili, 251–252
- Cheesy Vine Fruit Manicotti, 323–325
- Copper Shepherd, 315–317
- Forest Fromage Soup, 40–41
- Gnomebalaya, 164–165
- Golem Grub, 254–255
- Huntsman's Hoagie, 102–104
- Ocean's Embrace, 91–92
- Smoke Copper Spice Blend, 13
- Tea Witch Soup, 151–152
- Twinebrush Onion Soup, 311–312

corn, 10
- Cheesy Harvest Wands, 97

couscous
- Terra-To Salad, 176–177

crab meat
- Colossal Crab Cheese Dip, 95–96

cream
- Burnt Sugar Harvest Brew, 281–282
- Farvenor's Autumn Harvest, 297–299
- Forest Fromage Soup, 40–41
- The Meal, 290–291
- Melodius Mushroom Soup, 189–190
- Ocean's Embrace, 91–92
- Sea Dragon and Noodle Stew, 313–314

creamer
- Dwarven Float, 76
- Karn's Comfort, 273

crema
- Cheesy Harvest Wands, 97

creole seasoning
- Sea Dragon and Noodle Stew, 313–314

Crispy Lava Lizard Tacos, 264–265

Crispy Roasted Spuds, 70–71

cucumbers
- English
  - Terra-To Salad, 176–177
- Gruble Kebab and Cucumber Salad, 197–200
- Huntsman's Hoagie, 102–104
- Island Burger, 285–286

cumin
- Golem Grub, 254–255
- Stuffed Dragon Scale, 148–150

curry powder
- Golem Grub, 254–255

Cyclops Bane, 14

D

dairy substitutions, 3–4

dandelion petals
- Sea Dandelion Lemonade, 136–137

diabetes, 10

dill
- Gruble Kebab and Cucumber Salad, 197–200

dip
- Colossal Crab Cheese Dip, 95–96

Dryad's Crunchy Morsels, 326–327

dumplings
- Hen and Hearth Stew, 33–34

Dwarven Float, 76

E

edamame, 6
eggplant
   alternatives, 9
eggs, 4–5
   duck, 5
   flaxseed, 5
   psyllium, 5
   quail, 4
Everything-but-the-Dragon's-Hoard Scones, 195–196

F

Farvenor's Autumn Harvest, 297–299
fennel bulb, 9
finfish, 5, 6
Firebird Stew and Rice, 240–242
fish sauce
   Island Burger, 285–286
   Manticore Noodles, 283–284
flour
   almond, 7
   coconut, 7
   gluten-free, 7
   Gluten-Free Flour Blend, 19
   Hen and Hearth Stew, 33–34
   Nana's No-Wheat Bread (Gluten-Free), 26
   Not Your Papa's Bread Rolls, 24–25
   psyllium, 7
   rice, 7
      brown
         Gluten-Free Flour Blend, 19
      soy
         Gluten-Free Flour Blend, 19
Forager's Impy Rolls, 68–69
Forager's Pillows, 207–209
Forest Fromage Soup, 40–41
fruit, 8
Fudgy Brownies (Gluten-Free), 74–75

G

gardein, 5
garlic
   Adventurer's Comfort, 45–46
   Baked Apple Cheese, 300–301
   Boar Butt Sliders, 249–250
   Broccoli and Dire Bull, 295–296
   Changeling Chili, 251–252
   Cheesy Garlic Swirls, 72–73
   Cheesy Vine Fruit Manicotti, 323–325
   Colossal Crab Cheese Dip, 95–96
   Copper Shepherd, 315–317
   Crimson Berry Soup, 193–194
   Crispy Lava Lizard Tacos, 264–265
   Crispy Roasted Spuds, 70–71
   Cyclops Bane, 14
   Dryad's Crunchy Morsels, 326–327
   Firebird Stew and Rice, 240–242
   Forager's Impy Rolls, 68–69
   Gnomebalaya, 164–165
   Honey-Glazed Pink Lance, 133
   Huntsman's Hoagie, 102–104
   Island Burger, 285–286
   Lemony Toadstools with Salty Cheese, 27–28
   Manticore Noodles, 283–284
   The Meal, 290–291
   Melodius Mushroom Soup, 189–190
   Ocean's Embrace, 91–92
   Piggy and Onion Cheesy Melt, 222–223
   Rancheros Adventeros, 259–261
   roasted
      Forest Fromage Soup, 40–41
      Roasted Garlic Butter, 16
   Roasted Coral Bulbs, 134
   roasting, 15
   Sampler Spuds, 42–44
   Scrumptious Scholars Pasta Salad, 224–225
   Sea Dragon and Noodle Stew, 313–314
   Smoked Centicore Sandwich, 59–61
   Squashling Soup, 185–186
   Stuffed Dragon Scale, 148–150
   Surprise Fries, 86–88
   Sweet Dream Soup, 201–202
   Tea Witch Soup, 151–152
   Wanderer's Savory Porridge, 307–308
Garlic Confit, 17
garlic powder
   Copper Cockatrice Caprese, 22–23
   Grammy Linda's Spoon Tacos, 30–31
   Smoke Copper Spice Blend, 13
ghee, 4
ginger
   ground
      Golem Grub, 254–255
      Harold's Ginger Peppermint Tea, 114
      Red Ruby Spiced Cider, 184
      Sea Bullet Rice, 123–125
   Gluten-Free Flour Blend, 19
   Nana's No-Wheat Bread (Gluten-Free), 26
gnocchi
   Forager's Pillows, 207–209
Gnomebalaya, 164–165
Gold Coins, 153–154
Golem Grub, 254–255
Grammy Linda's Spoon Tacos, 30–31
grapes
   red
      Sea Moon Charcuterie, 128–129
gravy
   Chimera Roast and Root Veggies, 144–146

Forager's Impy Rolls, 68–69
Tag Along's Clouds and Cream, 276–277
Gruble Kebab and Cucumber Salad, 197–200

H

halibut
    Siren Fry, 106–107
Harold's Ginger Peppermint Tea, 114
Harold's Late Night Comforts, 278
Hen and Hearth Stew, 33–34
herbs, 10–12
High Elven Garden Tacos, 155–156
hoisin sauce
    Manticore Noodles, 283–284
    Surprise Fries, 86–88
honey
    Baked Apple Cheese, 300–301
    Bayberry Taffy, 98–99
    Boar Butt Sliders, 249–250
    High Elven Garden Tacos, 155–156
    Honey-Glazed Pink Lance, 133
    Island Burger, 285–286
    Nana T's Copper-Pop, 29
    Pixie Pie, 168–170
    Roasted Coral Bulbs, 134
    Scrumptious Scholars Pasta Salad, 224–225
    Sea Bullet Rice, 123–125
    Siren Fry, 106–107
    Stuffed Dragon Scale, 148–150
    Twinebrush Onion Soup, 311–312
Honey-Glazed Pink Lance, 133
hot sauce
    Firebird Stew and Rice, 240–242
hummus
    Stuffed Dragon Scale, 148–150
    Huntsman's Hoagie, 102–104

I

ice cream
    Blackberry Honey Crumble and Ice Cream, 328–329
Irish cream
    Dwarven Float, 76
    Tropical Cream, 105
Island Burger, 285–286
Italian seasoning
    Crimson Berry Soup, 193–194
    Gnomebalaya, 164–165
    Ole Bessy's Legacy, 37–39
    Roasted Thunderbird Thighs with Zucchini and Squash, 305–306
    Scrumptious Scholars Pasta Salad, 224–225
    Sweet Dream Soup, 201–202

J

jalapeños
    Crispy Lava Lizard Tacos, 264–265
    Huntsman's Hoagie, 102–104
    Phoenix Feathers, 253
    Siren Fry, 106–107
    Stuffed Dragon Scale, 148–150
jam
    bacon onion
        Piggy and Onion Cheesy Melt, 222–223

K

Kappa Cookies (Gluten-Free), 215–216
Karn's Comfort, 273
Kelpie Cookies (Gluten-Free), 135
ketchup
    Manticore Noodles, 283–284
kielbasa
    Tavern Classic, 49–50

L

lavender
    Pixie Pie, 168–170
    Twinebrush Onion Soup, 311–312
lemonade
    Sea Dandelion Lemonade, 136–137
lemon balm
    Wildwinter Tea, 214
lemongrass
    Harold's Late Night Comforts, 278
Lemony Toadstools with Salty Cheese, 27–28
lettuce, 10
    Dryad's Crunchy Morsels, 326–327
    Grammy Linda's Spoon Tacos, 30–31
linden flower
    Wildwinter Tea, 214
liquid smoke
    Moorhsum Cap Sandwich, 174–175

M

manicotti
    Cheesy Vine Fruit Manicotti, 323–325
Manticore Noodles, 283–284
maple syrup
    Red Ruby Spiced Cider, 184
masa harina
    Gluten-Free Flour Blend, 19
mayonnaise, 4
    100 Gold Chocolate Cake, 54–55
    Boar Butt Sliders, 249–250
    Cheesy Harvest Wands, 97
    Copper Cockatrice Caprese, 22–23
    kewpie
        Huntsman's Hoagie, 102–104
        Island Burger, 285–286
        Siren Fry, 106–107
        Smoked Centicore Sandwich, 59–61

sriracha
    Surprise Fries, 86–88
Meal, The, 290–291
Melodius Mushroom Soup, 189–190
milk
    almond, 4
    cashew, 4
    evaporated
        Hen and Hearth Stew, 33–34
    oat, 4
    soy, 4
    substitutions, 3–4
mint
    Gruble Kebab and Cucumber Salad, 197–200
mirin
    Surprise Fries, 86–88
monosodium glutamate (MSG), 8, 12
Moorhsum Cap Sandwich, 174–175
MSG. *See* monosodium glutamate (MSG)
mushroom juice
    Forager's Pillows, 207–209
mushrooms, 6, 8, 10
    Forager's Impy Rolls, 68–69
    Forager's Pillows, 207–209
    Lemony Toadstools with Salty Cheese, 27–28
    Melodius Mushroom Soup, 189–190
    Moorhsum Cap Sandwich, 174–175
    Ole Bessy's Legacy, 37–39
    Tea Witch Soup, 151–152
    Toadstool and Leaf Pockets, 292–294
mustard
    Boar Butt Sliders, 249–250
    Changeling Chili, 251–252
    Chimera Roast and Root Veggies, 144–146

ground
    Copper Shepherd, 315–317
    Smoke Copper Spice Blend, 13
    Tea Witch Soup, 151–152
    Scrumptious Scholars Pasta Salad, 224–225

N
Nana's No-Wheat Bread (Gluten-Free), 26
Nana T's Copper-Pop, 29
nightshades, 9
noodles, yakisoba
    Manticore Noodles, 283–284
Not Your Papa's Bread Rolls, 24–25
nutmeg
    Red Ruby Spiced Cider, 184
nuts
    Fudgy Brownies (Gluten-Free), 74–75

O
Ocean's Embrace, 91–92
okra
    Gnomebalaya, 164–165
Ole Bessy's Legacy, 37–39
olives
    garlic stuffed
        Scrumptious Scholars Pasta Salad, 224–225
    kalamata
        Terra-To Salad, 176–177
onion powder
    Copper Cockatrice Caprese, 22–23
    Grammy Linda's Spoon Tacos, 30–31
    Smoke Copper Spice Blend, 13
onions
    Twinebrush Onion Soup, 309–310
orange
    Red Ruby Spiced Cider, 184

orange peel
    Twinebrush Onion Soup, 311–312
    Wildwinter Tea, 214
oregano
    Adventurer's Comfort, 45–46
    Changeling Chili, 251–252
    Chimera Roast and Root Veggies, 144–146
    Copper Shepherd, 315–317
    Firebird Stew and Rice, 240–242
    Smoke Copper Spice Blend, 13

P
panko
    Siren Fry, 106–107
paprika
    Adventurer's Comfort, 45–46
    Changeling Chili, 251–252
    Cheesy Vine Fruit Manicotti, 323–325
    Chewy Gnome Bread and Cheese Sauce, 100–101
    Chimera Roast and Root Veggies, 144–146
    Copper Cockatrice Caprese, 22–23
    Copper Shepherd, 315–317
    Crimson Berry Soup, 193–194
    Forager's Impy Rolls, 68–69
    Forest Fromage Soup, 40–41
    Gnomebalaya, 164–165
    Golem Grub, 254–255
    High Elven Garden Tacos, 155–156
    Honey-Glazed Pink Lance, 133
    Huntsman's Hoagie, 102–104
    The Meal, 290–291
    Melodius Mushroom Soup, 189–190
    Ocean's Embrace, 91–92
    Ole Bessy's Legacy, 37–39
    Phoenix Feathers, 253
    Piggy and Onion Cheesy Melt, 222–223

Rancheros Adventeros, 259–261
Roasted Thunderbird Thighs with Zucchini and Squash, 305–306
Siren Fry, 106–107
Smoke Copper Spice Blend, 13
Stuffed Dragon Scale, 148–150
Sweet Dream Soup, 201–202
Tag Along's Clouds and Cream, 276–277
Tea Witch Soup, 151–152

parsley
Adventurer's Comfort, 45–46
Gruble Kebab and Cucumber Salad, 197–200
The Meal, 290–291
Roasted Garlic Butter, 16
Scrumptious Scholars Pasta Salad, 224–225
Sea Dragon and Noodle Stew, 313–314
Terra-To Salad, 176–177

pasta
gnocchi
Forager's Pillows, 207–209
The Meal, 290–291
ravioli
Sweet Dream Soup, 201–202
tri-color
Scrumptious Scholars Pasta Salad, 224–225

pastry, puff
Ole Bessy's Legacy, 37–39

paté
Huntsman's Hoagie, 102–104

peanut butter
Nana T's Copper-Pop, 29

peanut substitutions, 6–7
pepitas, 6
peppercorns
Smoke Copper Spice Blend, 13

peppermint
Harold's Ginger Peppermint Tea, 114

peppers
chipotle
Siren Fry, 106–107
Phoenix Feathers, 253
pickles
Huntsman's Hoagie, 102–104
Island Burger, 285–286
Stuffed Dragon Scale, 148–150
pico de gallo
Stuffed Dragon Scale, 148–150

pie
Pixie Pie, 168–170
Piggy and Onion Cheesy Melt, 222–223
Pillow Bread, 47–48

pineapple
Siren Fry, 106–107
pistachios, 6
Everything-but-the-Dragon's-Hoard Scones, 195–196
Twinebrush Onion Soup, 311–312
Pixie Pie, 168–170

poblano pepper
High Elven Garden Tacos, 155–156
Rancheros Adventeros, 259–261

popcorn
Nana T's Copper-Pop, 29

pork
belly
Braised Dire Bear Belly and Eggs, 205–206
Crispy Lava Lizard Tacos, 264–265
roast
Huntsman's Hoagie, 102–104
shoulder roast
Boar Butt Sliders, 249–250
tenderloin
Forager's Impy Rolls, 68–69

potassium chloride, 12
potato
Adventurer's Comfort, 45–46

alternatives, 9
Chimera Roast and Root Veggies, 144–146
Copper Shepherd, 315–317
Crispy Roasted Spuds, 70–71
Forager's Pillows, 207–209
Golem Grub, 254–255
Ocean's Embrace, 91–92
Ole Bessy's Legacy, 37–39
Rancheros Adventeros, 259–261
red
Tavern Classic, 49–50
Sampler Spuds, 42–44
Surprise Fries, 86–88

pretzels, 6
prosciutto
Sampler Spuds, 42–44

pudding
Chocolate Cherry Allure, 231–233

pumpkins, 9–10
pumpkin seeds, 6
pumpkin spice
Burnt Sugar Harvest Brew, 281–282
Farvenor's Autumn Harvest, 297–299

R

Rancheros Adventeros, 259–261
Red Ruby Spiced Cider, 184
rice
Arborio
Wanderer's Savory Porridge, 307–308
Firebird Stew and Rice, 240–242
Gnomebalaya, 164–165
Island Burger, 285–286
Sea Bullet Rice, 123–125
Roasted Coral Bulbs, 134
Roasted Garlic Butter, 16
Roasted Thunderbird Thighs with Zucchini and Squash, 305–306

root beer
    Dwarven Float, 76
rose buds
    Harold's Late Night Comforts, 278
    Twinebrush Onion Soup, 311–312
rosemary
    Adventurer's Comfort, 45–46, 47–48
    Changeling Chili, 251–252
    Cheesy Vine Fruit Manicotti, 323–325
    Chimera Roast and Root Veggies, 144–146
    Copper Shepherd, 315–317
    Crispy Roasted Spuds, 70–71
    Forager's Impy Rolls, 68–69
    Forager's Pillows, 207–209
    Forest Fromage Soup, 40–41
    Lemony Toadstools with Salty Cheese, 27–28
    Melodius Mushroom Soup, 189–190
    Moorhsum Cap Sandwich, 174–175
    Ocean's Embrace, 91–92
    Ole Bessy's Legacy, 37–39
    Piggy and Onion Cheesy Melt, 222–223
    Roasted Garlic Butter, 16
    Roasted Thunderbird Thighs with Zucchini and Squash, 305–306
    Smoke Copper Spice Blend, 13
    Squashling Soup, 185–186
    Tea Witch Soup, 151–152
    Toadstool and Leaf Pockets, 292–294
rum
    coconut
        Tropical Cream, 105

S

sage
    Baked Apple Cheese, 300–301
    Copper Shepherd, 315–317
    Harold's Late Night Comforts, 278
    Ole Bessy's Legacy, 37–39
salad
    cucumber salad
        Island Burger, 285–286
    Gruble Kebab and Cucumber Salad, 197–200
    Scrumptious Scholars Pasta Salad, 224–225
    Terra-To Salad, 176–177
salami
    Scrumptious Scholars Pasta Salad, 224–225
    Sea Moon Charcuterie, 128–129
salmon
    Honey-Glazed Pink Lance, 133
salsa
    Crispy Lava Lizard Tacos, 264–265
    Siren Fry, 106–107
salt, 12
Sampler Spuds, 42–44
sandwich
    Boar Butt Sliders, 249–250
    Forager's Impy Rolls, 68–69
    Huntsman's Hoagie, 102–104
    Island Burger, 285–286
    Moorhsum Cap Sandwich, 174–175
    Piggy and Onion Cheesy Melt, 222–223
    Smoked Centicore Sandwich, 59–61
sauerkraut
    Tavern Classic, 49–50
sausage
    andouille
        Gnomebalaya, 164–165

breakfast
    Tag Along's Clouds and Cream, 276–277
chicken
    Tea Witch Soup, 151–152
chorizo
    Rancheros Adventeros, 259–261
kielbasa
    Tavern Classic, 49–50
scones
    Everything-but-the-Dragon's-Hoard Scones, 195–196
    Scrumptious Scholars Pasta Salad, 224–225
Sea Bullet Rice, 123–125
Sea Dandelion Lemonade, 136–137
Sea Dragon and Noodle Stew, 313–314
Sea Moon Charcuterie, 128–129
seitan, 5
sesame oil
    Broccoli and Dire Bull, 295–296
    Island Burger, 285–286
    Manticore Noodles, 283–284
    Sea Bullet Rice, 123–125
    Surprise Fries, 86–88
sesame seeds, 7
    Island Burger, 285–286
shrimp
    Gnomebalaya, 164–165
    Sea Bullet Rice, 123–125
    Sea Dragon and Noodle Stew, 313–314
Siren Fry, 106–107
sliders
    Boar Butt Sliders, 249–250
Smoke Copper Spice Blend, 13
Smoked Centicore Sandwich, 59–61
soda
    root beer
        Dwarven Float, 76

soup
- Crimson Berry Soup, 193–194
- Firebird Stew and Rice, 240–242
- Forest Fromage Soup, 40–41
- Hen and Hearth Stew, 33–34
- Melodius Mushroom Soup, 189–190
- Squashling Soup, 185–186
- Sweet Dream Soup, 201–202
- Tea Witch Soup, 151–152
- Twinebrush Onion Soup, 309–310
- Wanderer's Savory Porridge, 307–308

sour cream
- Changeling Chili, 251–252
- Cheesy Harvest Wands, 97
- Copper Shepherd, 315–317
- Grammy Linda's Spoon Tacos, 30–31

soybeans, 6, 7–8

soy sauce
- Broccoli and Dire Bull, 295–296
- Colossal Crab Cheese Dip, 95–96
- Huntsman's Hoagie, 102–104
- Island Burger, 285–286
- Manticore Noodles, 283–284
- Moorhsum Cap Sandwich, 174–175
- Sea Bullet Rice, 123–125
- Surprise Fries, 86–88

spices, 10–12
- Smoke Copper Spice Blend, 13

spinach
- baby
  - Tea Witch Soup, 151–152
  - Rancheros Adventeros, 259–261

sprinkles
- Kelpie Cookies (Gluten-Free), 135

squash, 9–10

butternut
- Squashling Soup, 185–186
- Roasted Thunderbird Thighs with Zucchini and Squash, 305–306

Squashling Soup, 185–186

sriracha
- Island Burger, 285–286
- Sampler Spuds, 42–44

stew
- Firebird Stew and Rice, 240–242
- Hen and Hearth Stew, 33–34
- Sea Dragon and Noodle Stew, 313–314

Stuffed Dragon Scale, 148–150

substitutions, 3–12

sunflower seeds, 6

Surprise Fries, 86–88

Sweet Dream Soup, 201–202

T

tacos
- Crispy Lava Lizard Tacos, 264–265
- Grammy Linda's Spoon Tacos, 30–31
- High Elven Garden Tacos, 155–156

taffy
- Bayberry Taffy, 98–99

Tag Along's Clouds and Cream, 276–277

tahini, 7

tajin
- Cheesy Harvest Wands, 97

Tavern Classic, 49–50

tazatziki
- Gruble Kebab and Cucumber Salad, 197–200

tea
- Harold's Ginger Peppermint Tea, 114
- Harold's Late Night Comforts, 278

Wildwinter Tea, 214

Tea Witch Soup, 151–152

Terra-To Salad, 176–177

Thai chilis
- Cyclops Bane, 14

thyme
- Changeling Chili, 251–252
- Cheesy Vine Fruit Manicotti, 323–325
- Chimera Roast and Root Veggies, 144–146
- Copper Shepherd, 315–317
- Crispy Roasted Spuds, 70–71
- Forager's Impy Rolls, 68–69
- Forager's Pillows, 207–209
- Forest Fromage Soup, 40–41
- Hen and Hearth Stew, 33–34
- Lemony Toadstools with Salty Cheese, 27–28
- Moorhsum Cap Sandwich, 174–175
- Ocean's Embrace, 91–92
- Ole Bessy's Legacy, 37–39
- Piggy and Onion Cheesy Melt, 222–223
- Roasted Garlic Butter, 16
- Roasted Thunderbird Thighs with Zucchini and Squash, 305–306
- Squashling Soup, 185–186
- Tea Witch Soup, 151–152
- Toadstool and Leaf Pockets, 292–294
- Twinebrush Onion Soup, 309–310
- Wanderer's Savory Porridge, 307–308

Toadstool and Leaf Pockets, 292–294

tofu, 5

tomato
- alternatives, 9
- Braised Dire Bear Belly and Eggs, 205–206

343

Cheesy Vine Fruit Manicotti, 323–325
cherry
Gruble Kebab and Cucumber Salad, 197–200
Terra-To Salad, 176–177
Copper Cockatrice Caprese, 22–23
Crimson Berry Soup, 193–194
Crispy Lava Lizard Tacos, 264–265
Firebird Stew and Rice, 240–242
Gnomephalaya, 164–165
Grammy Linda's Spoon Tacos, 30–31
Stuffed Dragon Scale, 148–150
tomato paste
Cheesy Vine Fruit Manicotti, 323–325
Golem Grub, 254–255
High Elven Garden Tacos, 155–156
tortillas
Firebird Stew and Rice, 240–242
High Elven Garden Tacos, 155–156
tostadas
Stuffed Dragon Scale, 148–150
Tropical Cream, 105
turnips, 10
Twinbrush Onion Soup, 309–310

u
Uni-Fruit Cheesecake, 157–158

v
vanilla
100 Gold Chocolate Cake, 54–55
Bayberry Taffy, 98–99
Chocolate Cherry Allure, 231–233

w
Forager's Impy Rolls, 68–69
white
Ole Bessy's Legacy, 37–39
Manicotti, 323–325
Cheesy Vine Fruit Eggs, 205–206
Braised Dire Bear Belly and red wine
Wildwinter Tea, 214
Smoke Copper Spice Blend, 13
white pepper
Piggy and Onion Cheesy Melt, 222–223
Dwarven Float, 76
Copper Shepherd, 315–317
whiskey
wheat substitutes, 7
Wanderer's Savory Porridge, 307–308
Huntsman's Hoagie, 102–104
white
Island Burger, 285–286
rice wine
Terra-To Salad, 176–177
148–150
Stuffed Dragon Scale,
Pasta Salad, 224–225
Scrumptious Scholars
red wine
22–23
Copper Cockatrice Caprese,
balsamic, 8
(Gluten-Free), 26
Nana's No-Wheat Bread
apple cider
vinegar
vegetables, 8–10
vegan, 4
Fudgy Brownies (Gluten-Free), 74–75

x
xanthan gum
Nana's No-Wheat Bread (Gluten-Free), 26

y
yogurt
Greek
Gruble Kebab and Cucumber Salad, 197–200

z
za'atar seasoning
Gruble Kebab and Cucumber Salad, 197–200
zucchini, 9–10
Roasted Thunderbird Thighs with Zucchini and Squash, 305–306

Melodius Mushroom Soup, 189–190
Sea Dragon and Noodle Stew, 313–314
Twinbrush Onion Soup, 309–310
wonton wrappers
Colossal Crab Cheese Dip, 95–96
Worcestershire sauce
Cheesy Vine Fruit Manicotti, 323–325
Colossal Crab Cheese Dip, 95–96
Copper Shepherd, 315–317
Dryad's Crunchy Morsels, 326–327
Manticore Noodles, 283–284
Moorshum Cap Sandwich, 174–175